ALSO BY LESLIE MORGAN

Crazy Love

The Baby Chase:
How Surrogacy Is Transforming the American Family

Mommy Wars:
Stay-at-Home and Career Moms Face Off on
Their Choices, Their Lives, Their Families

THE NAKED TRUTH

A Memoir

LESLIE MORGAN

Simon & Schuster

New York   London   Toronto   Sydney   New Delhi

Simon & Schuster
1230 Avenue of the Americas
New York, NY 10020

First Simon & Schuster hardcover edition May 2019

SIMON & SCHUSTER and colophon are registered
trademarks of Simon & Schuster, Inc.

For information about special discounts for bulk purchases,
please contact Simon & Schuster Special Sales at
1-866-506-1949 or business@simonandschuster.com.

The Simon & Schuster Speakers Bureau can bring authors to
your live event. For more information or to book an event contact
the Simon & Schuster Speakers Bureau at 1-866-248-3049
or visit our website at www.simonspeakers.com.

Interior design by Lewelin Polanco

Manufactured in the United States of America

1   3   5   7   9   10   8   6   4   2

Library of Congress Cataloging-in-Publication Data

Names: Morgan, Leslie, 1965- author.
Title: The naked truth : a memoir / by Leslie Morgan.
Description: First Simon & Schuster hardcover edition. |
New York : Simon & Schuster, [2019]
Identifiers: LCCN 2019000817|
ISBN 9781501174100 | ISBN 9781501174117 (ebook)
Subjects: LCSH: Morgan, Leslie, 1965—Sexual behavior. | Divorced women—
United States—Biography. | Divorced women—Sexual behavior—United States.
| Man-woman relationships—United States.
Classification: LCC HQ811.5 .M67 2019 | DDC 306.70973—dc23
LC record available at https://lccn.loc.gov/2019000817

ISBN 978-1-5011-7410-0
ISBN 978-1-5011-7411-7 (ebook)

to the men who made me scream
and the women who let me cry

THE
NAKED
TRUTH

*A*t forty-nine, I got divorced after twenty years of marriage and motherhood.

I had work I loved. My delectable, seditious teenagers had more than silenced my biological clock (trust me). I had enough money stashed away not to worry about it much.

Even though I'd been married for most of my adult life, I had doubts about the viability of romantic relationships. Betrayal and neglect in my marriage had shattered my sexual self-esteem. I came up with the idea of having five lovers for a year. I was clueless about which ones, if any, I'd keep for good.

This is the story of what I learned along the way about love, sex, men, and myself.

Amazing to me even now, the events described in this book are real. A few important characters have been omitted and some have been combined, and some chronologies have been condensed and reworked for compression's sake. I re-created the dialogue as accurately as I can recall it. All names, as well as several geographic, chronological, and identifying details, have been changed.

REWARDS
OF A
STARVATION
DIET

I drove along the sweltering Pennsylvania highway like a demon, hoping to make it to the Philadelphia Airport in time. My flight took off in less than an hour, but suddenly, stopped cars littered the road like confetti. A summer traffic jam caused, I kid you not, by drivers slowing down to look at a couple walking two Jack Russell terriers. To have any chance of making my flight, I had to keep swerving my dented black minivan around idiotic drivers who did not have a plane to catch. And whose cars presumably had air-conditioning that still worked.

Despite the traffic and the heat, my heart felt light with joy, because for the first time in nearly twenty years, I was on a trip by myself, with no one in the car to fight with me. After ending an abusive marriage in my twenties, I'd just gotten divorced again. All I wanted now was to hang out with my two teenaged kids and our pets. Although it had been three years since I'd had sex, my wildest dream was to never get into a car, or sleep in a bed, with any man, ever again.

I pulled the van into the airport lot and parked in the first open space I found. I ran through security, my Rollaboard stuffed with books rattling behind me, checking the time on my iPhone as I went. I clattered past a Hudson News store and didn't recognize myself in the plate glass window. I had on a stretchy black top and my favorite Lucky jeans. Not surprisingly, my forty-nine-year-old reflection looked stressed, my forehead wrinkled, as if I were a once-sexy T-shirt that had become faded and crumpled after being washed too often.

But somehow, I also looked thinner, younger, prettier, more *myself* than I'd looked in ten years. I'd gotten my hair streaked blonde and was wearing lipstick again on a daily basis for the first time in two decades. I'm never going to look like Gisele Bündchen, but I'd lost about twenty pounds since the split, via what my girlfriend KC called "the divorce diet." All that anxiety about custody, legal bills, health insurance, and the leak in the bathroom ceiling had a silver lining after all: smaller jeans.

When I got to the gate for the flight to Long Island, in addition to sporting a layer of sweat, I was hyperventilating. I had ten minutes to spare until takeoff. I pulled the chrome handle on the industrial gray door leading to the jetway. It was *locked*.

"Fuck!" I yelled at the door. "Double fuck!"

The frosted-hair clerk at the gate spoke without looking up from her mauve fingernails flitting across the computer keyboard.

"Flight's delayed. Thunderstorms."

I looked quizzically at the jets parked outside the window behind her. The sky was blue and cloudless.

Feeling paradoxically pissed off *and* relieved, I whirled around, looking for an outlet to charge my phone, or at least an empty chair to collapse in after my Olympic sprint. To my horror, as if in slow motion, my purse knocked over someone's coffee on the high top charging station behind me. Black liquid poured over the table. I watched as it slowly dripped onto the industrial airport carpeting.

"Oh my God, I'm so sorry! Let me buy you another cup . . ."

My voice trailed off as I registered the man whose drink I'd knocked over.

Holy shit.

The drink's owner was, quite possibly, the best-looking man I'd ever seen. Cropped dark hair. Deep blue eyes. Two decades younger than me. A chill zigzagged through me as my eyes met his.

To my surprise, instead of being annoyed, he offered me a lazy smile. His eyes held mine, replacing my shiver with the warm cloak of a cashmere sweater. No man had smiled at me like that in years. Entire decades had passed during which I thought a man would never look at me like that again.

"You don't need to buy me another coffee," he protested, mildly, faint smile lines creasing his tanned cheeks.

The man had to be in his late twenties or early thirties. He looked like an executive dressed for business-casual Friday, a blue button-down shirt tucked into dark Levi's. However, his hands were bare and brown, rough and calloused, and he wore scuffed construction boots, as if he worked outdoors.

"Please? I feel terrible."

Did I sound like the mom who wanted to make everyone's skinned knee better? I tried talking again, willing myself to say something normal, clever even.

"Are you also on the flight to Long Island?"

Not the wittiest repartee, I know. But it worked, because it kept the conversation flowing.

"Yeah, I take it all the time for work." Mr. Blue Eyes sighed. "I'm based in Richmond, so I change planes here. This afternoon flight is always delayed."

He had a lovely baritone voice. He'd be good on the radio. Or a sex chat line. How would it feel to be naked in front of him? Why was I thinking about taking off my clothes in the middle of an airport? With a stranger half my age? When I never wanted to have sex again as long as I lived?

"Can I please take you to Starbucks? I would feel better getting you another coffee," I explained, squeezing my suitcase handle from sudden, excess adrenaline. I badly wanted him to say yes.

He looked at me, raising his eyebrows in assent. The repressed grin on his face reminded me of the expression my grandmother called "a cat with a canary in its mouth."

"Of course," he said politely. "Very nice of you."

We mopped up the spilled coffee with napkins from my purse

and then I looked around for the green Starbucks mermaid. Fortuitously, there she was, only one gate away. I carried two iced Americanos to a wrought iron table we'd snagged, squeezed between the pastry display and a concrete pillar. We were so close, I could smell him. And boy, he smelled good, like wood chips mixed with clean laundry hanging in the sun to dry.

We sat across from each other, awkwardly holding our cold plastic cups. The people in line for lattes and macchiatos snaked around us. A voice came over the airport loudspeaker announcing another flight delay, this one bound for Florida. A passenger in a pin-striped wool suit standing behind me groaned and shut his eyes in frustration.

"So what are you doing on Long Island?" he asked. His soft southern drawl sounded polite. And still amused. By my airport rush? By the coffee fiasco? By . . . me? I felt almost giddy that I'd entertained this man, whose name I still didn't know.

I smiled at him. Was I flirting? Did I still even know how? I hadn't had coffee with a man besides my ex-husband in twenty years. I hadn't even had coffee with *him* in at least ten.

"I have a beach house there . . . I just dropped my daughter off at camp so I'm going there to work."

I took a pull on my straw out of nervousness. Iced coffee flooded my mouth. I swallowed as quickly as I could.

"I'm a writer," I continued, racing to head off an embarrassing silence.

"Wow." He grinned again. He had straight white teeth with one slightly crooked bottom tooth. "That must be pretty amazing to work at something creative."

Was it possible that *he* was flirting with *me*? That seemed improbable. But he did sound curious. As if he wanted to know more about me. Something I also couldn't remember sensing from any man since I'd started having kids in my early thirties. My stomach fluttered. I was curious about him, too.

"What's your work?"

He looked back at me, his gaze softening as he met mine. God, he had beautiful eyes.

"I run a construction company, kind of. It's a small business my granddad started that we expanded together."

He glanced sympathetically at a frazzled woman carrying a screaming, squirming, red-faced baby. Her face looked as if she wanted to scream, too. I wondered if he had kids.

"Hey, that sounds kind of creative. In a different way. What kind of business?"

His looks and his voice morphed into the perfect combination of Abercrombie & Fitch model and every country singer on my Apple Music playlist.

"Um, it's unusual. Not your typical day job. I work in quarries. I guess the best way to describe it is that I'm in explosives."

I furrowed my brow at that one. Explosives?

"My specialty"—he paused and looked at me with unruffled blue eyes—"is drilling and blasting."

I coughed involuntarily, more like a gasp, trapping a half sip of cold coffee in my throat. I tried to swallow but couldn't. Then, against my will, I spit out the coffee, as well as a chunk of ice. It skittered across the wrought iron tabletop toward him.

I blurted out the first words that entered my head.

"I could use some of both!"

I blushed. *I cannot believe you said that!* a voice in my head shrieked. He looked like he was going to spit out *his* coffee.

Luckily, right then our flight was called over the loudspeaker directly above our table. I stood up as quickly as I could, hoping to disguise my mortification, and grabbed my Rollaboard handle. He stood up, too. Lost in the throng of passengers rushing the gate, neither of us even said good-bye. We boarded the plane separately.

I thought about Mr. Blue Eyes for the hour it took to fly to Islip. Did I have the guts to ask for his name, or give him mine? Once we landed at the tiny, almost deserted Long Island airport, I walked as slowly as I could to the rental car counter, looking for him, hoping he might be waiting for me.

He wasn't.

———————

But before I tell you how I tracked down the twenty-nine-year-old explosives expert I met in the Philadelphia Airport, and how we blew up two decades of marriage and thirty-six months of celibacy, first I have to go back in time and tell you about getting rid of my husband, Marty.

Please, don't think I'm being callous.

Trust me, my husband wanted to get rid of me, too.

———————

I felt sorry for Marty's butt. From behind, my husband's tush looked like two sweat socks, grayish and wrinkled from sitting in a gym locker for months. It was the peak of summer, and we were at our shingled beach house in Southampton, New York. My beloved of nearly twenty years, wearing brown swim trunks, trudged down our grassy hill toward the garage we were planning to turn into a bunkhouse for our kids and their friends. It had been almost two years since I'd seen his actual ass, but I could have drawn you a picture of what it looked like.

We'd been married that long.

Tigger, our white Lab mutt, was panting with his pink tongue hanging out, sprawled on the grass overlooking the pool, watching the kids swim as if he were the official lifeguard. Both sixteen-year-old Timmy and fourteen-year-old Bella were crazy about the pool and the ocean. Thank God Tigger didn't like swimming. There'd have been so much dog hair to skim off the water, I would have stuck a fork in my eye.

I made my way across the lawn to Marty, who was checking the Rolex he'd bought himself on his last birthday. We had agreed to meet here, next to the sliding garage door by the pool, because we needed a semiprivate place to talk as a follow-up to our last couples therapy session. The psychologist had given us an assignment: we each had to share the "critical success factor" we needed to make our marriage work. As much as I hoped we'd make some progress today, I dreaded hearing more details from Marty about the ways in which I didn't meet his needs.

Over the past two years, Marty and I had spent an hour a week in therapy, the most excruciating way an unhappy couple can spend money on each other. We had two children we adored, a gracious home, a cute Christmas card. But our love had developed a kind of gangrene. Even though I slept next to him night after night, I'd never felt so alone. Years had passed without his telling me I looked pretty, or that I was a good mom. I couldn't recall the last time I'd complimented him about *anything*. I suspected my husband of at least one affair, maybe more. In therapy, I had asked him, jokingly at first, and then pleadingly, to make a list of reasons why he'd married me. I'd been waiting two years for him to answer.

However, that day in Southampton, I played the highlight reel of our relationship as I headed to our rendezvous point. Our sweet, easy friendship in our twenties. How sweaty his palms got the first time we kissed. The six months we spent dating long distance, me in Chicago, counting down the hours until I flew to his bachelor apartment in Philly. How we both pretended he didn't have an engagement ring in his pocket as we traveled to a friend's wedding in the Czech Republic.

That morning in Southampton, Marty had just come back from working out at Big Dick's Boot Camp, where he hooked up with all his business buddies from New York and Philly who also had second homes here. The truth was, boot camp was a place to get away from us wives, to make up for too many late nights at the office and rich dinners with clients, and to network with the boys without making it seem like work. But it was cheaper and a shorter time commitment than golf, which took at least half a day and cost about twenty times as much, so I never complained.

As I got closer to him, I noticed a shimmer of sweat covering his forehead. He'd slathered 100 SPF sunscreen in white streaks across his bald spot, which now counted for most of his head. I always found bald guys attractive, but I'd never been able to convince Marty of that. He still snuck special hair-regrowth shampoo into the shower, assiduously turning the label toward the wall, as if I didn't know he used it.

He looked at me now with his Wall Street lawyer face, the expressionless mask he wore when he talked to anyone, including our children, his mother, and me. He examined us as if we were companies he was planning to take over and sell within a few years. As if he were trying to ascertain how much we were worth in dollars.

This was not the man I married on a beach in Maui twenty years ago. That man had worn a batik sarong in the Hawaiian sunshine. That man had played me an off-key solo on the mahogany guitar his parents had given him for his thirteenth birthday, to convince me that I was the most wonderful woman in the world to him. Tears had wet his eyes as he sang to me.

I hadn't seen a tear in Marty's eyes for at least a decade.

But you know what? I wasn't the same sweet, eager-to-please twentysomething woman Marty had fallen in love with, either. I was resentful about the compromises marriage and motherhood had extracted, and bitter that Marty had not made the same sacrifices for our family. I'd gained at least twenty-five pounds since our wedding day and I often didn't brush my hair until after noon; I didn't care how I looked to Marty or anyone. As hurt as I was that Marty did not seem to value my contributions to our family's well-being, the truth was, I never told him anymore that I appreciated his temperance and steadiness, his commitment to providing for us financially, or his love for the two most precious humans in the world to me. Marriage and parenthood had taken its grim toll on both of us, driving us apart rather than bringing us together, in insidious ways neither of us could have predicted on that sunny day in Hawaii when we held each other tight and promised we'd always be there for each other.

Today, we didn't have much time for reflection, because the kids would inevitably interrupt us within minutes, and we would invariably let them. Tapping into perverse, almost evolutionary survival tactics, the more desperately Marty and I needed time alone together, whether it was for sex (never these days) or arguing (almost always these days), the more insistently the kids interrupted us. As if sensing the deep trouble we were in as a family, we all colluded in disrupting and postponing our marital conflicts.

Marty pulled open the garage door with the purposeful air of a gardener searching for a rake, but I knew he was simply trying to avoid talking to me.

I took a deep breath to calm my heart rate, and cut right to the chase.

"Honey, we have to discuss this. Now. You've been avoiding this conversation all week."

A white Learjet roared overhead, some Hollywood or Wall Street tycoon coming in for the weekend. Marty's face stayed rigid. He didn't say a word.

"We have such a wonderful life," I went on, reaching for his hand, running my fingers over his wedding band. "The kids are incredible. I love you. I want this to work. But I can't do all the emotional heavy lifting alone. I need you to be here, too."

Hope-junkie me meant every word. As a writer, I believed that carefully chosen words, said the right way, could solve any problem. Unfortunately, Marty was a numbers guy.

He looked out at the forty-foot pines that held our hammock, and blinked uncomfortably. For him, this was a big reaction. At moments like this, I knew to blow air on the embers, to inflame the emotional flicker into something strong enough to get him talking, before he could figure out how to squelch his reaction.

"Come on, we haven't had sex in two years. *Two years?*"

I tried to lock on to those gray-green eyes that I had stared into lovingly more times than I could remember.

Tell me I still matter to you, I thought, examining his face as if I held an invisible magnifying glass.

"Honey, no matter how much I love the kids and our life together, I can't stay if I'm not still the most important woman in the world to you."

I felt as if I was begging him to respond. I *was* begging him to respond. Marty's Adam's apple clenched and he looked away again, this time at Timmy's baseball pitch at the bottom of the gravel driveway.

I went to put my arms around my husband. I wanted to pull him close, to feel the warmth from his body, to smell his sweat and sunscreen. But it felt more like I was grabbing him, pleading with him to react to me. To care.

"Please, honey! If you say I'm one in a million, I'll do anything to make this work. But don't you see I can't do this alone, with you ignoring me?"

He stood stiff as a corpse, refusing eye contact. His arms hung at his sides. Despite his shiny forehead, his body felt as if it'd been stored in a refrigerated meat locker. I pulled away.

Then, finally, he spoke.

"I don't like the way . . ."

Another jet thundered overhead. I held my breath. I was ready for whatever he had to unveil.

He started again. "I don't like . . . the way . . ."

He froze, as if surprised by the sound of his own voice.

"The way you hug me."

My head jerked up. Something burst in my chest. Maybe it was what was left of my heart. Sweet Jesus. *That* was his emotional breakthrough? His daring risk that would revive our connection? Like a pot boiling over, I unexpectedly became so furiously angry, I could hardly stop to inhale.

"We've been married for twenty years." The fury I'd squelched over a decade of Marty ignoring me made me so enraged, I was actually spitting the words at him. "The last time we had sex is a long-lost memory. And you say you don't like the way I *hug* you?"

Marty looked down at the hairs on his bare toes. The skin was translucent from years trapped in the custom-crafted wing tips every law firm partner in Philadelphia seemed to wear.

I had not planned to end our marriage that afternoon. But I couldn't bear one more talk like this. Ever. I had tried my damnedest to reach Marty, opening my psyche to him in the therapist's office, and giving him every drop of love in my body over our years together. In return, he'd kept his hopes, dreams, and body to himself, ignoring me on my birthday, Mother's Day, and our wedding anniversary. And I'd sunk to that level and repaid him with unrelenting anger and resentment. Suddenly, it was crystal clear to me: I never, ever wanted to be in a therapist's office, our car, our beach house, or anywhere else with this man, much less naked in a bed in his arms. And he didn't want me there either. Which obviously would make it tricky to stay married.

Heart racing, blood pounding in my temples, I realized in a rush that this wasn't a talk. It was *the talk*. Now I was the one with the poker face, even as the hollow of my stomach clenched.

"I think we have to admit that our marriage is dead, Marty. It died on its own. I'm not sure we can revive it, no matter what we do."

I searched my husband's face for heartbreak. Or fear, or even anger. Instead, what I saw was worst of all: relief.

Tears came to my eyes as I tried to pinpoint the exact moment our marriage had died. Maybe years before, when he first refused to kiss me on the lips when I had bronchitis, claiming he couldn't afford to get sick at work then. Months later he still averted his mouth every time I went in for a smooch. I should have known it was over then. Isn't the way a man kisses you a clarion bell for how he really feels?

Now he was talking again. His words made my head spin as if I'd stood up too quickly.

"Obviously, I haven't been in love with you for several years."

The "obviously" and "several" burned as if he were holding my palms to a hot stove. As did his blithe, matter-of-fact tone, as if everyone in Southampton and Philadelphia knew he hadn't cared for me in years. Maybe they did and I was a fool.

"It would be better, for me, if you moved out of the Rittenhouse place."

His voice rang toneless and rehearsed, as if he were explaining cash flows at an investors briefing, not asking me to move out of the home I'd raised our kids in. We'd fallen in love with it almost eighteen years before, an 1800s three-story redbrick town house with six sandstone steps leading up from the sidewalk to glossy black double doors with a brass knocker in the shape of a pineapple. We faced the southwest corner of Rittenhouse Square, a manicured oasis built in the 1680s, with flower beds surrounded by wrought iron fences and old-fashioned streetlamps, halfway between the Schuylkill and Delaware rivers. The famous bronze *Duck Girl* statue in the reflecting pool looked like she was walking on water, holding a mallard under her left arm. Timmy was born a few months after we moved in. We'd cried together the day we brought him home from the hospital, tucked like a doll in his immaculate new car seat, a yellow duck pattern on his baby blanket, so placid he didn't even cry when he woke up to nurse.

I wasn't sure Marty had thought of where the kids and I would go. He was acting as if the critical factor was how inconvenient it would be to move his suits. I was too stunned to respond. Unfazed, he carried on.

"And, ah, have you given any thought to how soon we can start seeing other people?"

I stared at his face through my tears, which were drying up pretty fast. Marty paused as the neighbor fired up his buzz cutter to trim the hedges between our properties. Then he leaned in so close to me, I could see the saliva in the corners of his lips.

"I'll start working on your severance," he announced, to my amazement, looking at the blue sky and clapping his hands as if we were executives at a board meeting finally getting down to business.

"My . . . severance?" I whispered. My voice, and all my faculties, threatened to fail in the shock of the moment. "Because, after two decades together, I'm fired? As your wife?"

"That's not what I said!" He took a step backward and held up both palms. "That's not what I meant! I meant . . . your . . . you know, your settlement."

"Fuck you, Marty."

It was hard to keep my voice low now.

"You and the horse you rode in on. I've tried so fucking hard to be a good wife to you. Despite the way you've ignored me. Despite that lingerie I found under our bed. There is no goddamn way I'm leaving our house and I don't give two fucks when you start seeing her openly. Keep the kids out of it, motherfucker."

The sound of a splash came from the pool, followed by Bella shrieking "Mom, heeeeelp!" as the kids roughhoused, oblivious to the fracture between us. I stood frozen for a long moment. I didn't feel anything. I stared at Marty, hard, one last time. Did he notice, or care, that I'd finally had enough? I couldn't hear the birds in the trees or the jets overhead any longer. I willed myself to walk to the pool to make sure the kids were okay.

Our marriage was over. For good.

In fairness, Marty did one nice thing. A week after that marriage-ending fight, when he was back in Philadelphia for work, late one night, my phone lit up with a three-word text from him. I miss us.

It was so damn sweet, two tears popped out of the corners of my eyes. But only two. I put my phone away without replying. One three-word text did not come close to making up for years of neglect and condescension. I was done.

The next day, Marty conceded, via email, that he'd move out of our house once the children went back to school.

Two weeks later, we told the kids we were splitting up. Marty drove out from his office to Southampton for one night, so we could break the news together. With a kid on either side, all holding hands, we clustered around the glass-topped table where we'd spent many summer evenings playing I Doubt It and Tunk and other absurd card games. I felt as if I'd swallowed Drano, but both kids looked at me, tears dripping down their cheeks, with a surprising measure of relief. With that intuitive kid sense, Timmy and Bella may have already realized, probably even before we did, that our problems weren't fixable.

Back in Philly in September for the first day of school, I took pictures of the children with their squeaky clean, carefully brushed hair, new backpacks, and first-day-back outfits. For Timmy, back-to-school meant a fresh buzz cut, shorts, and a T-shirt. Bella had spent days Snapchatting different ensembles to her friends. She'd finally settled on short-shorts and a loose white V-neck over a gray camisole. To me, their clothes looked exactly like every single thing they'd worn all summer. But fine. The pictures I snapped were in the top 10 percent of cuteness.

As I watched the kids trudge out the double front doors, I could smell the water the doorman from the apartment building next door had sprayed on the sidewalk with his hose. The water made the sidewalk smell clean and fresh, even though it did little more than wash away the top layer of grit. I slid the brass lock on the doors as Marty came downstairs lugging his Hartmann suitcase. He looked exactly like he had a hundred times before, taking off for yet another business trip. No emotion on his face, no reluctant body language to mark the fact that this wasn't just any old good-bye, this was *the* good-bye.

The kids didn't know Marty was moving out today, that this crisp morning marked our last occasion as an intact family. He planned to break the news once he'd settled into the house he'd rented a few blocks away. I did not object, although it felt like sub-terfuge, because now it was Marty's subterfuge, not mine.

I stood in the kitchen next to the butcher-block island, mo-tionless. He headed toward the back door. I remembered him half carrying me, in labor with Bella, out that same door to the hospital. If you'd told me, at that moment, that Marty would be leaving me and our kids behind in a mere dozen years, and that I'd be relieved to see him go, I would have said you had us confused with another less committed, less in love, less hopeful young couple. Divorce was never going to happen to us.

Marty paused to grab the suitcase handle. Without looking at me, in a chillingly nonchalant tone, he said:

"I thought I'd be married to you forever."

With that, he turned his back and walked through the sunroom filled with early-morning September light. He paused to get a better grip on the taupe suitcase handle. I held my breath. I waited for the words that would capture—and maybe set free—the sadness, the relief, the uncertainty, the love we'd felt together in this place.

In our sun-dappled living room, if he'd asked me to try again, if he'd taken my hand or broken down and told me I was one in a million, he'd do anything to fix what was wrong between us, told me he *wanted* to be married to me forever, I would have hugged him—if I could figure out the way he liked—and never let go. But I'd begged enough. Words had made no difference.

Instead he offered a weak wave. His left hand looked naked, his fingers oddly bare. I realized he had already removed his wedding ring. His back was still to me. He didn't turn around.

"See ya," he said.

He walked out the back door.

I stayed there for a few moments, listening to his luggage wheels squeaking. I crept to the French doors and watched him walk across the flagstone deck and past the cedar hot tub where we'd spent many evenings catching up at the end of long days, past my mermaid sculpture. I'd spotted the mermaid ten years before outside an antique store on Route 27 between Sagaponack and East Hampton. She was made from copper, gone to green with gold highlights. Her head was bowed over her gracefully curled tail. Her naked breasts were spectacular. I'd found the perfect spot for her, on the brick wall by the hot tub, under a red-leafed Japanese maple my mom had planted while she was still strong enough to garden. As I watched, Marty went down the steps and through our garden, surrounded by ten-foot-high, ivy-covered brick walls. I heard the back gate clang shut, and then the chirp of his BMW unlocking. *The opposite of love is not hate*, my mother once told me. *It is indifference.* I felt like my heart was out in the alley, packed inside my husband's suitcase. My future spread before me like the slate-gray Atlantic Ocean at the end of summer. Were there mermaids or sharks under the surface? I didn't know. All I was sure of was that I was done with indifference in my life.

Safe to say, the next several months sucked. As you might imagine—though I never did until it was my daily reality—separating my life, and my financial future, from a control-oriented lawyer with an ambiguous relationship to the truth was hell. I actually think, now that I'm on the other side, that all divorces are hell, no matter what anyone tells you. Amicable ex-spouses are urban legends, on par with boa constrictors coming out of bathtub drains. But at the time, I thought our split would be straightforward. Rather laughably, I actually said to my girlfriend KC that I thought Marty would make a great ex-husband, because he was unemotional and rational, and had always forgotten our marital spats quickly. Instead, I was surprised by how excruciating the transition was for the kids and me, and probably for Marty, too, although it was hard to tell since he openly started dating another woman six weeks after moving out. Paradoxically, those months were also boring, like a predictable but occasionally amusing sitcom about a lawyer divorcing his wife, hopefully played by Jennifer Aniston or Reese Witherspoon. If you could measure months in money, the transition was also astronomically costly, because, like wedding planners, divorce lawyers maniacally add zeros to their bills, knowing clients will pay without a peep.

But we survived. Somehow. Barely. And then, to my relief, it was finally summer again.

———————

Now we can go back to that June afternoon in the Philadelphia Airport. It was early summer, that brief window between the breezy last day of school and Philly's dog days of hellish humidity. I'd put Timmy on a bus to baseball camp at six in the morning, and then Bella and I drove to sleepaway camp in rural Pennsylvania. It was the first time the kids and I would be apart for more than a few nights since the August day Marty and I had broken the news to them that we were getting a divorce.

Bella and I stopped at a McDonald's off the highway to get French fries and vanilla shakes. When I restarted our Honda Odyssey, I realized I couldn't get the air-conditioning to work. Another thing for me to fix on my own. So we drove the rest of the way with the windows rolled down and the smell of fresh-cut hay filling the car.

In the cool, pine-scented Pennsylvania woods, I unpacked Bella's trunk. As she picked her cuticles, anxious and adorable in Daisy Dukes and One Direction T-shirt, I fluffed her pillow and sleeping bag.

"You're going to have another great two weeks here, honey," I told her as I smoothed the extra blanket at the foot of her cot. "Thank God this year is over. We both need a break. If I can make the last flight, I'm going straight to the beach. I need to get some writing done."

I kissed the part dividing her silky brown hair, taking in one last breath of her coconut shampoo, and said good-bye.

Then I drove to the airport. And knocked over that coffee. And tried to flirt. And hoped that a perfect stranger would be waiting for me when we both got off the plane on Long Island.

And found out he wasn't.

––––––––––

After leaving the Long Island airport in my maroon Kia Soul rental car, zipping east on Montauk Highway in the end-of-day traffic, I called my friend KC. In addition to being a former colleague from the Philadelphia *Star*, she was my divorce sounding board and impromptu dating coach. As the traffic thinned out, replaced by summer fireflies and giant sunflowers like fence posts lining the highway, I told her everything without taking a breath.

"KC, he was so, so, *so* cute! Do you think he was flirting with me? Can you believe he works in *drilling* and *blasting*?"

KC was a working mom, too, a few years younger than me, a blunt, no-nonsense, brainy South Carolina belle with a drawl more commonly heard offering iced tea in a Broad Street mansion drawing room than plotting circulation strategy in an urban newsroom.

We started out as colleagues a few years before, when my kids were in middle school and I was still a full-time manager at the *Star*, dreaming of becoming a full-time writer. We collided trying to save a failing division that corporate later unloaded. The day we met, she had on a brown giraffe print wrap dress, her blonde hair skimmed her shoulders, and her glossy peach-pink nails matched her lipstick. I trusted her as soon as we shook hands.

About two years before I left Marty, KC abruptly left her husband, Nick. He was a ruggedly handsome, smart, frustrated, subterraneously angry and deeply troubled Philadelphia detective she'd met the year after she graduated from Clemson with a degree in business. When he started getting physical—kicking their dog, grabbing KC's arm hard enough to leave purple bruises she showed me in the office supply closet—that was it. Overnight.

"My daddy always said he'd kill any man who laid a finger on me," she told me one day in her southern accent as we washed our hands in the women's restroom. "I'd kill Nick myself, but divorce and alimony are better than murder and prison."

A year after they split, she started dating online, which intimidated the hell out of me. I flatly refused despite her exhortations; I couldn't handle the frank inspection and rejection she faced every time she logged on. Plus, from my view, online dating seemed limited to the two narrow objectives society gave women: finding someone to screw once, or someone to marry and screw forever. KC was open to both. These days, I didn't know if I wanted either.

As I flicked on the rental car's cruise control, KC snickered into the phone.

"So, what's his name, honey? Where does he work?"

"Um . . . yeah . . . I . . . uh . . . I didn't get his name. Or the name of his company."

An exasperated, distinctly un–southern belle snort came over the phone line.

"You *are* kidding, right? This is Dating 101. *Get the goddamn name.*" She sounded as southern, and as tough, as Johnny Cash. "Why do you think guys used to ask six times, 'You're Leslie, right?'

back when you were at bars in college? You cannot track someone down without a name."

I passed an old Toyota pickup truck with jacked-up monster wheels. Montauk Highway narrowed to two lanes curving between potato fields. Only another twenty minutes to go.

KC paused to collect herself, like a boss frustrated by a wayward intern, digging deep for the patience to deal with my inept dating skills.

"Hey, look, there cannot be that many men"—she pronounced it *mayhhn*—"who work in that specialized a field. I bet you could find him."

KC made it sound like a threat, as if her next step were putting me in the pokey. Like if I tracked him down, she'd let it slide that I'd been too insecure to exchange names with a man I found attractive. She knew exactly how to push my buttons.

"All right, KC. I'll try. Stay tuned."

I got to the beach house shortly before nine o'clock. I closed my eyes in bliss, even though I was driving, at the sound of the tires crunching on the gravel drive under the canopy of beech trees overhead. I pulled into the parking cutout, and my heels crushed the wild mint as I carried my bag to the slate steps, filling the night with a sweet tang. I headed to the blue front door, which matched the hydrangeas in bloom so heavy their stems bent toward the ground. I found the spare key hidden on a nail under a loose shingle.

Inside, the place still smelled like spray-on sunblock from last summer. On the screened-in sun porch I used as an office, I unzipped my computer from its case and plugged the cord into the electrical outlet under the scratchy jute carpet. And then I began my online search, per KC's directive, relishing the quiet, dark house normally overrun by kids in wet bathing suits and sandy feet, clamoring for a bonfire and s'mores.

First, I found the company. KC was right, there was only one excavation company with Long Island and Richmond, Virginia, offices. But how to find one specific employee? I was looking for a needle in a haystack.

Then my brain kicked in: He had to be a senior executive in management, or sales and marketing at the very least, although he didn't look like a slick sales guy. From the executives section on the company website, I wrote down six names. (There was only one woman, Helaine something—the director of human resources, of course.)

Listening to the sound of crickets outside, I went on Facebook and Google to check pictures against the names I'd found. A few were easy to eliminate. Overweight. Old. Bearded. Finally, I discarded all but one name: Dylan Smyth. It seemed to fit him.

Then I turned to Facebook. I found Dylan Smyth *immediately*. I was so excited, I clicked "Add Friend" before looking. This guy lived in Detroit. His arms, which were crossed in front of his massive chest, were covered in violent tattoos. He was missing his front right tooth.

As quickly as I could, I canceled the request, hitting the keyboard frantically.

This quest was ridiculous. I was never going to find the real Dylan Smyth.

I took a break to unpack and brush my teeth. As my toothbrush whirred, I could hear a lone deer outside the bathroom window, crunching on the hydrangea blooms. I kept thinking about how to find him. *He's an executive. How do executives track each other down? Not through Facebook. Not through pictures on social media sites.*

I spit out my toothpaste and ran back to my office. I clicked onto the blue and white LinkedIn icon and typed "Dylan Smyth."

A fuzzy picture came up of a man wearing a tie. I recognized those blue eyes. It was the man from the airport. Definitely. The pen wobbly in my hand, I grabbed a torn envelope and scribbled down the mailing address in Virginia and the division's main switchboard number.

Now that I knew the town where he worked, I ran a tighter search. A picture of his college lacrosse roster came up. A jolt spiked through me as I looked at the screen. Even as a college senior, Dylan

Smyth had been *spectacular*. An athlete with cobalt-blue eyes and a sweet smile and that one crooked lower tooth. I looked for the year he graduated. It was six years after Bella was born. Which meant he was twenty-nine. Then I collapsed back into my black swivel chair and screamed loudly into the night.

For years, sex with Marty had been . . .

How can I put this?

Soul-crushing.

I'm not trying to be vindictive. I admit that, like most exes, at times I have imagined stabbing my wasband with a carbon steel chef's knife. But right now, I'm simply being honest. Acknowledging the truth about our sex life still takes me by surprise: it was never that good, and it wasn't Marty's fault. He was a sensational kisser. I was wildly attracted to him, and even in his late forties his body was thin and toned, with less than 10 percent body fat, on par with a triathlete twenty years younger. But something was always off between us physically, and I was too much of a hope junkie to realize it could destroy us over time.

The grim reality is that Marty never seemed to enjoy sex with me. This is still hard to wrap my head around. I've always had such a sweet tooth for sex, even sex with him, that I truly didn't notice he wasn't there with me emotionally. Not our first time, not on our wedding night, not on the balcony during our honeymoon in Amalfi. I still feel a queasy regret that I overlooked something so crucial to both of us, and to our marriage.

Marty and I met in our late twenties, at a conference I'd been sent to by a now-defunct financial magazine. I'd left my abusive first husband a year before, and I was still finding my sea legs. Marty and I were seated next to each other at dinner. We became friends first, two very different people occasionally grabbing a meal or going to a concert together when we happened to be in the same city for work. He lived in Philly, and I was in Chicago. After I'd known him for about a year, a voice in my head began whispering,

You should date someone like Marty, which to me meant someone easygoing, gentle, and stable, the polar opposite of my brilliant, volatile, self-destructive first husband. That man had told me I'd make a great writer one day, and indeed, he gave me unbeatable material for my memoir *Crazy Love* when he held loaded guns to my head and pulled the keys out of the car ignition as I drove our Volkswagen down the highway at fifty-five miles per hour. It's tough to discuss husband number one without getting sidetracked. Which is why, eventually, I left the *Star* and wrote *Crazy Love* about our relationship, and turned my experience into advocacy for abuse victims.

My past may have been messy, but Marty seemed like the key to the happy, secure future I craved. After a few months, that voice in my head replaced *You should date someone like Marty* with the more insistent, *Why don't you date* Marty? The voice was kind enough not to add, *You numb-nut*.

At the same time, Marty went on vacation to Anguilla with a woman he was dating. He looked down from his beach chair one afternoon to discover he'd written *my* name in the sand. As soon as he got home, he called me and confessed that story. After I hung up the phone, I dialed my childhood friend Winnie and announced, "I'm going to marry that man." Things moved quickly after that, and we exchanged vows in Hawaii sixteen months later.

But even when we initially dated, Marty limited sex to once every seven days. In my experience, most men seemed to interpret "early dating" to mean three-orgasm-a-day sexathons, making it hard to bend over to pull on socks without getting grabbed from behind. But Marty treated making love like medicine he had to take. The first night we slept together, I tried for a second round by climbing on top of him in the middle of the night. He had an erection, so I thought he liked it.

"What are you doing?" he asked groggily, sounding genuinely confused. "Stop. It's two a.m."

The next morning in his bed in his Philly apartment, I tried to wake him up with my mouth. What guy refuses *that*? But Marty did. At first, I thought he was simply shy. But over time I noticed that Marty never responded to my touch, or indicated that he liked anything I'd done to him sexually. What disturbed me the most was that he didn't, or maybe even couldn't, look me in the eye when we made love.

But here's the thing: Marty was stable and reliable, and tender in countless other ways that mattered far more to me than sex. For my thirtieth birthday, he took me for a carriage ride in Central Park because I'd told him I loved horses as a child. When Marty proposed (in Prague, at midnight, next to the Jan Hus fountain), he wept fat tears as he vowed to take care of me forever. I thought I was being mature by choosing reliability over passion. Maybe I was.

After our wedding, we settled into a routine that included making love often enough to have Timmy and Bella. Periodically, I tried to spice up our sex life, but eventually I gave up. I masturbated during the late mornings when he was at work and the kids were at school. I thought this acceptance was another sign of our maturity, of a happy union, of the sleeping-with-socks comfort of a long, mellow marriage. How important was good sex, anyway? Or any kind of sex? Maybe I could live without it. A married friend told me once, as we walked home from yoga, that when her husband was on top of her, to get through it, she imagined eating a tootsie roll. Very, very slowly. So I figured muted lovemaking, doled out a few times a month, was typical for most marriages, and a small price to pay for a stable family life with a kind, reserved man. Or so I thought for a long, long time.

However, once I backed off, Marty reacted as if thrown off by my no longer pursuing him for intimacy. For the first time in our relationship, he was the one initiating conversations about improving our sex life. Alas, his words were like 7-Eleven coffee, scalding and bitter.

"You need to be more spontaneous," he told me sternly, looking over his horn-rimmed reading glasses one Saturday night in our bedroom, after we'd made love for the first time in four weeks. "I want more frequent sex. Experiments."

"What kind of experiments?" I asked him. I'd do anything—read bad *Playboy* fiction out loud, wear a French maid's uniform, hang naked from our living room chandelier—if it would help us. "Give me a list of three things you'd like to try."

Marty looked as if I'd asked a question in Kiswahili, unable to answer me with specifics. I had no clue what he wanted, any more than he did. God, did I try, though. I booked an expensive overnight babysitter and an even more expensive suite at the Four Seasons and fucked him in the middle of the night. I bought new lingerie. I ordered a book from Amazon about what women like in bed, which he kept on his bed stand, the pristine spine forever uncracked. I screwed him in the daylight in our own bed for the first time since the kids had been born. I tried getting into the shower with him, but he told me he was in a hurry to get to a meeting at work and then ducked his soapy bald head back under the faucet.

One night, after another awkward tryst in our bedroom, he stared in frustration at my favorite painting of the ocean, hanging across from our bed. We'd been married for fifteen years. I wasn't sure I could take another fifteen minutes of feeling so badly about myself sexually.

"I think you may be frigid," he announced. Marty sounded like a surgeon delivering a diagnosis. For a second, I nodded, thinking of course that his erotic reticence was my fault, looking at those hazel eyes I'd trusted for years. I allowed him to blame me because he seemed so sure of himself. But me, frigid? I started having sex at fifteen. I first tried anal in the 1980s, when putting your tongue in someone's ear had passed for adventurousness.

"Marty, do you want me to pretend that I like what we're doing in bed, even if I don't? That everything between us is perfect?"

He nodded, as if to say *Of course, that would work fine*. But he hesitated before speaking, as if he couldn't bring himself to say the words aloud. Instead, he told me something that made me feel just as empty inside.

"We have different needs," Marty explained. "You're not meeting mine."

From then on, he repeated this every single time we had sex.

Stupidly, I kept trying to revive our sex life with myriad, inventive attempts to please him. This got harder as he added rules about what I could and couldn't do. I couldn't rub his leg when we sat next to each other on the couch, or put my arm around him in a movie theater, because it "tickled." He asked me not to leave the bathroom without a robe because my nude body made him "edgy." He wouldn't kiss me on the lips or let me know what sexual position was his favorite. He acted like a coach disappointed in my performance on the field after every blow job and orgasm. How could someone who supposedly loved me be so unkind? Eventually, being naked in front of my husband felt as warm and fuzzy as spooning a coat hanger. But I stayed married to him.

I'm one of those people who believe everything in one's life, including sex, starts with your mother. My mom passed away two years before Marty and I split, from breast cancer caught too late. She was having such a terrific time winning golf tournaments in Florida, she couldn't bother to see her doctor. By the time she did, the cancer had spread ferociously, to her brain, hipbones, and lungs. She died after being bedridden for only ten weeks in our guest room. But when she was alive, Mom was a brilliant, beautiful goddess.

Unfortunately, it was sometimes in the snake-haired medusa kind of way, especially after five or six rum and cokes.

Mom grew up in New York City in the 1950s, in my wealthy grandparents' emotionally frigid, folded-linen-napkin Upper East Side world with its vague but strictly enforced WASPy etiquette strictures. Especially confusing to me were the taboo subjects refined women of all ages avoid mentioning, as if they simply don't exist: money, sex, and any form of failure. Throughout my childhood, I never once heard Mom say, "Gee, I'm sorry I got shitfaced again last night," or "Gee, I love you," or "Gee, that's okay, no one is perfect." That would have been weakness, God forbid.

It was clear that the subject Mom least enjoyed was female

sexual biology. Not me. Starting when I was eight, during Mom's weekly set-and-curl hair appointment, I scrutinized women's magazines while I sat next to her under an unplugged hair dryer as big as a Flyers hockey helmet. Forget about *Cosmopolitan*'s taped up breasts and raccoon eye makeup. Instead, I combed the dog-eared salon magazines for the names of the products the frighteningly exotic models used. Foraging for fungible items to help puberty along seemed more achievable, and realistic, for a fourth grader than did cleavage and orgasm, whatever those things were.

One day, swinging my bare legs and waiting for Mom to finish beautifying, I saw an ad for Tampax. The swirly seventies-era font read "The Carefree Girl!" followed by a photo montage of a laughing blonde teenager in tight white hip huggers on a rowboat, splashing in a lake in an orange macramé bikini, and hiking athletically in terry-cloth shorts that were shorter than the cotton underpants I wore.

On the drive home in our white Cadillac, which was the approximate size of a houseboat, I mustered the courage to speak. My body felt as tense as a stretched-out bungee cord.

"Mom, what's a *tampoon*?"

I pronounced the word, memorably, as if it rhymed with *harpoon*.

Mom laughed with a clenched jaw and without taking her eyes off the road, fixating on the massive tusk-and-flag chrome hood ornament as if she were an addict eyeing a bag of meth. She said I was pronouncing the word incorrectly. She did not tell me the correct pronunciation.

"Leslie," she said instead, dismissively, as if she had ice cubes in her mouth.

Her tone implied: *Jesus H. Christ, how could such an imbecile have come out of my body?*

"Leslie." She said my name again, to make sure she had my full attention, which, I promise you, she did. "Only prostitutes use such . . . unmentionables."

Her tone made it clear I'd asked a horrific question, but not only had I no idea what a tampon was, I didn't know what a prostitute was, either. I shrank into the Caddie's velvet upholstery, wanting to disappear. Needless to say, Mom did not explain.

A few weeks later, I heard two boys talking on the playground about something called *a blow job*. Whatever it was, they made it sound kind of fun. That night, Mom was wearing black calfskin heels and a sleeveless Jackie Kennedy sheath as she peeled carrots over the sink for dinner. I stood next to her, holding out my palm to collect each carefully skinned vegetable and pat it dry with a strip of paper towel.

It seemed like the ideal private moment to ask her about the boys on the playground. I thought they were talking about water balloons, a new kind of hair spray, or a technological advancement in bubble gum. If I'd known the answer involved sex, I never would have asked.

"Mom, ah, have you ever heard of a blow job?"

She whirled toward me. The shiny metal vegetable peeler gleamed in her wet hand like a weapon. A few floppy orange strands flew toward my chin like miniature Frisbees.

Apparently, I'd made Mom *extremely* angry. God, not again!

"It's a disgusting *sex* term, *Leslie*." She emphasized key words with her teeth clenched. Her gold wedding band and diamond engagement ring glistened with tap water. "Where a girl *drinks* from a boy's *penis*. Only prostitutes do it."

I stared back at her, so taken aback I could breathe only through my mouth. I tried to digest (sorry) two unfathomables: (1) Mom was talking about sex; and (2) the concept that anyone—obviously not Mom!—chose to swallow *urine* directly from a boy's penis.

I still didn't know what prostitutes were either, but both times she'd mentioned them it had sounded pretty bad. I decided not to ask Mom any more questions. Instead I looked words up in the dictionary and tried to piece together the mechanics myself. I got as far as understanding that a prostitute was someone who got paid a lot of money to drink pee.

It helped significantly when a new girl from New York City with freckles and a turned-up nose sat next to me in fifth grade.

Winthrop Carter Winslow, a Mayflower descendant like Mom, was also from the Upper East Side. Winnie knew so many dirty words, I figured Manhattan must be the mecca of preteen sex education. This puzzled me, because growing up there hadn't much helped Mom's comfort with sex.

Winnie told me that a liquid besides pee could come out of a boy's penis. For a long time, I didn't believe her. She was also the first person to suggest that, in my own body, there was something else down there besides one hole for pee and one for poo. The day she told me this, I locked myself in the bathroom I shared with my sister, took off my panties, and bent over the toilet with a hand mirror. It was kinda dark and frightening down there, but sure enough, Winnie From New York City was right. There *were* three holes!

When I lost my virginity at fifteen with my first high school boyfriend, of course I didn't tell Mom anything about it, including how appallingly, disappointingly unromantic it was. I didn't even tell Winnie how much it hurt and how let down I felt afterward. Luckily, my mother's discomfort with sex didn't stick to me for good. However, I still have a hard time saying "tampon" without stuttering on the second syllable.

Mom got sick soon after Marty and I celebrated our eighteenth wedding anniversary. All she wanted was to watch golf on TV in the guest room where I'd parked her after her oncologist broke the news that the end was near. Marty set up the Golf Channel in Mom's room, which meant the world to Mom. And to me, although the taste was bittersweet, because it had been years since he had done anything similarly thoughtful for me.

I came down to wake Mom that June morning while the kids and Marty were still asleep. I'll never forget how still the room felt. I stood on tiptoe, looking at her under the peach guest-room comforter. Afraid to inhale, I willed her chest to rise. The room held the sacred hush of an empty chapel at ten o'clock on a weekday morning.

I called the hospice nurse from my cell phone outside Mom's room.

"If you think she's dead, she's dead," the nurse announced.

She was correct.

To my surprise, in the chaotic, grief-filled days that followed, flashes of relief lightened the inevitable shock and sadness. I felt gratitude that Mom had died without pain or drama, sure. But I also experienced waves of unexpected relief for . . . me. I'd be driving or loading the dishwasher, and I'd hear a quiet voice say, *It's okay to leave him now*. I hadn't known I'd stayed married to Marty in part to assuage Mom, to reassure her that I was taken care of by a good provider who loved me. Then, one night a few weeks after her interment in the family plot at Sleepy Hollow Cemetery, Marty asked me casually, "So, when are you going to be done with this grief thing?" as if my dead mother were something I needed to wash my hands of.

The last time Marty and I had sex was on a Friday night in July, a month after Mom died, two years before our marriage-ending fight in Southampton. Under the covers, our bodies performed the necessary functions, but emotionally, Barbie and Ken had a deeper connection. Of course, I had no idea it was the last time we'd have sex. Unfortunately, in real life, unlike in the swirling dark of the movie theatre or the pages of romance novels, there's no narrator telling you *This is the last time, sweetheart, enjoy it for all it's worth*.

The day after, I kissed Marty good-bye through the minivan window as the children and I left for almost a month in Southampton, a respite after Mom's passing. I'd pleaded with Marty to come with us, even for a few days, but he said he had to stay in Philadelphia. His entire firm was prepping for a biotech IPO scheduled for the first week of September.

The kids and I got back to Philly on a stifling August afternoon around five o'clock, two days before school started. Working late again, Marty didn't meet us. After I'd made the kids some fish sticks and tater tots in my typical supermom fashion, I went upstairs to unpack. Looking under my and Marty's bed for one of the cats who always got spooked by the long car ride, I saw a small red pyramid that, at first, looked like a dust bunny. Gingerly, I reached for it. I stood up and looked in my hand: it was an unfamiliar red lace bra and skinny thong. The fabric was twisted, in the way of lingerie taken off in a hurry. At first, I was puzzled. *When did I get red lingerie?* Then the answer dawned on me: *These are not mine.* I dropped them like someone else's used handkerchief, appalled that I had been cradling them in my palm. They landed on the wood floor, crumpled like tissue paper.

But then I picked them up, because I couldn't resist looking at the sizes. The thong was one-size-fits-all. The bra was 36D, two sizes larger than what I wore.

That night, Marty got home around ten thirty. The kids were in bed. I shut our bedroom door gingerly, the way you do when you put down a sleeping baby and you'd sooner drink chlorine than startle her. Busy taking off his shoes in the chair by his side of the bed, Marty took a few seconds to notice me standing in front of him. His eyes widened when he saw me.

"Yes?" he said, as if I were a secretary who had disturbed the boss with an ignorant question. I could hear cicadas rattling outside the French doors of our bedroom balcony.

My body shook with that trembling feeling you get when you cradle the toilet right before you throw up. Had another woman been in my bed? Had Marty been inside another woman in my bed? The dread interlaced itself with treacly hope that made my mouth taste like Sweet'N Low. Surely Marty had a plausible explanation. He didn't even like sex, anyway. So why would he have an affair? Maybe he'd failed to mention some houseguests?

"I found these under our bed," I said, as steadily as I could, standing in front of him, feeling tears pooling in my eyes. "They are . . . not mine."

Please, please have a good answer. I was desperate for a logical explanation, one that would still the queasy feeling in my stomach.

Marty looked back with the unflustered gaze of a crocodile motionless on a riverbank.

"I bought those for you, honey," he said, looking straight into my eyes, his irises clear and dark, not a titch rattled or guilt-ridden. He imitated my trembling cadence. "You are . . . so paranoid."

His mockery was like a chopstick thrust into my jugular notch. I was alarmed by how easily he lied. It sickened me as much as his infidelity. But this was *marriage*, to the father of my children, to a man I still loved, despite his betrayal. I needed time to figure out how to proceed, how much I could handle, how to protect myself. That night, we brushed our teeth together, standing in front of our his-and-hers sinks, as we had one hundred other nights before. Then we got into our bed as if nothing had changed.

It took me over an hour to fall asleep, my back to Marty, hugging my arms around my chest so I wouldn't cry. I never slept in our bed again without wondering who had been there, and what she and Marty had done together. I started to question every woman in our lives who had bigger breasts than I did. Was his lover that pretty younger mom I'd seen him talking to at the school auction? An old girlfriend? A legal secretary from his office?

Obviously, it was someone who had wanted me to find her cast-off lingerie. Or maybe both she *and* Marty had wanted me to find it, laughing about how clueless I was. Otherwise, why would she have left my house without her underthings?

I never asked Marty about the red lingerie again.

Risking his lying to me would be like pulling out that chopstick in my throat; better to leave it. I couldn't share my suspicions with anyone else, not even KC, or Winnie, who'd heard about nearly every diaper I'd changed. Speaking the words out loud felt too raw. Or worse: if I told anyone, it might make the truth, oddly, more true. If the red lingerie stayed inside my head, I could deny our problems and cherish the moments we were still a family. Thanksgiving dinner. Christmas Eve. Sunday mornings making blueberry pancakes. The kids blowing out the candles on their birthday cakes.

However, I couldn't lie to myself forever. Cheating is not the worst thing you can do to a spouse. I came to the same truth while coping with abuse in my first marriage: emotional abandonment is as destructive as terror and bruises. Withdrawing and making a person feel invisible, the way Marty did with his contempt for my fears, did far more damage than my suspicions about his infidelity. After the way he reacted to my discovery of the red lingerie, I couldn't contemplate sex with Marty without crying. Which, I promise, is not an aphrodisiac.

I didn't know what to do. We'd been married for almost two decades. I still loved him. Did infidelity mean he didn't love me? What else had he lied to me about? What on earth would we tell the children if we split? How was I going to pay for health insurance if we got divorced? Could we stay married if we never had sex again?

At the end of my weekly yoga class, I'd lie on my back in *Savasana*. The teacher always emphasized the pose as the most important time of practice, even though we were all just lying there. She said the posture signified rest and renewal, the end of one life and the beginning of another. My life made me feel like I was stuck in poured concrete. As badly as I'd ever craved anything in my life, I wanted someone to hold me and look in my eyes with love again. Most of all, I wanted Marty to. I let the tears roll down my cheeks onto my purple yoga mat because I knew he was never going to.

During the two years we stayed together after the lingerie discovery, there were other red flags in my and Marty's marriage, of course, problems more subtle than our lack of sexual connection. Behind our shiny front doors, we became adept at compartmentalizing the petty bickering over who made the bed each day, or how long a delay was acceptable before returning a spouse's phone call. ("Sometime before I die," was what Marty once told me.) It was harder, for me, to dismiss years of his forgetting Mother's Day, the business trips he scheduled on my birthday, the time he took the necklace he'd bought me for our anniversary and gave it to his mother because he'd forgotten her birthday.

As if I were swallowing gum, I sucked down my feelings on the nights he walked through our front door three hours late. Or when I took out the trash and found him sitting in his BMW, in our alley, finishing a call while I'd been waiting at the candlelit dinner table for an hour, wondering where the hell he was. How ironic that during this time I wrote a book, *Mommy Wars*, about work-family balance. Yet I showed up solo to Timmy's baseball games, most kiddie birthday parties, and the annual parent-teacher conferences, and I got into bed each night next to a man who refused to come home before nine o'clock and never asked how my and the kids' days had gone.

No one could see this from the outside. Our marriage appeared so idyllic that the Philadelphia *Star* featured us, and our redbrick town house, on the cover for a real estate broadsheet on the gentrification of Rittenhouse Square. The inside spread showed off the house's inlaid floors and fireplaces. When the issue first came out, Marty plastered the reprints across the coffee table in his law firm waiting room. He also hung a framed copy in our entrance hall. I cringed at how matronly the woman in the photo looked. I wore a pink pseudo-Chanel top over a striped black and pink skirt, my makeup carefully applied, my hair styled in a conservative blonde bob. I looked like I was auditioning to be a politician's wife. We had our arms draped lovingly around each other's waists, but as the photographer clicked away I kept thinking how unfamiliar it felt to have Marty hold me, how long it had been since I'd smelled his neck.

Whenever I passed the *Star* cover Marty had hung in our hallway, which happened about twenty times a day, the worst part was looking at that woman's face staring back at me: a plastic pink-lipstick grin forming a half-circle under mascaraed eyes. I appeared vaguely confused, like an Alzheimer's patient thinking, *How did I get here again?* I felt baffled by the woman I saw. Whom was she trying to convince that this was the perfect life?

Then came the day the radiologist's office called. I was washing the breakfast dishes after taking the kids to school.

"Ma'am, there's a spot on your annual mammogram we need to check out," the scheduler said in a practiced, kind voice she probably learned in cancer training school.

Instead of bursting into sobs as I held a wet sponge in one hand and the phone in the other, instead of feeling scared and horrified at the possibility that I had breast cancer like my dead mother and would die an ugly death leaving two motherless young children, I hung up and dialed Winnie, my voice giddy with . . . *joy*.

"Hey, Win, the radiologist says I have a mark on my left breast. If I have a double mastectomy, I'll have a really good excuse to never have sex with Marty again, right? I'll never have to have sex with *anyone ever again*!"

My voice cracked like I'd had too many glasses of champagne. There was a long moment of silence as Winnie took this in.

"Les," she finally said. "Listen to yourself. You'd rather die than have sex with your own husband?"

She made a good point. What had happened to me that I could be glib about cancer?

The lab eventually confirmed the black spot on the film was a false positive. Of course, I was relieved. However, Winnie's complete silence on the phone following my crazy no-sex-ever-again confession, her shock at what marriage had taken from me, made me cringe more than the mammogram contraption squeezing my flesh. Like a bell I couldn't unring, it echoed inside me as months of fruitless couples therapy went by, and I realized I was never going to have sex with Marty again, because one day, when I mustered enough courage, I was going to ask him for a divorce.

———————

"Found him!" I crowed triumphantly over the phone to KC the next morning, taking a sip of Citarella's French roast from my *Little Miss Sunshine* mug. I was out on the slate deck with the Southampton rays warming my skin. KC was already at work. After leaving the *Star*, she'd become the CEO of an international save-the-world nonprofit with a long acronym like SFFRRAWNGO. I could never quite remember what it stood for.

"Congratulations, you cougar." She pronounced it *couga*.

"His name is Dylan," I crowed. "How old do you think he is?"

"Any American male named Dylan was born in the late eight-ies. He's probably not even thirty. You got his number and address, I assume? A young explosives expert is exactly what you need. What are you going to do? Call him?"

Even with her southern accent, the girl could talk fast.

"No way," I said. "I'm going to send him a card and tell him if he comes out to Long Island again, I'd love to take him for a boat ride. You know, to show him how nice the area is, since he only comes here for work. Totally innocent."

Which is exactly what I did.

Later that day, I dropped the stamped note, handwritten on a watercolor reprint of an idyllic beach scene, in the Southampton Village mailbox next to the library on Sea Road.

Three days later, I was at the drugstore dropping off an allergy prescription for Bella, whom Marty was putting on a plane to fly up to the Hamptons the next day. Timmy would join us in a few weeks once baseball camp ended. In the bright red aisles, Man-hattan teenagers who looked like swimsuit models in ninety-dollar Tory Burch flip-flops were buying sunscreen.

My phone rang. I froze when I saw an unfamiliar area code. Could it be . . . Dylan Smyth? I contemplated the screen, as dazed as a red-eyed stoner, as the call went to voice mail.

I abandoned my cart and hurried out to the car in a far corner of the parking lot. I sat there with the windows rolled up so no one but me could hear as I listened to the message on the rental car speakerphone.

"Hi Leslie, this is Dylan . . . Dylan Smyth."

My heart did a somersault.

"Uh . . . hey . . . yeah. Of course I remember you."

His voice, at first, sounded laid-back and sexy. Then he cleared his throat.

"I got your letter today. I really liked meeting you. I would like to take you up on that offer. The boat ride, I mean."

He slowly counted out the ten digits of his cell phone number. Then he said, and spelled, his email address. Twice. Each.

I listened to his message six times. My favorite part came a few seconds before he hung up, when he added one final note: "Please call me. Soon." I loved the urgency of "soon" and the way his drawl cracked like that of an anxious teenaged boy. Which he practically was.

Although I was elated to hear from Dylan Smyth, I forced myself to wait twenty-four hours before returning his call. I didn't want to come off as overeager. Plus I needed a full day and night to calm myself down.

The next day at sunset, after collecting Bella from the Islip airport and getting her settled at home, I drove to the Coopers Beach parking lot. The beach was deserted. Alone in my car watching the waves break, I picked up the phone. My hands shaking, I tapped the numbers Dylan left on my voice mail. It took me three tries to get the sequence right.

He answered after two rings. I had no idea what to say. I forced the words out.

"Dylan, uh, hi, this is . . . Leslie?"

I sounded like an ICU patient whose breathing tube had recently been removed.

"You know, Leslie Morgan. From the airport?"

I felt as if I had swallowed a tennis racket.

"Ahhh . . ." I heard on the line. It sounded like he was smiling over the phone. My chest unzipped. It seemed so unfamiliar, so *nice*, that a man who was not a relative, a waiter, or the plumber wanted to talk to me.

"Leslie, um, thanks for calling me back."

He sounded as anxious as I felt.

"I was hoping I'd hear back from you. It was funny when I got your note. At first I thought it was an early birthday card . . . my birthday is coming up. Then I realized it was *you*."

There was silence. I attempted to take a normal breath. The intensity of male energy, after a twenty-year absence, felt as revitalizing as inhaling smelling salts.

Then he said, "Wait a sec—I need to pull my truck over. I'm on my way to see my daughter."

He spoke easily, like he'd already told me he had a child, as if we had a casual intimacy with the particulars of each other's lives. I pictured Dylan, sitting in his truck, pulled over on the side of a Virginia country road, windows down, his tanned forearm hanging out the driver's door.

"Nice," I said, even though he seemed young to have kids. "How old is she?"

"Five. She's . . ." He sighed. "Amazing."

I was about to ask how long he'd been divorced when he cut me off.

"I want to be honest here, Leslie. My wife and I are separated. She's still in our house with my daughter, and I rent a condo near my office. I don't think we're gonna make it over time, but I care for her. I love our daughter. I still have dinner with them every night."

Dylan paused as a truck rumbled by. Dating a married man was not something I'd ever considered doing. Separated, however, was okay, especially because he was being up-front about his marital situation, and I wasn't technically divorced yet myself. I sat motionless in my car, stunned by how transparent he was being. And he wasn't done.

"The thing is, Leslie, I didn't date much in college. I'm from a small town. I was shy and playing lacrosse all the time. She was my first girlfriend. It felt right at the time, but now . . . We've been separated for about six months. I got married too young. I'm figuring out what to do. How's that for a lot of honesty from someone whose coffee you knocked over in an airport?"

I'd been pressing my cell phone so hard against my head, my ear felt like a slice of Velveeta smashed between my skull and the phone.

"Hmm . . . actually, I'm into honesty, Dylan." I tried out saying his name. I liked the way it sounded. "I haven't had much of it in my life lately."

Taking a deep breath to relax, I decided to be as blunt and bold as he'd been. *Leap and the net will appear* was one of my favorite new sayings. I leapt.

"So, have you ever been with anyone else, besides your wife, since you got married?"

"Fair question, I guess." Dylan didn't sound uneasy anymore, either. "The answer is yes. Last year. Someone at work. Which was stupid."

He laughed painfully, like he had rocks in his throat.

"When I ended it, she called my home. My wife said if I ever did it again, she'd leave. We live in a small town, like I said. My mom and dad own a house up the block from us. My job, my kid . . . my wife would take everything. So, we're doing this separation thing so that both of us have time to figure out what we want."

"Oh, that's pretty extreme."

"You have no idea, Leslie. My wife saw this therapist on *Oprah* who says I have to give her my phone and computer passwords and she can check all my emails and texts twenty-four seven. You know, because I betrayed her, and this is how we rebuild our trust."

"Wow. I'm not sure that's the way to rebuild trust, Dylan."

"Tell me about it. And trust—I can be trustworthy. But that's our second-biggest problem, not the first. The real problem is I cannot live the rest of my life in a monogamous relationship. I'm too young for that."

Another truck roared by in the background.

"Anyway, I want to let you know something else about me. It's about you, actually. You realize I'm younger, right?"

"Um, yes."

By twenty years, Dylan. I didn't say that part. I hoped he didn't know how much older I actually was.

"I've always wondered about older women. A woman like you. I'm twenty-nine. Is that a problem for you?"

Was he kidding?

"No, it's actually a plus, Dylan. A big plus."

Dylan laughed.

"God, you're beautiful, Leslie."

Me?

Me?

Me?

I couldn't remember the last time Marty had told me I looked pretty. Possibly never. It felt as priceless as finding a red diamond to hear a man—a younger man, beautiful himself, someone who'd met me only once—tell me that.

"You look like you're from Manhattan," he added.

I stopped myself from bursting out laughing. Dylan Smyth surely didn't know it, but that's the one compliment every woman from Philadelphia secretly dreams about hearing.

"My rule is that no one gets hurt here," he continued. Clearly, he'd thought about this, and had already decided that he wanted to sleep with me. "Not you. Not me. Most especially, not my daughter. But I want to see you. I come to Long Island for monthlies, the second Friday of the month. Can we meet then?"

That was in two weeks. It was obvious what we were going to do when he got here. I took a deep breath and exhaled two decades' worth of sexual frustration.

"Dylan, I can't imagine anything I'd enjoy more," I said.

If my grandmother could have seen my face as I hung up my phone, she would have said I was the cat with a canary in its mouth now.

Was I thirteen again?

For the next two weeks, every weekday afternoon around five thirty, Dylan Smyth called me from his Silverado on the drive home to have dinner with his daughter. It was like high school, when a boy calling me was the apex of my week. One night, I actually wrote *I ♥ DS* on an old Citarella receipt while talking to him.

Even though we hadn't met up yet, I felt like this was *Gone with the Wind*, with me playing Belle Watling, the wise madam who intuits that men need someone to listen to them, even more than they need sexual variety. I was learning a lot from Dylan about unhappily semimarried twenty-nine-year-old men. Plus he had a very arresting phone voice.

"You are helping me so much, Leslie," he told me one evening, his pickup truck stopped by the side of the road so we could finish our conversation before he pulled in the driveway. "It's like that Zach Brown song, 'God didn't make me a one-woman man.' And Zach Brown is married with something like five kids and he sings all the time about how much he loves his wife. Can't I love my wife and want another woman, too?"

If my own husband had asked me this, I would have wanted to cut his vocal cords. Maybe I was being naive, but as far as I could tell, Dylan had no desire to hurt his wife. He'd gotten married a few months after college and become a father right away. He wasn't even thirty years old. He'd had sex with three people. I'd be going crazy myself. Maybe anyone would be. And although perhaps it was unethical for him to pursue me, given that he might stay married, I saw that as his choice and his conscience to wrestle with, not mine.

I didn't know how much I was helping him, but I was pretty sure he could help me when he came to Long Island, which was in four days, six hours, and twenty-seven minutes. First, though, I was going to have to buy at least one new bra. Mine were all worn-out beige with sturdy straps, married-mom armor bras, not a seductive stitch of black or lace anywhere. However, except for an excuse to buy new lingerie, I didn't want anything material from Dylan Smyth. I did not want his money. I certainly didn't want to make babies with him. I didn't want to ride in his pickup truck. Or go out with him on Valentine's Day. Or wake up in the morning next to him.

I didn't want any of that from Dylan or any man.

I'd married two husbands full of confidence, hopeful and in love, and both marriages had eventually made me feel as if my hands were nailed to a Formica table. As KC often says, *Marriage is a sucky institution for women*. The last thing I wanted was to be someone's wife again. But I also was looking for far more than a one-night stand. What I needed is hard to admit because it sounds egotistical, but it's the truth and it goes a lot deeper than mere ego: I wanted men to desire me. I wanted to feel good about myself, attractive and valued, after the heartbreak of my early abusive marriage followed by almost two decades of Marty's sexual negativity and betrayals.

How could that be too much to ask?

———————

A Victoria's Secret dressing room is not the ideal place to rebuild one's sexual self-esteem. Especially at forty-nine. A few days earlier during plank pose, a yoga teacher had poked my abs and told me to suck in the small, flesh-covered pouch of marbles near my belly button. "That doesn't suck in," I whispered back, humiliated. But surprisingly, in the Victoria's Secret dressing room, my potbelly, framed by sixty dollars' worth of black lace push-up bra and matching lace thong, looked passable. Possibly even cute.

On the drive home, it occurred to me, with a jolt, that Dylan might expect oral sex. A wave of anxiety made my gut flip. It had been three years since I'd given a blow job. Had I forgotten how? Did I ever really know how? Fortunately, you can Google anything. I couldn't wait to get back to the beach house and my computer.

Once home, surrounded by pink Victoria's Secret bags, I typed "How to Give a Blow Job" and waited for guidance from the universe. Awash in paranoia, I actually looked around to see if anyone was monitoring me. Of course, no one was. But I felt like Mom was slut-shaming me from heaven.

I scrolled down a page of links to porn sites. A blog by a former dominatrix caught my attention. I double-clicked. The first thing she wrote was, "Ladies, your grandmother was wrong. The way to a man's heart is not through his stomach. It's through his dick."

She said the key to a good blow job is a good hand job. I'd never thought of it that way. This didn't improve my situation, though. Personally, I always found giving a hand job even harder than giving a blow job. But the sheer practicality of her advice reassured me. I felt like writing notes in pen on the back of my hand.

The subsequent, far more valuable, bullet point was, "If he likes what you're doing, don't stop."

Absolutely. I could remember that one.

Her final tip was the best one. "Every man will tell you that enthusiasm for his dick, his most prized possession, is *the* critical success factor for an outstanding oral sex experience."

After three years off the job, *enthusiasm* was not going to be my problem. My shoulders unclenched. Maybe this would be okay.

My phone buzzed with a text from Dylan that afternoon as I was writing in my sunny porch office. I looked down at the screen. It was the name and address of the hotel he'd booked. I looked the place up online. It was one of those boutique suburban chains, a Sheraton dressed up to imitate an expensive New York apartment, thirty minutes from my beach house and thirty minutes from his Long Island office.

I clicked through the website photos of conference rooms, vast inviting terraces, an indoor pool, and various suites. I tried to picture the two of us alone together in bed in the rooms. I had never met someone in a hotel to have sex. I couldn't imagine what it would feel like. Sleazy? Anonymous? Smoking hot?

Was I really going to do this?

The next morning, I woke up early, too fired up to sleep. I took Bella to the beach, then spent all day getting ready, because I had zero ability to concentrate long enough to write a sentence or do anything mundane like pay bills or fold laundry. I showered and shaved my legs and underarms. Walking through the living room, I caught sight of myself in the mirror over the fireplace and started hyperventilating, imagining what it would be like to see this man again. I gave myself a pedicure and painted my toenails fuchsia. I soaked my skin in body cream that smelled like bergamot oranges. I practiced deep breathing.

Was this finally happening?

I checked my phone in between ablutions.

This is crazy! read a text from Dylan. Then he sent a smiley emoji. I can't wait.

At five o'clock, I dropped Bella at her friend Alice's for a carefully orchestrated sleepover. Alone at home, I changed into my new lingerie and pulled on my favorite sleeveless black sundress and sandals. Right before I left home, and twice in the car, I touched up my eyeliner and lipstick.

I hoped I looked good enough, but honestly, I had no idea what he was expecting me to look like.

I was so jittery, I drove five miles under the speed limit, clutching the steering wheel like a grandma. A dump truck honked at me, and I flinched like it was a gunshot. At the postmodern hotel portico, I parked a few spaces from the entrance. Practically tiptoeing, I made my way into the air-conditioned lobby, sat on a Creamsicle-orange love seat, and began hyperventilating again. My fingers quivering, I texted Dylan.

I'm here but I can't breathe.

He sent me another smiley emoji.

Be right down.

Watching the elevator doors, I tried to steady my heart rate. It wasn't easy.

Then, the elevator pinged, announcing its arrival in the lobby. The two doors opened and there he was. Dylan walked toward me like Brad Pitt in a slow-motion movie scene. He was shorter than I remembered from the Philly airport. His eyes were bluer.

"Hi," he said awkwardly as he stopped in front of me. He put his hands in his khaki pockets and then took them back out. I laughed, unable to move, frozen to the fuzzy orange couch like a panicky four-year-old waiting for shots at the doctor's office.

He took my hands and pulled me up for a hug. His body felt strong and warm against mine, his brawny back slippery with muscles under his soft cotton shirt.

"It's nice to see you again, Leslie," he said, holding me at arm's length, smiling like he was trying not to break into a huge grin. We were both obviously so happy to see each other, like teenagers on a first date, that my anxiety dissipated, replaced with a surge of adrenaline that made me feel as if I'd heard my favorite song on the radio.

We drove in his rental car to the closest restaurant, the Cheesecake Factory. I wanted to sit next to him in our teal Naugahyde booth, so our legs could touch and my forearm could brush his accidentally, but that felt geeky, so I sat across from him with my hands clasped together on the table to keep them still. To any outsider, it might have looked as if we were simply acquaintances. Not two people twenty years apart in age who met randomly at an airport and were going to shamelessly rip each other's clothes off in a hotel room in less than an hour.

I couldn't follow our conversation thread. Maybe there wasn't one. My effort went into breathing normally and proffering small talk about his work and my writing. We ordered, dishes arrived, and we ate. I didn't taste a bite.

Then the pace screeched to super slow motion. We drove back to the hotel. We got into the elevator. He pushed the button for the ninth floor. The air in the elevator felt suctioned up by our silence. We walked down the hallway to his room.

Inside the twilit hotel suite, the door banged shut, and we turned to each other a few feet inside the room. I dropped my purse on the floor. He cupped my face in his hands. Then, for the first time in years, I was being kissed, slowly, softly. And kissed. And kissed. His mouth was delicious.

Without stopping, we moved to the couch by a window. His hand inched up the soft inside of my left inner thigh.

I folded my hands over his to stop him.

"Dylan, wait a minute. I need to go slowly. Because . . ." I paused, my cheeks flushed like a child with fever. "I haven't had sex in over three years."

I was afraid of how he'd take this news. I needn't have worried. His cobalt eyes lit up like he was getting an expensive present.

Incredulous, he asked, "You're a MILF *virgin*?" Whatever a

MILF was. He took my hands and held them, looking honored. Then his face lit up. "A virgin with about a hundred times more experience than me."

He took me in his arms and started kissing me again. After a few minutes, he reached under my dress and paused with his fingers under my lace thong.

"Can I take this off?" he asked. I nodded wordlessly. I didn't trust my voice.

I unbuttoned his shirt and slipped my hands inside. His tanned chest was hard and smooth, the kind of skin I remembered from making out with eighteen-year-olds in high school. I would have been happy to kiss him and bury my head in his neck and slide my fingers over his muscular pecs for the entire night.

Dylan Smyth had other ideas. He pulled me up to stand about halfway between the king bed and the couch. In one fluid movement, he reached for the hem of my black sundress. Before I could stop him, he'd lifted the dress straight up over my head.

I froze. I was standing in front of him wearing only my black heels and the black lace Victoria's Secret bra.

The lighting in the room came from two flattering yellow wall sconces. But embarrassment made the hairs stand up all over my body. Had he ever seen a woman my age nude? I had given birth to two eight-pound, full-fucking-term babies. My belly showed the telltale signs. I'd nursed both babies as well, and at times my breasts looked, from my view at least, like wet paper towels.

It felt as if a strobe light were scanning my body, accompanied by a police megaphone booming, *Step away from the old wrinkled lady now!* I looked down at my saggy breasts in my bra and the cellulite on my belly. I wanted to scream in horror and cover myself in shame.

He took a step back. "Oh. My. God," he said.

What was he thinking? Was he going to leave, even though it was his hotel room?

"Oh my God, Leslie," he said again. "You . . . you have a spectacular body."

Me? The same person Marty told, again and again, *you don't meet my needs sexually*? The one whose husband insisted she wear a robe so he didn't have to see her naked? I did *not* have a spectacular body. How could he see it that way?

I felt like Dylan might be joking. Were we even looking at the same physical entity? I started to tremble involuntarily. How could I possibly trust this stranger, even if he was the best-looking man I'd ever kissed?

"Leslie, you have to know this."

He paused and looked right at my face. He grabbed my hip-bones and squeezed them, and then moved his hands behind me to cup my ass with his palms. He drew me to him, and then buried his face between my breasts. I could feel him getting hard against me. He took a deep breath and then let out a full-body sigh. He looked up, his eyes blue and sincere.

"You have nothing to be embarrassed about."

He'd read my mind.

"Your body isn't perfect," he said, cupping my very imperfect breasts. "Although maybe it was when you were eighteen." He smiled, and ran his hands slowly down my rib cage and over my hips, as if he wanted to absorb my skin with his palms. "Your life . . . makes you even more beautiful. Every inch of you."

Dylan slowly slipped his hands under his waistband to show me the line of dark hair disappearing under his boxers. He un-zipped his pants and slowly pulled the boxers toward the floor. And let's just say, I got over my embarrassment.

———

Later, I lay naked in Dylan's arms on the titanic hotel bed, which spread like an ocean around us. At some point he had turned off the lights. The hotel room was now filled with bluish gloaming twi-light. My body sank into the soft mattress as if I'd spent an hour in a eucalyptus-scented sauna. I felt delirious with sex, sore in all the right places, smelling salty like Dylan's saliva and sweat and more. Although here's a secret: the sex itself was awkward and fumbling, and I didn't even get close to coming. I was so anxious I couldn't get wet. Dylan didn't know how to get me wet. We were as tense as you'd expect two strangers in a hotel room would be. None of that mattered. I was overjoyed to be having sex again, even mediocre sex. And apparently, Dylan didn't know the difference.

His responsiveness and enthusiasm made up for his inexperience. At one point, prior to the actual, much-anticipated consummation, as we were kissing and I was in general marveling at how tanned and smooth his torso was, I noticed a whitish scar on his right shoulder. Without thinking, I leaned down and kissed it. I flushed for a second. Was that the kind of thing I'd do to my kids if they had a boo-boo? To my relief, Dylan lay still as if he enjoyed it, closing his eyes to absorb the sensation more fully. So I let my lips travel down to his right nipple. I kept them there and sucked gently, all wet and warm the way I liked it, using the tip of my tongue for emphasis. This made Dylan shudder and moan. Which was unexpected and very nice. What came next was even nicer.

"Ahh," he said. "No one has ever done that to me before."

And I thought: really? Wow. He was actually more the virgin than I was.

We lay there, nude under the cool sheets in the shadows, his muscular arms wrapped around me, for what felt like hours. I wanted the night to last forever. I pressed my butt and the backs of my thighs against his smooth abs, soft penis, and scratchy pubic hair like I was trying to use my skin to memorize the contours and unfamiliar sensations. I'd forgotten how good it felt to be in a man's arms, and the indescribable feeling of having a cock inside me again.

"You haven't missed a beat, babe," Dylan said in a husky voice from behind me, hugging me tighter, burying his face in the hair at the nape of my neck. "I've never been with a woman who enjoyed sex as much as you just did. Have you always been like this?"

The answer was so complicated, I didn't even give it a try. I had no desire to darken the moment with tales of Marty's twisted attempts to shame me sexually. Instead, I rolled over and pressed my naked body against his naked body and kissed him.

Dylan kissed me back. Then he whispered, laughing a little, "You're pretty pleased with yourself, aren't you?"

I closed my eyes and buried my face in his neck. I couldn't stop smiling.

Because I was.

At about ten the next morning, Alice's mom dropped off Bella. I sat on the living room couch, in a daze, drinking black coffee. My lips felt like ripe raspberries, bruised and swollen. I was still wearing my new bra and thong under my pajamas. Every few minutes, I caught a delectable whiff of Dylan. He was like perfume on my hands and skin. Every inhale was like taking the last toke of a joint before entering rehab. I was not planning to shower until I saw Dylan again. I hoped that would be soon. However, it had felt too awkward to bring it up at midnight when we'd said good-bye at his hotel room door, so I'd said nothing.

Seeing Bella, I remembered that mothers usually greeted their daughters after sleepovers.

"Did you have a nice time, honey?" I forced out the correct words. Bella didn't notice how stiff they sounded.

"Yeah, Mom. It was great." Her words echoed like they were reverberating through that voice distortion machine the kids' favorite radio station used to disguise a caller's identity. "How was your night, Mother?"

Bella was looking at herself in the mirror, twisting a strand of hair, not paying attention to me. Which was good, because I could feel myself blush pink and freeze.

I managed to squeak out, "Um . . . I went to bed early!"

All through that day, I felt as if the barista had slipped an extra espresso shot into my latte. The sky was a shade bluer; I could make out individual blades of grass on the neighbor's front lawn.

After lunch, Bella and I drove to Coopers Beach. I pulled the car headfirst into a space overlooking the sand so, as the kids and I joked, the car could have an ocean view, too. I got out to sniff the

salty air. Bella grabbed her beach bag, adjusted her Ray-Ban avia-
tors, and went off to find Alice.

It was a sunny, breezy weekday in June, and Coopers Beach
was packed. The adults on the beach were almost all moms, with
a few grandparents, babysitters, and nannies sprinkled about. Kids
of all ages were spread out on towels and splashing in the surf. At
first, the most noticeable men were the skinny teenaged employees
trolling the parking lot for cars without the coveted "Southampton
Village Resident" decal assiduously displayed on the rear window.

And then I noticed . . .

The lifeguards.

Now, the Town of Southampton usually staffs three to four lifeguards at each twenty-foot-tall white lifeguard chair. This means
that I probably saw over a thousand Southampton lifeguards wearing their signature red swim trunks over the course of twenty years
of marriage. The waves here are rough. There are frequent riptides.
Lifeguards are a necessity. Part of the scenery, so to speak.

Not today.

Apparently, in my married state, I had failed to notice that lifeguards are tanned young men who work without their shirts on. I
did now. Despite Dylan, I was not yet looking *for* men. I was looking *at* men. I was not ready to fall in love again. I wasn't entirely
sure if I was ready for any kind of lasting intimacy with a man. But
I was definitely ready to fantasize about it.

Instead of heading home to write, I decided to stay at the beach.
I stumbled to an open square of sand and spread out my towel. I
felt the tiniest bit drunk. Hanging out at Coopers as a spanking
new divorcée who'd had sex again for the first time in three years
felt like watching a soft-core porn movie. I had the bizarre sensation of seeing the world in color for the first time.

There was one dark-haired, tanned lifeguard who kept turning
my head. I casually moved my towel a few feet (okay, several yards)
closer. I couldn't tell if he was eighteen or thirty-eight, but he was
dazzling. Tousled dark hair, a deep tan, ripped calf muscles. Bi-
secting his washboard abs was a narrow, vertical strip of dark hair

leading into his red bathing suit. I hoped my sunglasses hid how much I was staring.

The lifeguards were not the only men on the beach with their shirts off. There were dozens of them! I did not stop smiling for four hours. Although I'd spent decades of my younger life as a feminist railing against male objectification of women, and two wrongs definitely don't make a right, objectifying those lifeguards felt as refreshing and innocent as a glass of lemonade. There is no way to prove this, but I think a few of those shirtless men were looking back at me in my pink and black bikini. I wanted them to objectify me; I *hoped* they were objectifying me.

Then, as I walked back to the car in a daze, a twentysomething jogger with washboard abs (did every man under thirty have them today?) ran toward me. Our eyes met briefly. He whispered "Hi" as he passed, leaving a trace of twentysomething sweat wafting after him.

Where had all these men been for the past two decades? And me. Where the hell had I been?

But even more entertaining than spying on lifeguards and joggers was imagining seeing Dylan again. With his shirt off. He had worked a form of magic on me. It was like being given a bite of a sandwich, and realizing I'd been starving. Ravenous to be held, to be loved, to let a man inside me. To my surprise, the first reward of a starvation diet is that when you're famished, everything tastes amazing.

Dylan didn't call me for several days. This struck me as strange, since we'd been talking nearly every day for weeks, and I felt closer to him now that we'd had sex. But since I was out of touch with modern hooking-up protocol, I didn't reach out to him. Then he sent me a text that read Leslie, I'm dying to see you again, can you meet me in Baltimore? We set a date via text, I booked my flight, and he sent me the address of an Inner Harbor hotel. I picked out a white eyelet minidress and bought a new set of white lace Victoria's Secret lingerie.

I was even more excited to see him again, because I wasn't as frazzled or disbelieving as the first time. My body hummed with the sensation of being on the verge of having sex, craving every kiss and touch. I kept finding myself at my desk, or washing dishes, daydreaming about what we were going to do this time around. I had dozens of questions to ask him, things I wanted to talk to him about, and a list in my head of small sex acts, like kissing his nipples, that I guessed he'd never experienced before, that I would introduce him to. I could not believe how lucky I'd gotten, to meet, and then track down, this exquisite, smart, open younger man who wanted my body, but didn't seem to want anything more.

Then, twenty-four hours before my flight, he sent me a text:

I need to talk to you today. I'm sorry. This will probably be the last time.

What? Why? I had been counting the minutes until I could see him again. My brain couldn't grasp that the first time with Dylan might turn out to be the last time. But my heart, rocking behind my ribs, got the news loud and clear.

This time, I didn't force myself to wait to call him. I drove all the way to East Hampton, to Georgica, my favorite beach, to cushion whatever news he had for me. I parked in the public lot squeezed between two hotel-sized beach houses. Then, once again, I dialed Dylan Smyth's number from a sweltering car overlooking the ocean.

"Dylan, hey, it's me. Can you talk?"

"Yes. Thank God you called."

I heard him get up to shut his office door.

"Leslie, I'm dying inside. This weekend I took my daughter camping. I kept looking at her playing in the creek, and I couldn't stop thinking about you, and it all felt wrong because I'm still technically married and my wife would destroy me if she found out. I felt so damn guilty about seeing you, wanting you, and worrying about my wife, it was hell."

He sighed and then inhaled deeply.

"If I didn't like you, it'd be easier. If it weren't for my situation, I'd come see you every week at the beach. But . . . my daughter is so little. And I like you. It'd be easier if I didn't. You're not the one doing anything wrong, but I kind of am. I don't think it's going to work with my wife, but I have to stop seeing you now, or I'll be in trouble because she'll catch me one way or the other. I'll call you again if I figure this out. But now—I can't do this right now."

I sat in my car, windows rolled up, as my heart crumpled in on itself. The summer humidity made the sweat pool in the crook of my collarbone. Despite the heat, I felt cold with dismay. In one measly night, Dylan had made me feel sensual and feminine again, like the blissed-out model with her eyes half-closed in perfume ads. I wanted *more more more* of Dylan Smyth, not *none*.

"Hold on, Dylan, give me a minute to take this in."

Maybe I should have seen it coming. Perhaps he was simply jettisoning me now that he'd gotten a tryst with an older woman on his conquest belt. Many people believe that's all men want from women, anyway, and maybe they're right. What I thought likelier: Dylan Smyth couldn't trust that I wanted only sex (and respect) from him. He probably worried that over time, I'd want things he couldn't give, wheedling blow jobs and pussy for money and security. And, if spurned, I'd retaliate by blowing his cover and calling his wife, like stereotypically angry, vindictive women allegedly always do.

I wasn't the kind of woman who would ever want to hurt Dylan or reveal what we'd done to his wife; I'd been on the other side, and I didn't want to make the situation any messier than it already was. But also, the idea of Dylan divorcing his wife for me made me dry heave. I wanted to be held, and yes, to be fucked, by a sexy, younger, unthreatening, uncomplicated man. But anything vaguely resembling a commitment jolted me like hitting a pothole on the highway.

Damn it. How many older men, fresh off divorce, sought shallow sexual relationships with pretty, pliable, twentysomething women with impunity, with approbation, with a nod of under-standing from our culture? Why couldn't I do the same? Was our culture really that hypocritical, that sexist, that traditional? Once in my life, I wanted to act like a man and get away with it without society's criticism or ostracism.

I pushed the button on the driver's-side door to roll down my windows to catch a gust of ocean air. I felt like a kid watching her ice cream cone fall onto the sidewalk after one lick. No more Dylan. No more cute crooked front tooth. No more stolen late-afternoon phone calls from his truck on the side of the road. No more sex. It was too much to lose all at once.

"Dylan, okay, you have to do what you feel is right. But tell me one good thing. Something I can remember when I'm missing you. A memento of how you woke me up after so many years of being asleep, of being dead to men. I don't ever want to forget how you made me feel."

There was silence on the other end of the line, and I could hear the waves crashing. He sighed like an hourly employee about to head to an assembly line shift at a job he despised. Then Dylan made a husky sound under his breath, the same rueful noise he made when I first knocked over his coffee in the airport a month before.

"Oh, Leslie, there are so many things about you that any man would go crazy for. I love your body—your shoulders, your stomach, your blue eyes, your blonde hair. You have the softest skin. Your lips . . ." He blew out a big puff of air, as if gathering strength to cram ten bullet points into one paragraph.

Then he laughed, a chip of joy mixed with the regret in his voice as he began again.

"You have the most spectacular ass. Don't you ever let anyone tell you it's too big—it's perfect. I loved being your first after so long. I can't believe what it's like to be with a woman who lets me know what she likes. I'll never forget you.

"But I guess the best thing I can say is that . . . Oh, Leslie, it's that you remind me of my wife. In all the best ways."

I was so appalled by this, I couldn't respond. Dylan meant it as a bittersweet compliment, the biggest one he could think to give me. But to me, being compared to his wife was almost an insult, the most confusing accolade any man could have offered me at that moment. After a long silence, I said, "Okay, Dylan. Take good care of yourself." I hung up the phone and threw it on the passenger seat. I drove home, alone, his words echoing in my head.

In a raw twist of timing, forty-eight hours later, I returned to Philadelphia for my and Marty's final divorce hearing, to officially become an un-wife.

The date had been set for months (getting legally divorced in Pennsylvania takes *forever*). According to my lawyer, it was not the kind of appointment you reschedule. So instead of coming back to Philly blissed out by a Baltimore sex-fest with Dylan, I flew home alone and cried in the Odyssey in the airport parking lot before heading to family court. I wasn't sure if I was crying over Marty or Dylan or both and it didn't matter; I felt filled with *endings*, sad about the past, while also excited about the future, a tumultuous emotional combination.

This was the official, legal end of my and Marty's union. I'd walk into the courthouse married, and walk out a divorcée. I had the sensation of being weightless at the prospect of getting our divorce finalized, because for years I had thought I was handcuffed to Marty and his condescension. I also felt dirty, ashamed of our marital failure. I dreaded dissolving my marriage in front of a judge, a stranger who'd never met us, who didn't care what our children's names were, and whom we'd never see again.

Everything about the day felt peculiar. It was like the black-and-white beginning of *The Wizard of Oz* right before the twister comes. The barometric pressure drops, the farmhands look at Dorothy quizzically, and she knows something's off with Toto and the horses and the wind, but she's not sure what, exactly, is about to happen, or whether it's going to be pleasant, painful, or both.

My lawyer texted me directions to a seldom-used underground court entrance to avoid the long lines filled with people called for jury duty.

An impressively large security guard by the metal detector remarked to us, "Y'all here to get married?"

"To each other?" I quizzed him.

"Yep. You both look so happy. Like you're gonna live happily ever after."

My lawyer and I locked eyes and burst out laughing. On the day I was getting divorced, how could anyone mistake me for a bride? My wedding date and divorce date were like that old joke about boats, that the two best days are the day you buy your boat, and the day you sell it. The guard had it backward. I was happy to be getting unmarried, not married.

We took the elevator down a floor, emerging into a narrow, semidark hallway outside a half dozen subterranean courtrooms. My lawyer left to locate Marty's lawyer. Marty himself, wearing a gray suit, pressed white shirt, and blue tie as if he were heading to a job interview, stood in silhouette at the end of the hallway, checking his phone. I felt nauseated at the idea of exchanging pleasantries with him.

My attorney believed that given Marty's fury and the months of petty motions his lawyer had already filed, even after today's proceedings it could take months to settle custody, divide our assets, and resolve several complicated issues related to Marty's partnership. Marty didn't want me anymore, but he also didn't want to let go of any of our married life without a fight. I couldn't figure out why a man who hadn't been in love with me for years would still want to punish me for not wanting to be with him any longer. It felt like another layer of betrayal, as excruciating as his laughter when I found the red lingerie. Instead of approaching our divorce with *Hey, we had a good run, thanks for bearing and raising two awesome kids with me, have a nice life*, Marty's stance seemed to be *You fucking bitch, you deserve nothing from me and if I get my way, the kids will hate you and you'll be eating cat food at seventy-five*.

My mom had been through a messy divorce, too. Her and Dad's relationship had begun like a 1950s fairy tale, at the Brattle Theater candy counter in Cambridge at a time when American men wore felt hats and skinny black ties and women wore cashmere sweater sets. Mom fell for him, a poor Oklahoma boy from an uneducated Baptist family, and broke off her engagement to her brother's boarding school roommate. Mom's salary as a special education teacher paid for Dad to go to Harvard Law School, which led to his long corporate career and judgeship. I'd grown up watching her whitewash Dad's lack of sophistication by throwing bridge parties for the law firm associates, presenting stunningly at social events as a snappy sexpot in her 1970s halter dresses, and beating the partners at golf and tennis outings, all while raising us unaided while Dad spent twelve-hour days at the office. And we kids had not been easy to civilize.

Then, after thirty-two years together, pretty much as soon as she'd raised us and gone back to being a teacher full-time, their relationship collapsed. My father decided he wanted to start over with a younger woman. I didn't have a choice when it came to loving Mom. Dad apparently did.

Mom was fifty-five. I was twenty-two. In my mother's WASP world, gentlemen did not leave their wives. She was the first woman in her family to stare down divorce. I heard her crying behind her bedroom door, stunned and shamed by Dad's abandonment.

Even worse was something I didn't know at the time: Dad tried, mightily, to mangle my mother financially, despite her years of support. Dad had a pension and investments. Mom earned less than a tenth of his judicial salary teaching autistic children. Despite her parents' wealth, she hadn't inherited enough to live on. I suspect Dad thought he'd get away with landslide penury because he was a judge. Mom fought back. She confronted his fiancée at social events, bringing the woman to tears. She called his former law firm partners at their offices. During billable hours! It got *ugly*.

I myself, having recently graduated from Harvard, was working at *Seventeen* magazine in New York and was fiscally responsible for the first time in my life. "Responsible" is a relative term, since I earned only seventeen thousand dollars a year, but still. In my sophomoric flush of independence and feminism, I thought Mom cowardly to ask for alimony, to fight to keep the house she'd raised us in, to beg my father for financial support. Oddly, I thought she'd have been a better heroine by going it alone. Like, I don't know, Ophelia or Juliet, who, I should note, both killed themselves.

I didn't realize at the time how important economic independence was, or that she was fighting for respect, not simply a monthly check. At the time, I believed Dad's version. But eventually, a family court judge awarded Mom a generous settlement. When I was older, I came to despise my father's choices, and respect Mom for gritting it out in order to take care of herself. It took guts, pragmatism, and self-respect. It was not until I had to face Marty in divorce proceedings that I realized how strong, and alone, my mother had been.

Twenty-five years after my parents split up, as I eyed my soon-to-be ex-husband, I wished I'd had Mom back, to teach me how to muster some of that same grit. I didn't think my dead mother would understand about Dylan or the lifeguards. I have no evidence she ever experienced an orgasm herself or even enjoyed sex. I'm sure Mom would have cheered me on, regardless. The details were different, but like she had been, I was fighting for my future.

As I stood waiting to go into family court, a woman came out of the bathroom, a gray ghost in the dark hallway. Something about her struck me as familiar. She was tiny, barely five feet in high heels. To my surprise, she walked toward me.

"Leslie, is that you?"

I still couldn't see her face clearly, but I knew her voice. It was Rebecca, the kids' former favorite babysitter. Rebecca had recently graduated from Yale and started working at a child protection agency in downtown Philly, which explained why she was in family court. I never imagined seeing her, or anyone I knew, here, much less that she'd be the only other person in court. She probably didn't know we were getting divorced. How could I explain so many years of disappointment in thirty seconds?

Her smile sank when she saw my face. And then, as if she completely understood, she wrapped her arms around me wordlessly and held me tight, the same way she held the kids when they were afraid of the dark.

"We're getting divorced," I whispered in her ear. "Please don't say hi to Marty. He's been such a dick."

She held me at arm's length, grinning. "Marty who? I don't even think I'd recognize him. Go get 'em. You got this."

She gave me a pat on my tush and click-clacked away, not even looking at Marty, who had crept up behind us and was standing near a long wooden bench, looking at his cell phone again. I'm sure he didn't even know who Rebecca was, even though she'd been in our house a dozen times and slept in our bed when we were out of town together.

After I signed approximately 327 legal documents, I was officially single again. A divorcée. The judge barely acknowledged us. Our paperwork, critical and painful to me, seemed to scarcely register on his daily radar. Marty stuck out his hand to shake mine after we signed the last document, as if we were business associates who'd closed a routine financial transaction. As repulsed as if his hand were a rattlesnake, I shook my head no, unable to speak, and rode the elevator up to the exit alone.

My lawyer had instructed me to dress blandly, so I had on a black blouse, an old flowered skirt, and black heels. Despite my shoes, and the fact that I felt like I'd been run over by a Mack truck, I needed the long walk home in the afternoon sun to put space between the sadness of signing my divorce papers and the house that held my favorite family memories. The summer breeze cooled me off, and although I was still sad, the grief was like watered-down iced tea, weak from ice cubes melting. The melancholy faded away.

A man, about forty, passed me on his bike, heading downtown. He wore a short-sleeved, gray Penn dental school T-shirt and faded jeans. He had strong forearms and windblown brown hair. Something in his face prompted me to smile at him.

A minute later, he circled back. He stopped and leaned his ten-speed bike over on one foot. He had on black Puma sneakers, the kind that cool soccer players wore back in high school.

"I have to tell you," he said, looking at me with basset hound eyes. "I'm not trying to pick you up. But you look so pretty bopping along in your skirt and heels. I had to stop and tell you," he repeated. "You look . . . happy inside. Have a wonderful day."

I stood there holding my purse—as dumbfounded as Dorothy when Glenda tells her to click her heels three times—as he got on his bike and pedaled away.

"I have someone lovely to set you up with," a woman's voice chirped out of my voice mail two days after I officially became a divorcée.

My stomach twisted. This had happened a few times before, as word had trickled out to acquaintances that Marty and I had separated. I knew what was coming. I called her back anyway.

She lived in a large stone house in the Philly suburbs, a stay-at-home mom who had been in my class in college. She'd worked in the mayor's office for three years in her early twenties, then married, quit work, had four kids, and climbed aboard the school-charity-kids carousel with a simplistic gusto I envied but could never match. Her toenails were always painted the coral shade my grandmother favored. The last time I saw her was in Chico's before Marty and I separated. I was trying to use a gift card my mother-in-law had given me, but there was not a single hot outfit in the entire color-coordinated nursing home. My neighbor had filled two dressing rooms with clothes. "My favorite store!" she'd exclaimed.

Today she picked up after two rings. After perfunctory pleasantries, she started telling me about a man named Dave.

"He is so sweet. I knew him from the mayor's office. So sad they split up, but you know how it goes. Of course you do!"

I made a murmur of assent into the mouthpiece.

"He's about your age. Dean of the law school at Widener. He asked if I knew any nice women. You were the first one I thought of!"

She sounded like she was handing me a five-carat diamond. Like she expected me to put out my hand and say, "Thank you so much for this priceless gift," because *of course* I must want to get remarried again as soon as possible to avoid the ostracism, loneliness, and financial and social uncertainty of being a single woman, struggling and stigmatized.

I wanted to groan at the barely masked pity. As a gleefully married woman on the other side of the invisible divorce divide, she could not possibly know that the last thing I wanted was another husband.

"Hey, that is so nice of you!" I told her. "I'm not really dating now, but I'll let you know if I am."

After I hung up, I went to the kitchen computer to Google this Mr. Perfect to be sure I was right in my assumptions. He looked like a clone of Marty. Bald—which, granted, I like. But he was not sexy bald. On the law school website, he looked embarrassed about having no hair. His pinched mouth and frowning forehead telegraphed arrogance and superiority, probably fine qualities for a legal giant. But to me, he resembled the kid on my block growing up who liked to rip wings off flies. Plus he was at least ten, maybe fifteen, years older than I was.

How was any divorced woman in the fiftyish range supposed to feel when this was the attitude of the sisterhood—that after years of sacrificing our careers and independence for our families, a downgrade in husbands was the best we could hope for? I felt the same way when women told me not to fight Marty over money in the divorce. "It's not worth it," almost everyone said, as if imparting great wisdom. *But we are worth it*, I wanted to protest. Statistics prove that women who don't fight for their share of marital assets and alimony almost always experience a significant, demoralizing drop in standard of living, which often force us to look for another man to marry for economic stability. Without a fair financial settlement after divorce, it was nearly impossible to recoup decades of lost earnings and career immobility, even for a woman like me who'd kept working part-time in exchange for flexibility so I could be my kids' primary caregivers. I had no regrets about putting my children first and only a few about supporting Marty's career moves, weekly travel, and late nights out with clients. But now, what good would it do to have gone silently, to be the smiling, submissive ex-wife, to let Marty take the lion's share of our assets, future income, financial freedom and security? Instead, I hired a lawyer and fought hard so that I could take care of myself, and my kids, for the rest of my life.

Precisely so I could find someone who treated me better than Marty. And in the meantime, I wasn't going on a single damn date with a man like the guy on the computer screen. I bet five million dollars no one told Marty standing up for himself wasn't "worth it." Or tried to set him up with a woman fifteen years older.

Now, every time a well-meaning but clueless married friend attempted to send me on a blind date, it was as if she assumed there were two options for a fiftyish divorcée: a serious downshift in lifestyle and economic security, or remarriage to another man as similar as possible to the ex-husband I had jettisoned. It was as if, because I was divorced and past my prime by society's carbon dating, another serious heterosexual relationship was my best (or only) option, and that I was searching the globe to find another Marty, only somehow older and even less attractive. *I've already had that*, I felt like saying. *I never, ever want that again. Don't you think I'm worth more than that?*

It was sufficiently debilitating that my own husband made me feel worthless for years. But now, to have female friends reiterate my lack of value felt like heavy artillery shelling my self-esteem. How could other women be so unimaginative and uninspiring, to think I still wanted what I'd already rejected, a life of being treated like a maid by someone I'd given my heart and body to for twenty years? Don't all women have the right to feel beautiful and treasured, at every age?

Maybe they'd accepted a reality I couldn't stomach. After her divorce, a good friend from Minnesota with an MBA from Harvard Business School considered paying thousands to a high-end matchmaker who worked with men who all made more than $250,000 a year. Trish had long, blonde hair and green eyes, and was a successful management consultant at an international firm. I wanted to date her myself.

"You're wonderful," Trish told me the group's founder announced after her ninety-minute interview. "Exactly the type of woman I'd want as my best friend. But I need to reject you."

She'd be hard to place, the woman explained.

"Because you're smart, with an impressive education. Because you're independent and striking. Because you barefoot water-ski at fifty."

Trish was stunned. So was I when she told me what the matchmaker said next.

"All my male clients will want to go out on a date with you," the matchmaker explained. "They'll love you for about three months, the novelty, your mind, your fire. Then, they'll come back to me and ask for someone more 'traditional.' These types of men say they want a partner. In reality, they don't. They want someone to make their world prettier, to ride in the backseat of their life."

Ugh. Were there any men out there who appreciated women as equal partners? Was I insane to think men could play a positive role in my life over the long run? All I knew, for certain, is that rather than sell out again to a man like that, I'd sleep in my California King bed by myself forever. Alone.

———

Beams of sunshine spliced through the interior of the empty Starbucks where KC and I sat on polished dark wood stools. KC looked every inch the corporate woman in strappy white sandal heels and a tight white sleeveless BCBG power suit that I could not have fit one leg into even back in third grade. We were sipping iced coffees while I waited for the minivan's AC to be fixed, finally. I brought her up to speed on the details of Dylan's abrupt departure, the divorce finalization, and the latest inane blind date offering. Then I plunged into what I'd really been considering. It was so audacious, I wasn't sure that even KC would understand.

"I can't go on blind dates with losers and I can't ever let one man let me down like Dylan did," I told her. "I am not—"

I paused, keeping my voice low, as if I were plotting a drug deal.

"Not that sad, submissive, sexually cauterized *wife*. I'm a woman who loves men. The way they smell. The way they talk. The way they fuck."

KC raised her eyebrows in surprise, and then nodded in agreement, her mouth full of lemon square. She knew I was just gathering steam. Forget about keeping my voice low; we were generals charting *life* and Starbucks was our war room. "Marty only loved me when I met his needs. Marriage was a gilded jail cell. I need to focus on me for a change."

"Hold on," KC said when she was done swallowing. She riffled through her purse for a pad of yellow legal paper and a pen. "I'm going to write this all down."

"Number one. I can't look for another husband, or even a serious relationship right now," I told her. "I'm too fragile. Too pissed off about how Marty treated me. Too hurt and vulnerable and warped inside. But I need men in my life. I can't figure out what I want from men in some kind of sterile vacuum of self-help books and yoga."

KC tilted her head at me, scribbling with a black Sharpie.

"Here's what I want: one year, a bunch of men, no commitments. All guys like Dylan. Sweet, cute, smart, transparent, nice. Just fucked-up enough to be interesting, but not too much. Crazy about me. No affair-seeking sleazebags. Any race, religion, profession, location. Aged . . . hmmmm . . . thirty-five to sixty-five. No assholes. Men who make me feel amazing about myself. I'll have enough men in my life that I won't get too attached to one. Then, after a year, I'll figure out what I want long-term."

Pondering this, she looked out the Starbucks plate-glass window at a Philly city bus letting off passengers at the corner. She put down the yellow legal pad on the table between our coffees.

"So girl, you're sayin' the amusement park is open for business."

I tried not to spit out my coffee, causing a small cold squirt to shoot up my nose. KC's salty verbal bluntness, delivered in her buttery southern accent, always created a shocking juxtaposition. She handed me a napkin with the green Starbucks mermaid on it. When I recovered, I elaborated.

"I want two boyfriends in Philly," I explained. "And three in other places. So . . . five. Five seems like the right number. Then I can lose one or two and still have a majority left."

"All at the same time, right? No monogamy or exclusivity?"

"None of those rules. I want to explore men like I'm Queen Isabella conquering the Americas."

Channeling her inner Wall Street numbers cruncher, KC probed the weaknesses of my plan. She lectured me about condom usage. We decided to tell my kids that I was dating a bit, not looking for anyone to marry, and to keep it at that.

"We need a title for this project, honey. Hmmm . . . How about the Five Boyfriend Plan?"

"But, they're not gonna be *boyfriends*, KC."

"Well, we have to call them something. Fuck buddies, boyfriends, baby daddies . . ." She was smirking behind her coffee cup.

"Those are all terrible. I don't know what to call them."

"Wait," she interrupted. "One more thing. Do you tell the five about the others?"

"Oh, God, KC, I don't know."

Those were the only issues that stumped us both. We decided neither mattered.

Then I told her Dylan's parting compliment, about how I reminded him of his wife, which I hadn't been able to bear confessing before. She laughed so hysterically, I thought she might fall off her bar stool.

"Stop, KC." I felt like bending back her pinkies the way my brother did when I was eight. "Why did he have to ruin it all by saying I was like *her*? That's the last thing I want any man to think about me."

"Oh, come on, girl. Forget it. He made your year. Fixed up everything Marty tried to destroy."

She took a draw of her cold brew.

"Marty tore you apart, tried to annihilate every bit of self-confidence you had about yourself as a mom and a woman and a wife. He didn't hit you, but what he did—the way he neglected you emotionally, *neutered* you sexually—no decent man does that to a woman. You need repair, honey. Hot sex with a twenty-nine-year-old was precisely the medicine the doctor ordered. Even if he was using you, even if you never see him again. And trust me, there's a Ram truck full of men like him watching you every day. Waiting. You're such a MILF."

"Dylan told me in the hotel room that I was one of those MILKs. I was too embarrassed to ask what it meant. What is it?"

"It's a *thing*, Leslie. Men—boys, really—who like older women, especially moms. You've had your married-blinders on for too long. Those young'uns have probably always checked you out. Isn't it fun?"

"Um . . . I guess. Yeah, sure. But what does MILK stand for?"

KC tittered. Two stools away, a girl in her twenties with a silver cross stud in her nose looked at us suspiciously.

"MILF. Not MILK. With an *F*. For Vitamin F. Mom-I'd-Like-to . . ."

"Wait. Are you serious?"

"That's what they call it. Google it. There's even MILF pornography."

She raised her carefully threaded Charleston eyebrows.

"And . . . you've done it, too?"

"Yes, ma'am. Probably half of the guys I met on Match were *babies*. Every one of them was hot, ambitious, and superconfident. That's the only type bold enough to go after an older woman."

"Why? What do they see in us?" I lowered my voice to a whisper. "Don't they want to be with other twenty-nine-year-olds?"

"Far as I can tell, an older mom—an attractive, confident older babe—is erotic and captivating. A dare to them, maybe? Plus, no pressure. We don't want to marry them or have babies or vet how much money they make. Do you remember being twenty-nine? We were bounty hunters, trolling for a mate who'd give us a diamond ring and a house with a picket fence and a bunch of babies. Women like that are too intense for men who aren't ready to settle down."

Miss Nose Stud gave a splutter of disgust.

"Also." KC paused. "One of my young guys told me that older women are much better in bed. Experienced, confident, eager in ways that younger women aren't." She gave our audience of one a wink. All of a sudden I imagined Whole Foods, Starbucks, the airport, the sidewalk as hunting grounds for a wrinkled wannabe sex goddess.

"But KC—was twenty-nine too young? How young can I go?"

"Twenty-one. Keep it legal so the sheriff doesn't come after you with his shotgun. Don't ask questions. After what you've been through, you deserve it."

She was right. I did.

Hey Leslie. Thanks SO much for all the Facebook love, much appreciated.

The afternoon following my coffee with KC, an email popped up from one of my high school boyfriends, Jake Bryant.

In high school, we all dressed the same, the boys in polo shirts, we girls in gauzy white sundresses and Guess jeans. (It was the eighties.) We all went to the same three bars and drank the same liquor, always St. Pauli Girl or Cold Duck or anything we could decant from our parents' liquor cabinets without getting caught. All the girls dated the same boys. I'd break up with one boyfriend, and he'd ask out my chem lab partner the next day. Winnie and I lost our virginity to the same older guy, Lyon Nash, a few months apart. Without killing him or each other, although a few times we came close.

All our boyfriends grew up to be the kind of men I think women are lucky to marry. Nice guys, still wearing Polo shirts, more contentedly mated than I had been. At least that's how it looked on Facebook and in person every few years when I saw them at high school reunions or at a random classmate's Fourth of July barbecue.

Except Jake Bryant. Jake never went out with Winnie or my

other friends. He never got married. He never had kids. And I had never slept with him.

Jake was a year younger than I was. When we'd dated my senior year of high school, I'd been reluctant to be his first lover, for reasons I can't fathom now. He was a tall, rangy basketball player who wore his black hair short and spiky, known around school for awing our English teachers with his creative writing. Plus he was the only junior brave enough to sneak into Philly's punk rock music clubs. What struck me most vividly about Jake from the beginning were his eyes, gray-blue in striking contrast to his black hair, and with a naked shine to them like a newborn's drinking in the first moments of life.

Basically, all Jake and I had done back then, physically, was kiss. Okay, plus a little of what my middle school health teacher liked to call "heavy petting." We'd gone off on many other adventures, including a crazy last-minute ski trip on a school snow day. I spent a weekend teaching him how to drive my stick shift Chevy Chevette, and shortly afterward witnessed his first car accident, on his sixteenth birthday, his maiden voyage driving his parents' station wagon. Mostly, we talked, shared our dreams to be writers, and listened to his edgy mix tapes in my Chevette, holding hands with our eyes shut. After Princeton, he became a writer, too, which led to documentary film production, which gave us an excuse to keep in touch on a semiregular basis. His black hair now had streaks of silver, but he still wore it short, looking like Joe Strummer, the front man for the Clash, that great mix of tough and sweet that I'd always found irresistible.

Apparently, other women shared my taste. Jake lived in New York and dated mostly models and actresses. A few years back he'd been on six or seven dates with Katie Couric, one of New York's most notorious cougars. Rumors had it that a celebrity rag had run a picture of the two of them that read "Joe Strummer still alive and dating Katie!"

These days, Jake lived in Greenwich Village and had a writer's cabin in the Connecticut woods. I'd met his latest girlfriend a few times. Like most former models I knew, she was paradoxically haughty and insecure. At a reunion two years ago, she stood under the basketball hoop in our high school gym, looking elegant but unapproachable with her arms crossed over her chest, giving us looks like we were all waiting to stick our tongues down Jake's pants as soon as she went to the bathroom.

"What the hell is he doing with *her*?" Winnie asked after they left.

Jake's latest film had recently come out, a droll exploration about the ways men face (and avoid) growing older. It was nominated for a Sundance Film Festival award. Jake and I had Facebooked a few times recently about the movie.

So when I got an email from him that June afternoon, I wasn't surprised. At first. Jake's email read:

Your re-post of the award nomination seems to have worked. For a brief, shining moment, I was #4 on Amazon's Best Documentary! I credit you, naturally. I'm speaking at the Philadelphia Film Academy this fall, followed by a screening party near Rittenhouse Square. Invite attached. Anyway, would love to see you at either or both events. Or if not, I'll be around that whole week so maybe we could have lunch or a drink. One way or another, you're going to be forced to watch the movie . . .

Hope all's well,
Jake

Well, well, well. This was a little friendlier than normal. Three separate invitations in one email, two months in advance? Did Jake still have that same girlfriend? Every time I'd seen him since graduation, he'd been with a woman guarding him like a German shepherd, and so I had no inkling whether Jake still had feelings for me. Probably not, especially since thirty years had passed since the last time we made out. But you did hear about old flames connecting via Facebook all the time. Maybe Jake had heard through the high school grapevine that Marty had moved out. Perhaps he'd finally had enough of his girlfriend's jealousy. Maybe, pushing fifty, Jake Bryant and I would get another chance to try all the crazy things we'd missed out on in high school.

Naked this time, of course.

––––––––––––

"I'm your therapist for life," Sara had said, almost two decades before, the last time I'd seen her in person before she moved to California. "Call whenever you need me."

Sara was the therapist I found in the wake of my physically abusive first marriage. I saw her twice a week for six months of intensive sessions that felt more like cheerleading than analysis. *Go Leslie! You can overcome this! You're a rock star!* She didn't literally make up chants for me, but our sessions felt that upbeat and confidence inspiring. She'd forbidden me from too much introspection, instead spouting wisdom that still echoes in my head today: *Your ex-husband is the one who needs psychoanalysis for trying to destroy you; all you did was fall in love with a troubled man.* She was like my fairy godmother, sprinkling advice that served as mental magic spells. *Promise yourself you'll never accept abuse again. Instead of a broken boy you think you can fix, look for a man who shows you kindness, respect, and love.* For the first several years with Marty, I thought I'd found one.

I decided to start working with Sara again long-distance. I had few regrets about divorcing Marty, but before embarking on something as audacious as acquiring five lovers at forty-nine, I needed a professional opinion from a woman I respected. What did I require from a man to be happy over time? Did I even need one to be happy? All I knew for certain was that I never wanted to get trapped in an unfulfilling relationship again.

At the start of each session, Sara searched for a single adjective to describe that day's precise shade of blue coloring the Pacific Ocean outside the living room window of the high-rise condo she shared with her husband of thirty years. She did this to remind both of us of how blissful life could be. She also always popped open a Diet Coke can to kick things off.

"Cerulean blue today." *Click*, went the Diet Coke tab. She took a sip. "Ahh, that's good."

She'd laughed out loud in our first session when I told her about my five-boyfriend plan. Today she had feedback.

"So, I've been pondering your idea. I see two areas for improvement."

Sara never said I had problems; they were always *opportunities*.

"One, you've never had any difficulty connecting with men." She paused. "You need to focus on picking better ones, men who can meet your needs in the long run. That's the mistake I see so far in your love life."

"I'm with you, Sara. Tell me more."

"You grew up in an alcoholic home. Fundamentally, this means that the people who loved you, who were supposed to take care of you, didn't protect you. It is why you're so independent, and yet paradoxically susceptible to abuse and manipulation by those closest to you. In close relationships, we all look for what feels like 'family' to us. In your case, that's problematic. Even though it's great progress that Marty wasn't physically abusive, he was emotionally abusive. In some ways, equally as destructively as your parents and your first husband."

She paused in that wise therapist way, to let her words sink in.

"But Sara, how do I love any man again, and not let him hurt me? I feel so vulnerable right now, given what I went through with Marty and in life in general. I cannot survive another abusive relationship. I'd be better off alone, for the rest of my life."

"Perfect segue to my second point. You wouldn't be better off alone. There's great value in trying, and failing, and trying again. Most people think the biggest emotional risk in relationships is loving someone. It's not. Especially for you. You're great at loving with abandon, opening your heart and soul to your mother, your kids, your friends, and both husbands. For you, the biggest risk is letting yourself be loved by a man. That's your next giant step. You need to allow a good man, or five good ones, to love you back."

I hesitated to say anything. She was right. I tried to absorb it all. Sara understood me like no one else. She'd uncovered the rationale behind my crazy dating plan.

"Sara, what if all I want now is to fuck a lot of hot younger men who adore me? Is there anything twisted about wanting *that*?"

"Leslie," she replied with a hint of admonishment. "You are a grown-up. You don't need my or anyone else's permission. It's your body, so you make the rules. Trust your instincts. They may lead you into unexpected situations and relationships, but they'll never let you down."

I let out a full-body sigh of relief. "Okay. That's what I thought. Just checking."

"There's a Spanish proverb that goes like this." Sara paused. "'God says, take what you want. Then pay for it.' There's gonna be some pain, Leslie. In love, there always is. But still, take what you want. If that's five 'boyfriends' or however many"—she paused to let out a chuckle—"go for it. Know that you are strong enough to take risks and pay the price, because that's how a good life is lived."

Could I handle naked hotel yoga? I'd flown to Ohio for a speaking engagement, and now I was alone in a beige hotel room in Cleveland. I had a free hour before getting dressed for a luncheon keynote in the elegant ballroom downstairs, raising money for Ohio's oldest domestic violence shelter by telling my *Crazy Love* story.

I needed to unwind before baring my soul to eight hundred strangers. I plugged my phone into the hotel TV and flicked on a yoga travel podcast. Which was exactly when, rustling through my suitcase, I realized I had no yoga clothes to change into; I'd forgotten to pack them.

Standing nude and alone in front of the burled wood hotel mirror in the middle of Ohio, I suddenly felt a wash of tension, an inner voice so loud it sounded like a loudspeaker had been miked into my brain, telling me to put on a robe to cover myself up. Why? A twenty-year-old memory spliced through me. It was from my early days with Marty. One night as we crawled into bed in his apartment, he'd left a love note under my pillow that proposed a new tradition.

Every year, let's have a Naked Week. Seven days. No clothes. Madly in love with you.

The next morning, as Marty brushed his teeth, I lay naked on his black-and-white zebra pattern carpet, holding the soles of my feet like a bug on its back, stretched into Happy Laughing Baby, studying my toenails. I felt like a happy laughing baby myself, in love with Marty and how free I felt with him.

I heard Marty open the bathroom door. For a second I thought, *Close your legs*. Happy Laughing Baby Pose invites exposure, even when you're fully clothed. But I thought his note meant Marty actually liked my nakedness. *He loves you and your body, he wants a whole week of you naked, a whole lifetime of you nude, don't zip up the cleft*. So I didn't.

I felt a ripple of air as Marty walked by, wrapped in a navy blue towel. He stopped moving. He looked at me, and my vagina, on his rug. He uttered one word, five letters that I can still hear today.

"Gross."

I curled up into a ball instinctively. I was too shocked to respond.

If Marty had laughed, I would have joined in; we would have been laughing together. Some yoga poses do make the human body look inherently awkward. Maybe the vagina is funny-looking, too, at least to some people. Before that moment, I had never thought of my most special body part as anything but fascinating. A bizarre, incredible trick of nature, the maker of orgasms and babies. Miraculous and beautiful in its own way, like the pearled inside of a conch shell.

I never did naked yoga in front of Marty again. I packed the memory of those five letters in a mental suitcase, ignoring his dismissive crudeness, trying to balance his rejection of my body against how thoughtful he seemed to be in other ways, how steady and stable and uncomplicated he appeared on the surface. After we married, I gradually began covering up my body whenever I was around him. Instead of our getting closer, invisible walls grew between us. We never practiced Naked Week. Starting that day, bit by bit, the part of me that loved my body and all the fabulous things it could do—make a baby, feed a baby, master Wheel Pose in yoga, have a mind-blowing orgasm—shut down. Marty hadn't prized any of that female magic. Sure, he valued me as a woman who produced babies, a wife with Ivy League credentials and social skills who assisted his career, a woman who took care of the home and the kids and used the correct salad fork at his firm holiday party. Marriage to Marty had shut down the parts of me that made me me. *You become what you don't leave*, my mom told me once. That's exactly what happened.

So the question now, twenty years later, was: how did I find my body and myself again?

At first, I was afraid to look in the mirror, which took up most of the wall. It felt like twenty years since I'd seen myself completely nude. I told myself, as kindly as I could, *Reality is your friend*. So while stretched in an inverted V shape for Downward-Facing Dog, I snuck a peek.

Wait a minute! I was nearsighted. I had to see myself as others saw me, or it'd be cheating, fooling myself. I found my glasses on the TV console and slipped them on.

Oof. Stretch marks. Cellulite on my legs. Flapping skin on my upper arms. And belly. Ugh. My nipples, which had pointed skyward before I nursed my kids for a year apiece, now pointed down as if reaching for my toes.

Wait. See yourself through Dylan's eyes. Maybe if I tried, I could see myself the way he had in that other hotel room, during our never-to-be-repeated night together.

I looked again and saw pretty parts in the mirror. Golden shoulders. The clavicle, and the ribs around my breasts protecting my heart, were strong and attractively bony, at least to me. Upside down, the spiky blonde hair on my head looked surprisingly good.

Don't zoom in on the flaws, I advised myself, the way I would Bella when she compared herself to her skinniest friends. I remembered a study I'd reported on years before, data that showed a trick American men play on themselves when they look in the mirror. Unlike women, men see a stronger, more muscular body than they actually have. They smile and suck in their beer bellies, as if they're still twenty-four. American women do the opposite, magnifying the parts of our bodies we hate, falling victim to a body dysmorphia brought on by years of seeing airbrushed models in *Sports Illustrated* swimsuit editions and thousands of Photoshopped glossy ads for products we don't actually need.

Imagine you are better than you are. Trick yourself like men do.

I tried it.

I paused in Eagle Pose, a twisty one-legged position where you wrap your arms and legs around each other, turning your body into a figure-eight hourglass. I felt as if I were noticing myself for the first time.

Wow, I had curves. My waist cut in nicely. My hips flared out. The skin wrapping my hipbones and ass was as smooth as it had been when I was eighteen. The triangle of blonde pubic hair seemed . . . discreet and tasteful, seductive, promising.

I saw a grown woman in the glass. Not a sexy twentysomething body that you'd find strutting on the Victoria's Secret catwalk. But even through my prescription lenses, the body I saw was curvy, soft, and appealing. This was *me*. If my forty-nine-year-old body still turned me on, it was a short hop to imagine it had done the same for Dylan, and could do the same for other men, if I (and they) were so lucky in the future. Not every man on the planet. But definitely one or two.

The woman in the mirror smiled at me.

Or maybe even five.

DRILLING
AND
BLASTING

L ike warmth from an invisible sun, I felt someone's gaze as I walked to the drugstore after an early Sunday morning jog around Center City. I was sweaty with snarly hair, wearing a black camisole over a pleated, aqua-colored athletic skort. I looked up and down the sidewalk. Empty. Then I noticed movement across the street. A thirtyish man, walking a speckled hound dog, was staring at me. *Staring.* I gave a little wave. He grinned sheepishly, caught in the act.

What did he notice that I couldn't see? Neighbors and parents I'd known for years passed by these days without recognizing me. Everyone said I looked taller after I got divorced, which was puzzling, because I wasn't, of course. Did I really look so different now that I wore lipstick and had lost a few pounds? Or was something else going on?

Being noticed these days—as if catching my reflection in a societal mirror—felt like that shock of getting splashed with sprinkler water on a hot summer day. Especially when the attention came from men. I'd spent my life evading male interest, starting at fourteen when construction workers leered at me on the sidewalk, and later when older male colleagues invited me to one-on-one lunches and dinners even though we had no business to discuss. Avoiding flirtatious men and unwanted sexual advances signaled my commitment to my career and husband, while sending a message that I was trustworthy to female coworkers and moms I liked and whose respect I needed.

Now, being shamed or pressured into short hair, loose dresses, and modest one-piece suits at the pool struck me as a perverse form of objectification. Not a pornographic type of diminishment—women as crude sex object—but the opposite, women as *non*sexual object. Up until now, it had seemed dishonorable, or antifeminist, to take pride in my body, to enjoy it hedonistically, or even to be at home in it. Today, that fleeting second of being noticed by a stranger across the street made something in me hum with the joy of being female.

In line to check out at the drugstore, I spotted Tara, one of my favorite moms from the kids' school. Tara's husband had gotten an MBA at Harvard alongside my Minnesota friend Trish. For years, we saw each other every week or two at charity fund-raisers or parties for the kids, but our paths hadn't crossed in months. After mutual friends heard about our divorce, I got left off dinner and cocktail party guest lists I'd been on for years. No one was intentionally trying to hurt me. Yet how could friends think a recent divorcée *wanted* to be excluded from social activities?

Today, Tara had on the mousy summer uniform I'd worn for nearly two decades: knee-length khaki shorts and an old button-down oxford. Maybe Tara had dressed this way, and eschewed makeup, long before she had added a wedding ring to her ensemble. But to me, her outfit looked like a sandwich board across her body declaring I'M MARRIED. No longer a woman, exactly, but instead a *wife* who had abandoned paying a nanosecond of attention to how she looked to the outside world. A person who deemed it unnecessary, or a betrayal of her role as loyal partner/mother, to scrutinize her physical appearance. Which of course was her choice, none of my business. I knew there was power in not wearing makeup, not bowing to traditional norms of female beauty. However, I got the feeling Tara was clinging to her identity as a mother in the absence of other selves: she was pushing one of those shopping carts that has a plastic kiddie car attached, even though she had no children with her today and, furthermore, her children were teenagers.

"Leslie!" She practically yelled in her Main Line accent when

she saw me. "It's been so long!" Her face broke into a smile, showing her cute overbite, as if seeing me was the whole point she'd
gotten up that morning. "How are you, honey?"

Despite her WASPy-ness, she was always as enthusiastic as an
Eagles cheerleader.

Then she looked down at my skort. She wrinkled her brow.

"Are you going to play . . . tennis?" she asked. She looked
around for my racket.

"Nah, I'm getting toothpaste." I smiled at her.

Thank God I didn't have K-Y or condoms in my cart.

"Why are you dressed like this?" she blurted out, genuinely
confused.

I didn't answer. I was fairly certain that even if Tara understood
that I dressed to feel attractive, *visible*, she couldn't admit, to me
or herself, that she sometimes felt invisible, too. There was something taboo about women, especially privileged women like me
and Tara, acknowledging marriage's disappointments and the need
to feel valued by our culture outside the house. After all, there are
many greater challenges and hardships in life. Tara and I both had
grabbed, literally, *the* gold ring, by marrying men who were ideal on
the surface, seemingly kind, smart husbands who paid their taxes,
made a good living, coached peewee soccer on the weekends, and
came home to us every night. Men whose biggest flaws seemed to
be that they played too much golf, left their socks on the floor, or
stayed a few hours too late at the office. How could we be ungrate-
ful that they ignored us? How dare we criticize the men in our lives,
or the lifestyle they made possible? These topics were at once too
personal and too complex for pharmacy checkout counter chitchat.

"Hey, Tara, it's always so good to see you. But I gotta jet. Coffee
sometime?"

"Sure," Tara said. Abruptly, she grabbed me for a hug. She held
on and whispered in my ear, "And by the way . . . you look terrific."

As I walked out the automatic doors, she stood by the self-
checkout register, still looking baffled by the way I'd changed. By me.

Not even half a block later, another woman called my name.

"Leslie!"

A platinum blonde in black Jackie O sunglasses and supertiny, supertight white shorts and wedge heels waved furiously at me. Her baby-blue T-shirt read PEACE LOVE BORA BORA in huge white block letters. Although it was barely ten o'clock on a Sunday morning, she had on full makeup, a Gucci purse, and four-inch wedge heels. Who was it? I stumbled into a teakwood bench on the sidewalk outside the kids' favorite ice cream parlor as I squinted at her. Then it came to me: Patti, a mom from Bella's first swimming class.

"Hey, skinny!" she said after she squeezed me in an enthusiastic hug. She was from Staten Island. Not to stereotype New Yorkers based on their borough, but everything about her was flashy and over-the-top. However, she'd taken Bella home for play dates with her youngest son at least a dozen times, and her heart was as big as her hair.

"The divorce diet," I explained. She was divorced, too. She put her glossy red fingernails on my forearm in sympathy. We traded the usual rapid-fire mom updates: *How are the kids? Going anywhere fun for vacation this summer? We should grab coffee sometime!*

"I gotta go," she said, looking at her Cartier. "My new exercise class."

"What? No more yoga?" This was a thunderbolt. Patti was the one who dragged me to yoga in the first place. "What are you doing now?"

"OMFG the best barre class ever!" she practically screamed in the glaring midmorning sunshine, throwing her arms wide open. *"Look at my legs!"* She pirouetted so I could see her cellulite-free upper legs and butt cheeks. I had to admit, her ass looked so good I wanted to caress it myself right there on the sidewalk.

"Look at these shorts! I can wear a thong bikini again!"

I stood in front of Patti and her perfect forty-five-year-old butt, speechless. I'd never worn a thong bikini. I hadn't put on short shorts since the summer I turned thirteen. But I realized something astonishing: I wanted an ass like that. What had happened to me? Had I become, practically overnight, a shallow, antifeminist

Playboy Bunny? Or was I on my way to being a true feminist, loyal to my own rules, for the first time in my life? It was surprisingly hard to know for sure. Then I had an even more startling thought: who cared?

Head spinning from all these thoughts on wifery and woman-hood, I headed home, where I found Bella in the kitchen drinking lemonade.

"Why do you have on makeup, Mom?" she asked.

I felt like saying, *You, too?*

It took me a second to find the answer in its simplest form.

"It's actually that I used to feel so unpretty. I want to look good now."

"But Mom, you went to *Harvard*. You're a feminist. A domestic violence advocate. Why do you want to look pretty? Why do you want men to notice you? Aren't you better than that?"

Her face looked disappointed, even hurt, by this facet of my postdivorce personality.

"Honey, my life is not all about looking good for men on the sidewalk. Although I do like that part."

Bella smiled, showing her dimples.

"It took me a long time to figure this out, that a woman can be smart and sexy at the same time. There's no disrespect in it. I wear lipstick and eyeliner and short skirts when I'm by myself. Even when I'm writing or doing stuff here, when I look in the mirror, I like to look nice. I'm not dressing up only for men. It's for *me*."

What I felt like saying was *I lost who I was for so long, now I need to be visible, even to myself*. That was the truth.

––––––––––

Back to my regular life with regular yoga. The kind with clothes. I was late to afternoon power hour. As usual.

I blasted into the studio foyer in a pissy froth, trying to morph my facial muscles into yoga-zen tranquillity. Your image mattered at Down Dog, Philly's hottest, and coolest, yoga studio. Inside the exercise space itself—hot and humid already, the way I loved it—I beelined toward the back corner. I had come to Down Dog for so many years that I had my favorite spot, the way ninety-year-old men claim benches in Rittenhouse Square. My place in back was closest to the bathroom. Best situated to catch the ribbon of fresh air that slithered in through the bolted emergency exit. Farthest from the teacher, so when a sophomoric guru spouted a bit too much faux wisdom ("your heart is your most intuitive muscle"), I could safely mutter back "Shut your clabwabber!" without getting busted.

Today my corner spot was taken. Motherfucker. That space was MINE. MINE. MINE.

I felt like cursing out my mat-stealer. I stared at him instead. Yes, him. It was rare to have a man in yoga, let alone a gorgeous, burnt-honey black man. Both his hands were folded, steeple-style, across his T-shirt. Which I couldn't help noticing were covering a big and barreled chest. His left hand was absent a wedding ring; check mark there, no more married men for *moi*. He looked to be a few years younger than me, but within KC's *Keep it legal* admonishment. Bulky arm, shoulder, thigh, and calf muscles. Tight waist and abs. A tattoo on his upper right tricep read FAITH. He diffused my zombie death stare by shooting me a beneficent, curious grin as the three ohms that signaled the official beginning of class rang out.

I spied on Gorgeous Yoga Man throughout practice. I'd taken the space right in front of him, slightly to his left, along the wall (which I needed for balance, given how tiny my dwarf feet were— they'd stopped growing in fourth grade, probably from the trauma of asking Mom about blow jobs). During *Savasana*, I lay a foot away from him, synchronizing my breath with his steady inhales. Good, sweaty karma. The connection felt sensual.

I was supposed to be clearing my mind, but instead I plotted how I could talk to him. After class, I'd start with "Nice practice, huh?" If I had the guts.

I dove for the bathroom as soon as *Savasana* was over. I had to fluff my sweaty hair and put on lip balm to bolster my courage. I came out, nonchalant and casually coiffed, but shaking with adrenaline underneath.

He wasn't there. How could he have gotten away so fast? If he had noticed me, wouldn't he have lingered to try to meet me, at least for two minutes?

I must have been wrong about the karma. I made a sad face to no one in particular, since it would have been too goofy to call KC right at that moment to confess my failure.

The truth was I also felt relieved. Trying to hit on men, making the first move, was *hard*. Before leaving Marty, I'd never once in my life asked a guy out. I'd never told the universe, or myself, *I want that one*. When I was dating in my twenties, it had seemed more socially acceptable, which at the time felt absolutely imperative, to let men come to me, then to pick the best of that subset. And where had that gotten me? Two decades of a marriage that had felt like a feather pillow held over my nose and mouth. It felt exhilarating to realize I could pursue men on the open market, rather than waiting to see who came to me.

However, despite KC's coaching, I lacked the bravado to shoot that first arrow. Disappointed *and* relieved, I trudged outside into the golden summer afternoon, walking past the cavernous redbrick Reading Terminal, the country's oldest farmer's market.

And there he was: my spot-stealer waiting to cross the street.

Before fear paralyzed me, I sidled up to him at the red light. I shifted my yoga mat to my other shoulder to make it obvious I'd gotten out of the same class.

"Good practice, right?" I managed to blurt out.

He whirled around as the cars streamed by. His eyes widened when he saw me.

"Oh, yeah," Gorgeous Yoga Man said, smiling a little. "More of that blissful torture, no? You were right beside me, weren't you?"

I swear he looked at my ass as he said that.

"Yup. Along the wall," I said. My heart was racing. I tried to remember KC's pickup tactics for dummies: act relaxed, keep the conversation flowing, and give him a chance to talk. "Have you been practicing long?"

"Two years," he answered, his eyes locking onto mine.

Whoa. Gorgeous Yoga Man had magnificent eyes, a deep brown-green with golden flecks. Light brown freckles bedecked his nose and cheeks. The sounds and colors of the buses and buildings around us faded away.

"Really?" I forced out, trying to appear normal. "At Down Dog? I've never seen you here before."

I would have noticed you, my friend. Even when I was married.

"Yep. I usually go to West Philly. But my son has a summer league baseball game near here in an hour, so I hit this studio today."

He had a son like mine who played baseball? A connection.

The light turned green. We crossed together. The late-afternoon sun turned the crosswalk into a golden path.

Once on the far sidewalk, he put down his gym bag and leaned up against the wall of a Subway sandwich shop. His body blocked the pedestrians who rushed by, creating a protective little triangle for me, like a branch sticking out from a riverbank forming an eddy of calm water.

"Where does he play?" I asked.

"Oh, he's a rising sophomore at St. Joe's."

"My son plays, too. He's the pitcher. At Friends."

GYM threw his head back and laughed. "Oh, I know him. Number Four? That boy who cracks the bats?"

"That's him." I laughed. *Namaste*, universe.

"You're married, right?" he blurted out, taking me by surprise. Before I could react, he said, by way of explanation, "Because you're such a beautiful woman. You have to be married."

Ah, slick. But I liked the way he said it.

"I *was* married." I smiled, to show I was *over it*.

"I'm Damon," GYM said, sticking out his hand for a shake. It was warm and dry, solid and thick.

I had his name. Now I had to give him my number. KC would give me an A+ on this one. I reached into my bag for my card.

"I'm Leslie. Here's my card. Have fun at your son's game. Hope they win."

He reached into his wallet and fished out his card. It had the University of Pennsylvania seal in raised blue and maroon lithograph. His full name was Damon McKenzie.

I was surprised to recognize the last name.

"Did you grow up here?" I asked. "My kids' preschool teacher spelled her name the same way."

"That would be my mom," he said, smiling like he was the luckiest kid on the planet to be her son. "Mrs. McKenzie."

His eyes, which were actually a froggy green mixed with brown and gold, shone in the fading twilight.

I had to leave quickly, before I tarnished this flawless scene by accidentally spitting on him or farting loudly.

"I'd like to see you again, Leslie," he said.

"Damon, I would, too."

He put out his hand once more. This time, when our palms connected, he held on a beat longer. I felt dizzy when I looked in his eyes. I let go and walked up the cobblestone sidewalk, my back to Subway and the most beautiful straight man to ever hold Tree Pose, practically dancing.

———————

I didn't want a new husband, but a new ride—that was a different story. The dented Honda minivan had kept me and my kids safe for twelve years of carpool lines and road trips, but driving it now felt like piloting a wet mattress, soggy with the tears of an entire generation of unhappy, unappreciated wives forced to drive minivans. I wanted to puke every time I got in it, and not from the smell of stale dog vomit.

However, before I could ditch the Odyssey, I had to prove I owned it. One of the legal documents Marty, the judge, and I had all signed that bizarre day in court was a piece of paper that said the Odyssey was now mine. But the car, like everything we owned, was in Marty's name. I couldn't register the car, much less sell it, without the title. My expensive, brilliant lawyer had neglected to get

Marty to sign the title over to me. The same husband who couldn't come home in time for dinner with us for two decades was spending six weeks parasailing in Nice and hiking Mont Blanc. He'd torture me before signing it, if he ever actually did sign it, anyhow.

So I went to the DMV headquarters, feeling like a kid secretly trying to shoot the moon with the queen of spades tucked in my sweaty hand. At eight o'clock, I stood obediently in the hot morning sun waiting for the DMV's dingy concrete block headquarters to open, amidst North Philadelphia's boarded-up apartment buildings and auto repair shops with spray-painted signs. Once inside, I sat on a yellow plastic seat next to a plastic plant, both bolted to the floor, feeling like the cheap fluorescent ceiling lights were frying my brain. After forty-five minutes, my number was called.

I walked to the designated cubicle and laid my cards across the Formica counter: the unsigned title with Marty's name in bold letters, the divorce decree, and the page of our terms sheet with "Leslie shall keep the Honda Odyssey" highlighted in yellow. The clerk was an expressionless African-American woman in a faded 76ers T-shirt, who looked like she could be anywhere from twenty-eight to forty-eight years old.

She looked so bored she could hardly keep her eyes open. I didn't blame her.

"Can't do it," she said after a minute of studying my three documents. "Title needs to be signed over to you by the owner. Sorry."

She pushed them back. I took a deep breath.

"It was a nasty divorce, ma'am."

When I said "ma'am," she raised her eyebrows like she knew I was sucking up to her, which I was.

"You wouldn't believe what I had to go through to get him to sign this document," I said quietly, pointing to his signature on the terms sheet.

"It cost me more than a year's pay to get these papers. He'll never sign the title. I'll have to take him to court. It'll take another year and cost more in legal bills than the car is worth."

Then I waited. She stared back for a solid five seconds. I didn't blink. Inside I was whispering *please please please*. But I knew not to beg. After her reaction to my "ma'am," I didn't want to risk triggering her bullshit monitor with any more flattery, for fear my hopes for a new car would go straight into the DMV trash can.

She shook her head as if to say *They don't pay me enough for this crap*, then started typing into her computer.

"I'm gonna do it," she muttered to herself. "But I'm gonna cover my ass, too."

She typed away, checking the divorce decree date and the judge's signature.

"What's your address? Full name? Driver's license number?"

I gave them all to her, afraid to exhale.

"We're gonna say this was his gift to you," she said, not looking at me. "So you don't have to pay any taxes on the transfer."

A tiny smile fluttered across her lips.

Then she held up the title and ripped it right through Marty's name. She kept ripping until the pieces wafted down to her desk like confetti.

I looked around to make sure no other employees were watching.

"Thank you so much," I whispered, leaning into her. "You have no idea what this means to me."

She looked at me with eyes the color of Hershey's chocolate syrup.

"I was married for eighteen years," she said quietly. "He tried to take everything I worked for. My car. My house. My kids. So honey, I do understand. You'll get that car title—in your name—in the mail in ten days."

Sure enough, I did.

Gorgeous Yoga Man reached out three days later. I read his first text with delight: Hey, L! Great to meet you! Checking up on you. After a few rounds of texting banter, we started talking on the phone at night. At first, the topics centered on our kids. He had a daughter in addition to his son. He was a writer, too, in his spare time, and one evening he recited several of his spoken-word poems. He was good.

"Do you want to go to yoga and have dinner together?" I forced myself to blurt out one night when we both lying in bed, separately of course. I didn't dare use the word *date*. I got the feeling that traditional dating had gone the way of the cotillion during my long stretch of married life.

A few days later, Damon drove from his job at Penn, parked his faded silver diesel Mercedes in my alley, and got out of the driver's side with a slow grin that made me feel like my ribs were melting. We walked the mile to the studio together for the late-afternoon power hour, talking so intently I was surprised when we arrived at Down Dog; it was as if we had floated there. In the back corner of the studio, we put our mats next to each other. In the quiet of *Savasana*, I reached for his hand, and he squeezed mine and held on until the teacher broke the silence a minute later. We ambled home to my place afterward, still sweaty in our yoga clothes, for a hot tub soak and late dinner on my back deck.

I made my favorite salad with avocado and dates, and grilled salmon steaks. When we were planning the evening, he'd mentioned he couldn't eat meat or drink alcohol. He didn't explain why, as if it was important, yet private and complicated, as if he'd converted to Islam or made a similarly profound life change. I didn't press. We went in the hot tub after dinner and he said he needed to keep his T-shirt on. Again, he didn't explain why.

Sitting with our legs on the edge of the tub, in an awkward silence, I slipped my arms around his neck and leaned in to kiss him. Making the first move may have been bold, but it seemed like the natural thing to do. I slipped my hand down to the small of his back and let the tip of my tongue cross between his parted teeth. He kissed me back, his lips wet and sweet, as the fireflies glowed in the yard around us.

"You look beautiful, Leslie."

He kissed me again, as if to show what he meant, closing his eyes. Then he opened them and unwrapped my hands from his back and neck. He took my palms and pressed them up against his, pushing back.

"I have to tell you a few things," he said. His voice was low and blue. "Things I haven't told you before. But I'm not ready yet."

"Okay," I said, confused. "Let's dry off. We can talk another time. Whenever you're ready." I gave him a quick kiss to show I wasn't kicking him out, just giving him space.

I walked him to his car in the gloaming twilight and watched him drive away, feeling naked and exposed as I stood there in my wet bathing suit, totally confused.

———————

Now that I had the Odyssey title, the next step was selecting which set of wheels and metal symbolized my future. I'd never bought a car for myself, by myself. It couldn't be that hard. The sticky wicket quickly became: which symbol?

That weekend, back in Southampton, I saw a sixteen-year-old blond boy driving a baby-blue convertible Bentley in the July sun. A middle-aged, suspiciously tan mustached man in a yellow Ferrari winked at me. I eyed more Porsche Cayennes and Boxsters than I could count. Southampton seemed to specialize in vehicle up-grades that were unrealistic for a divorced almost-fifty mom with two kids to put through college. Plus, I'd never coveted a flashy ride. I'd owned two vehicles in my life. My automotive priorities had always been affordability, reliability, and how many car seats you could fit across the back row. Just as I'd never eyed men with bold ambition, I'd never once thought, *God, I'd like to drive that car.*

Then one day, I saw a curvy black two-door with a flared hatchback parked outside a fudge shop. It had the rings that looked vaguely like the Olympic symbol. I texted a picture to Timmy at baseball camp.

"Mom, that's an Audi TT," he wrote back. Subtext: *My mom is utterly clueless.*

Next, I turned to the Google. According to Kelley Blue Book, I could trade in the Odyssey and replace it with a preowned Audi TT, as long as I could come up with a small chunk of cash to close the gap. With all the articles I'd been writing, I could swing it. *You're worth it*, I told myself.

I began trolling the Internet for used TTs. They were hard to find. None in New York. One in Pennsylvania. Then I found a three-year-old white model with twenty thousand miles on the odometer. It was at a dealership in Nashville. A flirty salesman with a deep southern drawl named Phil put his iPhone on the dash for a FaceTime test drive. The engine purred like a lioness when he took it up to a hundred miles per hour. *What the hell*, I thought. I sent a check to Tennessee.

———————

"May I speak to Leslie?"

My phone had lit up with the caller ID of a local Philly television station.

"It's Beth Critton. I've booked you a few times—"

"Oh, hi, Beth. Great to hear from you," I interrupted. I figured she wanted a quote about a recent high-profile domestic violence murder-suicide in an oceanfront Victorian on the Jersey Shore.

Instead, she explained she'd heard that NPR had canceled a moms roundtable I'd contributed to semiregularly. She invited me to do weekly on-air segments based on my mommy blog. Three minutes of live pithy parenting advice in exchange for free publicity. Of course I said yes, even though it meant traveling from Southampton to Philly each week.

The TV station staff wore jeans and blazers and got regular haircuts, in contrast to the wonky NPR crew, whom I also loved, in a different way. Each week, as I waited outside the green room for the on-air cue for my segment, I felt like I had transferred to a party school after a year at Yale. Everyone in Philadelphia, including my kids and all their friends, seemed to catch my segment. Which gave them a lot to give me grief about.

"Mom, come on," Timmy said one day after we'd caught the replay of my latest topic. He shook his buzz-cut head at me. "You, a parenting expert?"

We both laughed. He had a point.

As I prepped to go on air my second or third week, I stood by the plastic blue and white watercooler. The adjacent cubicle had previously been unoccupied. That day a very cute human, with chestnut hair, big brown eyes, and razor stubble, was working there. The nameplate next to his computer said Marc Jessup.

Of course, KC loved this when I called her to dish. "Marc with a C? Classic eighties baby," she snorted.

With a smirk that she couldn't see over the phone, I promised to keep her posted.

———————

Wrapped in oversized beach towels, Damon and I sat next to each other in the glow of the fire table. He'd driven in again, we'd gone to yoga, and we'd eaten dinner on my deck before getting in the hot tub. This time, he made the first move, putting his arms around me and kissing me.

"Your lips are so soft," he said. After we'd kissed for a few minutes, he sighed. "Okay, I'll tell you my story. You sure you're ready?"

I nodded and squeezed his hand. He leaned forward and put both his elbows on his knees, staring out at the fireflies in the backyard without seeing them.

"First, I was in prison. It was a long time ago. I had a football scholarship to the University of Virginia, right out of high school. Charlottesville. The South, you know?"

He looked at me ruefully. A mosquito bit my upper arm. I ignored it, afraid to look away.

"At training camp, one night in this bar parking lot after second practice, a few of us got in a fight with some other kids. I was the only one arrested."

"Oh, Damon, how awful." It was all I could say.

"I was the only black kid. Nineteen eighty-three. Virginia, right? The local lawyer wanted a thousand-dollar retainer. My mom couldn't cover it on her teacher's salary. Coach couldn't help me since it was summer training and I wasn't officially enrolled yet. So I went to jail for eight months. Lost my scholarship."

"Oh, God," I said. "That must have been heartbreaking."

Damon and I had both graduated from high school the same summer. The police stopped me as well, in a small-town speed trap when I was driving to the shore for Beach Week with a keg full of beer in the back of my parents' station wagon. The small-town officer—older, white, gruff—had asked if I was heading to college in the fall. When I told him I was going to Harvard, he let me leave without a ticket. "Good luck," he said. I remember him smiling at me through the car window, as proud as my own father. I can only imagine how differently he would have treated me if I'd been black and male.

"Moms cried for a week," Damon said, taking my hand in both of his. "No scholarship. No college. She'd been so proud when I got into UVA. And dang, it's hard to get a job with an arrest record. After a few years working odd jobs, manual labor, I got lucky."

A family friend told him about a loophole: university job fairs didn't check applicants' arrest records. After that, he interviewed only for academic jobs. He'd gotten hired at the Penn physics research lab. Unable to risk interviewing for another job, he'd worked at that one without ever considering leaving.

"The other thing. I don't like to talk too much about it. But the reason I can't eat meat or drink, or take my shirt off in yoga or your hot tub? I had a massive heart attack seven years ago. I died, but the EMTs brought me back. Open heart surgery, though. Changed everything for me. Everything."

He paused and sighed. "I might as well show you."

He lifted his wet T-shirt up over his head.

Above his slim waist and six-pack abs, a ten-inch scar split his massive barrel chest. It looked like a brownish-red railroad track across his heart.

"Docs say I'll never really be the same. Yoga is pretty much the only exercise I can do. And sex . . . kinda off the table. I'd love to kiss you all night, but that's probably all I can do."

He smiled, but his green eyes looked terribly sad.

To my surprise, I experienced a flare of kinship sparked by his confessions. Despite appearances, and my high-end Rittenhouse Square and Hamptons real estate, I'd lived my own version of parking lot fights and prison, although according to a decidedly more privileged, lily-white script. Damon's confessions washed away the shame of my family alcoholism, domestic violence in my twenties, and the divorce from Marty.

I didn't want to fetishize his past. We weren't the same, not even close, but both our lives had been derailed at a young age, his by racism and prison, mine by relationship violence, although arguably, Damon had paid the higher price over time. But the compassion I felt for him helped me accept myself as well. I never again wanted to hide my scars, to wear a Chanel top and pastel lipstick and pretend to be any man's plastic toy with shellacked hair and sensible heels. I wanted to be me, to make my own rules, to follow my own path, to be loved for myself. Damon's honesty made me feel like I could. Compared to my Lilly Pulitzer neighbors, the Martha Stewart moms at the kids' school, and even the twentysomething lifeguards I fantasized about, it felt more real to be nestled next to someone who'd traveled a road longer and harder than mine.

I leaned back into him and kissed his chest, right above the scar.

"Oh, Damon, that's all okay. I'm glad you told me. I'd love to kiss you all night, too."

So we did.

———

Crunch crunch crunch. I ran down the slate steps of the beach house to see if the biggest gift I'd ever given myself had arrived. Sure enough, a box truck was backing onto the gravel of our Southampton driveway. The driver, whose potbelly and wrinkles made him look seventy when he was probably my age, got out of the cab stiffly, carefully placing each scuffed brown work boot on the truck running board. He had a red pouch of tobacco sticking out of his wrinkled Wrangler jeans pocket. He asked gruffly, all good ole southern boy, "You Miss Leslie?"

"Yes," I told him as we both walked to the back of the truck. "Do you have my divorce present in there?"

He seemed taken aback by my effusiveness, and nodded without saying anything. After all, to him this was a routine delivery. He pulled down the six-foot corrugated metal ramp on the back of the truck. He leaned in to propel himself forward as he walked up the steep incline. He paused before he rolled up the back door, playing the Wizard of Oz behind the curtain.

"Ready?"

The door made a gritty rattling sound as he pulled up the handle. Sitting there in the darkened box truck, like a new pony in the backyard on Christmas Day, was a gleaming white Audi TT. The circular logos on the hood made it look as if the car were smiling at me.

The driver jumped down, landing with a heavy thud. Before he could take a step back, I hugged him hard. His T-shirt smelled like sweat, whiskey, and chaw. "Thank you so much," I managed to blurt out as a few tears sprung up in the corners of my eyes, embarrassing me and probably him, too.

After I let go, he shook himself awkwardly, smiled a little, and fished the key out of a small brown leather pouch. He climbed back into the truck and turned the TT ignition. A sweet rumble echoed inside the metal walls. He inched the car down the ramp and left the engine running while he got out a clipboard with yellow carbon papers for me to sign. Then he reached in and turned off the ignition. In the ensuing midmorning quiet, he held out the key.

"Congratulations," he said, dropping it in my palm as if he understood the freedom the car represented. The weight of the key in my hand surprised me.

Use your independence wisely. That was the message I'd read on a fortune cookie I'd gotten the last time the kids and I had ordered Chinese takeout. I'd taped it onto my computer. Buying the TT was as good a way to symbolize my independence as I could conjure.

He climbed back into his cab for the long trip back to Nashville. As the empty box truck started to ramble down my drive under its shady canopy of beech trees, he cranked down his window. "Babe," he yelled over his shoulder, his grin showing stained teeth. "You're gonna be the coolest MILF in the Hamptons!" I loved it when any man called me *babe*. And if older, male rednecks knew what a MILF was, I'd been a worm living under a rock.

Then I slid behind the wheel, cranked up the engine, gunned it a few times, and zipped to the grocery store in my official MILF mobile.

A few weeks into my TV gig, while still getting down the new routine, Marc Jessup and I nearly collided in the break room after my segment.

"Hey, I'm going down," Marc said, pointing to the elevator. "I'll walk out with you."

We rode down in awkward elevator silence. He was shorter than I was, and skinnier in a geeky, unathletic way I nonetheless found so attractive I could hardly look at him. We both turned right in the marble-and-chrome lobby, heading toward the back entrance. The TT was delicately squeezed into a spot on the narrow Philly street behind the studio. Marc stopped on the sidewalk as I pulled out my key and chirped the remote security system.

"Whoa, nice car," he gushed. He walked around it and whistled. "Costs more than the balance on my student loans. You have to take me for a ride," he said, raising one eyebrow flirtatiously. "One day."

I laughed. This was getting interesting.

"Hey, I'm getting coffee around the corner," he said, holding out his hand as if he were asking me to dance. "Wanna join me?"

"Sure, Marc."

I clicked the TT remote to lock the car, and we walked kitty corner across the street to La Colombe. It was empty at this hour. The barista, who looked like she could be Rihanna's twin sister, seemed almost happy to have something to do. I wondered how we looked to her.

"Black coffee?" Marc asked after I placed my order. He slid a ten-dollar bill across the counter. "Thank God. My old girlfriend took this crazy mix of cream and hazelnut flavor. I could never get it right. Ugh. Black is so easy."

I pushed the ten back to him.

"Save your money for that student loan," I told him, smiling.

He nodded. "Thanks, babe."

Babe? He kept talking. "Every penny counts."

He put the bill back in his jeans pocket while I paid for our coffees.

"But you miss her, right?" I said, trying to pretend that twentyish men called me *babe* every day. "Otherwise you wouldn't be thinking about her coffee."

He grinned. "Yup. Cried like a baby the day she left. She got a big job in California. She had to go. It's been two years, but I still talk to her almost every day."

We moved to the pickup counter. Through La Colombe's four-foot-high speakers, Sheryl Crow crooned, "You're my favorite mistake . . ."

"Why didn't you go with her?"

"Complicated. She was older. She wanted kids. Only a few years to squeeze them in. I was right out of college. Everything was good between us, but we were at such different places in our careers and our lives."

The barista put our steaming coffees on the counter. Mine was so hot, I could hardly pick it up.

"When her job offer came, we both knew it was time to end it. But when you love someone, it never feels right to let go."

Wow. If he'd been in his twenties, and she had only a few more years to have kids, she must have been at least ten years older. Maybe fifteen. Was he one of KC's MILF fans? Obviously, he wasn't afraid of loving someone older. Or talking about it. Did that explain why he'd been flirting with me?

He walked me back to the TT. We stood on the Philadelphia sidewalk, generously festooned with gum and trash. He talked, I listened, and we finished our drinks. He took my empty cup in his free hand. Our fingertips touched briefly and I felt a jolt of connection.

"And now? Anyone special?" I asked him.

"I'm trying to be good," he said, looking straight into my eyes with a mischievous grin.

I slipped into the driver's seat and turned the key. In the rearview mirror, I watched him watch me drive away, holding both recycled cardboard coffee containers, an inscrutable half-smile on his perfect twenty-whatever lips.

———————

Before I knew it, it had been more than a week since I'd heard from Damon. Then I had a three-day trip to Orlando to speak at the Delta Gamma national convention. I texted him when I got home, the day before the AAU baseball nationals, to ask if he wanted to watch it with me.

Oh, I'm sick as a dog. Haven't been to work or yoga. Gonna have to miss the finals this year.

I offered to bring him homemade soup, medicine, books to read. Whatever he needed.

I don't want you to see me like this, he texted back. I don't want anyone to see me like this.

I gave birth to a child in the U Penn hospital lobby, I wrote. I've changed over 1,000 diapers of the humans I love most in this world.

Hahaha. Let me feel better. Imagining you holding my hand in
yoga is all I need now.

Okay, Damon. Have it your way!

That was that.

———

Philadelphia Airport security. A man behind me, wearing a black
and gold Pittsburgh Steelers cap, flashed me a grin. He had large
blue eyes, paler than Dylan's, though. I started blushing and spun
away.

After years wrestling my way through security, pushing strollers overloaded with baby supplies and actual babies, airports had
now, to my surprise, become vast pickup bars. In case you've been
blind like me, let me enlighten you: airports are stocked with men
like trout in a pond, mostly traveling solo, easy to approach with
casual questions about destinations and delays. Although not all
the men in airports were quite as attractive as this man, whom I
was too shy to even smile back at.

I took off my boots to go through the metal detector. The man
with the Steelers lid plopped his bag onto the conveyor belt. He
wore a Florida Georgia Line T-shirt and jeans. He was younger—
late thirties, I'd guess—and muscular. Strong hands. No wedding
band.

I heard KC's voice in my head, telling me to turn my body toward him, to smile back. So I did.

"Nice socks," he said, after our eyes met. He looked down at
my stocking feet as other passengers pooled behind us.

Everything I was wearing, including my boots and jeans, was
black, my usual travel uniform. What did he mean?

I glanced down. Under my black suede boots, I'd thrown on
electric pink, purple, and orange socks that looked like I'd stolen
them from a five-year-old, which I probably had.

"Thanks," I managed to force out, red-faced.

Once I was on the other side of the conveyor belt, I was so frazzled I put my boots on the wrong feet.

I wish I were joking.

"Hey, have a nice flight," he said, hoisting his bag over one shoulder while looking at my mismatched boots and grinning as I stumbled away.

What was wrong with me? A cute guy. Single. Friendly. And I couldn't say more than one word to him, and then make a fool of myself like a kindergartener dressed up in her mom's high heels. Would I ever get good at flirting with men?

I had almost an hour until my flight left. The terminal was small, a cul-de-sac with only ten gates. Maybe I could find him, have another crack at this, and redeem myself enough to face KC.

I walked from gate to gate, pulling my black Rollaboard, clutching my business card in one hand. *You can do this*, I told myself.

Oh God. There he was. Standing next to the red and white checked Five Guys burgers sign with two friends. All unusually muscular, dressed similarly in jeans and T-shirts.

I walked up to them, like an eighth grader trying to sit at the cool kids' cafeteria table, punchy with adrenaline, hoping the men could not see my knees trembling.

"Hi again." I smiled. So far, so good—two words in. Like an inane cheerleader–cum–fairy godmother, I tried to reassure myself.

All three men stared at me like cows in a pasture watching traffic go by. *No one can tell you are sweating*, I said silently. Then I started really sweating.

"So, where are you guys headed?" I managed to ask. I could smell the salty potatoes sizzling in the Five Guys fryer.

The man with the brilliant blue eyes stepped away from his friends. Maybe he could tell how hard this was for me.

"We're from North Carolina," he said. "We had a business trip up here."

The cashier called out, "Number four sixty-nine! Number four sixty-nine!"

"Ah. Sounds good." That was all I could squeeze out. I rocked back on my heels, feeling I'd matured to at least sixteen years old, talking to a new guy at the school dance.

"What kind of work do you do?" I succeeded in asking, as a bead of sweat trickled between my breasts.

"We're Marines. Marine Special Operations Command. We led a weeklong training off the New Jersey coast. We do it a few times a year."

"Ah, sweet."

No wonder he was frighteningly fit. But not as verbal as this conversation required. It was up to me to keep this paltry exchange going.

"I'm heading to Alaska. For work. My first trip there. Have you been?"

"No. Long flight, huh?"

This was worse than a blind date. I fought the urge to wipe my forehead, which was covered in a light coat of perspiration. Time to pull the rip cord.

"Well, it was nice meeting you. Have a safe trip home."

Then I remembered KC's admonition: give him your name. Duh.

"My name's Leslie, by the way." He took my card, slightly crushed from my sweaty grip.

He didn't say anything. His two friends stepped toward me.

"Hey, we want your card, too," one said, with a hint of a leer tossed in.

Oh my God, I didn't want every man in the airport calling me! The idea was horrifying and humiliating. Blue Eyes shot them a glare.

"Oh, never mind. We'll . . . um . . . look at his," the friend added meekly.

I smiled and turned away. Quickly.

Well, I did it, at least. I gave him my name, although I didn't get his. I walked away, dodging families with strollers and businessmen with briefcases, dragging the Rollaboard behind me like a bedraggled stuffed animal. I rued how absurd this whole five-boyfriend strategy was. How had men weathered this humiliation, asking women out, since we were teenagers? I'd never thought how hard it must have been for them.

I went to my gate and looked around for a place to charge my phone. When I glanced up, the Steelers man was in front of me, a big grin on his face. This time, he held out his business card in a muscular, calloused hand.

"Sorry about my friends," he said in his soft Carolina twang. "Leslie, I'm Chris. Chris Bailey. Nice to meet you. It was good of you to come find me. I thought I'd return the favor. Thank you for your card. Here's mine. I wrote my cell phone on there, too. Next time I come back, I want to take you to dinner."

It was easy to smile at that, so I did.

"I never do this kind of thing," Chris said, smiling down at me. "I'm really shy. But I mean it."

"Sure," I said, putting out my hand. He shook mine. I could see the soft brown hairs on his forearm.

"Take care, Chris. Nice to meet you."

I watched him walk away, looking over his shoulder at me, smiling.

Chris Bailey stopped halfway across the shiny terrazzo airport walkway.

"I changed my mind," he called back to me, pronouncing the last two words like *mah mahnd*. His words carried over the waiting area, filled with molded gray plastic seats, moms with toddlers, dozens of travelers, all suddenly staring at us. He continued, as if now that he'd gotten a head of steam, he couldn't stop.

"Two dinners!" Chris Bailey put both arms in the air in a V shape. His voice echoed across the airport hangar. "I'm taking you out for two dinners next taaahhm!"

I wasn't sweating any longer. I was beaming. It felt like the whole airport was watching, thinking middle-aged-girl-meets-hot-young-guy who makes her feel good about herself again, awww . . .

Okay, maybe KC was right. Maybe I could do this. Wait—I *was* doing this. And it was fun.

Dozens of buzz-cut soldiers in green and brown camo were scattered around the ski resort lobby as I hunted for coffee the morning after my keynote address at the district attorney's domestic violence conference outside Anchorage. It was summer, even in Alaska, so there were no skiers. The hotel had been empty when I went to bed the night before. Now clumps of uniformed men covered every couch, spilling out to the stone patio and outdoor fire tables. Was this an inside joke from God?

To find out, I approached a comparatively ancient man in his forties sporting what looked like a commanding officer's stripes.

"Yes?" he said with a serious face, as if addressing the First Lady of Alaska. "Ma'am?"

The "ma'am" got me smiling.

He smiled back. He was shorter than I was, with a sturdy build and buzz-cut gray hair, and a gap between his two front teeth. My favorite imperfection in a man. My grandfather had a tooth gap, too. I'd fallen for Marty's tooth gap the first time he smiled at me. Until the day, ten years into our marriage, a new dentist mentioned that of course, Marty should get the gap capped.

"But honey, I love your gap. It's the best part of your smile," I told Marty when he came home that night. "Don't take away the gap!"

I hadn't been joking. Yet, a few weeks later, one night while we were eating our dinner salad, the gap was gone. Marty didn't say anything about it, as if my view had been irrelevant to his decision.

"Our transport planes from Japan to Ten Thousand Pines in California had to be diverted last night," the captain explained. This resort was the only place within three hundred miles that could accommodate so many men. "We've got six in each room."

I raised my eyebrows at that. However, despite waking up in a rustic paradise surrounded by hundreds of buff, unencumbered single men, before I could even think about flirting with anyone, I needed time alone to recover from the flayed-skin feeling I got after delivering my keynote about surviving relationship abuse in my twenties. I thanked the captain and went out to my rental car. Alone.

I drove down the curvy Seward Highway from Anchorage to the Kenai Peninsula, searching for a hike despite the light rain that had begun to fall. I passed so many bald eagles and moose that I stopped keeping count. A familiar ache rippled through me as I wished that Bella and Timmy could see this place, too; I felt this way every time I traveled without them. The road sliced through indigo, snow-covered mountains that looked like the Rockies had a hundred babies who had moved out west to find room to thrive.

I parked next to three moose as big as pickup trucks, placidly munching catkins and tall reed grasses. Across the road, a glacier melted like a huge inverted white triangle. The morning air was cold and damp; it was like I was inside an igloo, which I kind of was.

At the entrance to the path, I laced up my hiking boots under a dew-covered, Plexiglas kiosk holding a map of the Resurrection River Trail. Inside, under a graphic showing an orange sun rising over a jagged purple and blue mountain peak, the cautionary notice read:

TRAVEL ON THIS SECTION OF TRAIL IS FOR THOSE WHO SEEK RISK AND SOLITUDE, ARE SELF-RELIANT AND WANT A CHALLENGE.

I set out along the rocky, two-foot swath of path. Could those words describe me? I craved risk and solitude as I sought resurrection, of myself, of who I'd been as a little girl and an independent twentysomething woman before I'd fallen in love with Marty and started losing little bits of myself trying to become his ideal wife.

After an hour on the rugged, rocky path, my thought pattern veered from philosophical to practical: *You are alone, in Alaska, hiking a rainy trail marked with a sign to scare people off.* There had to be moose and bears and bobcats lurking behind the white spruce. I had seen zero other hikers and only one small metal trail marker once I left the trailhead. How long would I survive alone if I got lost out here? Maybe I wasn't so brave.

The map had starred a spectacular view of a glacial lake within four miles. Where was the turnoff? All I could see were rocks and bushes. Fir tree branches overhead surrounded me like a dark green circus tent. Despite the cool, wet weather, I was sweating. My thirty-two-ounce Nalgene water bottle was half-empty. Turning back seemed prudent.

But I didn't. I pushed on, stubbornly, for another thirty minutes, despite my sweat and doubt. I rounded a bend. A twelve-foot-high boulder blocked the path.

"Fuck," I said out loud to the rock face. It looked like it had been there for several centuries. Was I supposed to climb it, or go around? There were no blazes or arrows. The rock took up the entire path. Thick, scratchy rhododendron and scrub spruce trees flanked each side.

I decided to climb the boulder.

I scrabbled up, digging my hiking boots into shallow toeholds and scraping the skin off my knuckles and palms. I could barely breathe from the exertion of hauling my body straight up a slippery rock in the rain. This was crazy. I was crazy.

"Screw you, universe," I said under my breath. I gave myself one last push and almost fell over the top of the rock. I lay with half my body across the crest, my legs dangling behind me.

Laid out before me like a Patagonia catalog cover was a panoramic view of an ultramarine glacial lake, ringed by endless dusky blue snow-capped mountains. I felt gutted by the beauty before me. Easily the most spectacular sight of my life. Off to the right was not just a rainbow but a double rainbow.

For once, I wasn't afraid of heights.

I stared at the lake and the mountains and rainbows, hung my head, and laughed out loud. At myself, at my self-doubt, at my inane inability to see that this was the point of pursuing a path of risk and solitude. My attempts to curse the universe had been met with splendor, regardless of my shitty attitude and bloody knees.

"Okay, Okay," I said out loud. "Thank you, universe. I get it. This is the right *fucking* path."

I stood at the edge of the newsroom under six TV screens and high-tech studio intercoms. I'd been back from Alaska for a week. The scrapes on my legs and knuckles had just finished scabbing up. Marc leaned back in his swivel chair, holding a pen between two fingers like a cigar.

"I'm heading to New Orleans this weekend," he told me. "First time. Ever been?

"Yep. It's great," I gushed, distracted. It was a challenge to memorize my talking points while simultaneously breathing normally in the face of his cuteness. His jawline was straight as a ruler. I couldn't remember what kissing a man with an unlined cheek felt like. I kept my eyes averted from his two-day beard and chestnut-brown hair. I'd start mouth breathing if I got too close.

"It's New York with a funky soundtrack." I believe I managed to sound relatively calm. "The Laundromats all have bars and live music. What's the big occasion?"

I looked back at my note cards. The topic was how to talk to your kids about cheating. Cheating on tests and the SATs. Not the other kind of cheating, thankfully.

"Saying good-bye to my twenties," Marc said ruefully. He sat back and looked up at me with big brown eyes. He appeared genuinely sad.

I burst out laughing.

"You *infant*. You're going to love New Orleans. Have a blast."

Back home that afternoon, I got a Facebook friend request, from . . . Marc Jessup?

A few minutes after I accepted, he messaged me.

"I want to send you updates from my trip," he wrote. "And, btw, you looked super hot today."

I flushed, flattered but hesitant to respond. Professionalism. We worked together. Sort of. We watercoolered together. But . . . I was not technically an employee. Right? And did Marc have any idea how much older I was?

He didn't send me a single picture from New Orleans, though. The next week when I figured he'd be back, I sent him a private, intentionally innocuous, FB message.

> *How was your New Orleans trip? Did you eat beignets? Go on the Voodoo Tour?*

Marc didn't reply. Maybe he was violently hungover, sleeping in a New Orleans gutter.

Right after my TV hit that morning, I had to go to a funeral for a college classmate and golf buddy of Mom's at the gothic Cathedral Basilica of Saints Peter and Paul, where Benjamin Franklin's and Grace Kelly's memorials were also held, albeit almost two hundred years apart. I dressed in my standard funeral outfit, a black silk kimono dress and patent leather stilettos. Which I also wore to the station before the funeral.

Marc was staring fixedly at his computer screen while I looked at my index cards by the watercooler, studiously not noticing me even though my kimono sash was six inches from his shoulder. Why had he ignored my Facebook message? Was he dissing me? One more data point proving men were the more mercurial gender, even though that's what they always claim about us.

I shrugged to myself. Maybe I'd ask him about New Orleans after the segment. I tapped one of my heels. I hated mustering up the mojo to chitchat with anyone before going on air, anyway. I felt jumpy every single time. My topic today: is a school's dress code good for teenagers, or harmful to their individuality? As for my own dress code, it was the first time I'd worn an actual dress to the station. I wondered if Marc noticed.

I rocked back and forth on my heels, jittery, waiting for the red "On Air" light to flicker off so I could slip into the studio. Marc still hadn't said a word to me. Then he cut his eyes to me. Or rather, to my legs in their opaque black hose. His gaze stayed frozen on my calves as if he were about to start sketching them. A long stare. Then, while still rubbernecking at my legs, he raised his eyebrows. It gave me goose bumps. The good kind. A man noticing my body still felt novel to me. I was probably the only female in Philadelphia who crossed the street to get *closer* to construction workers.

When I came out after my hit, Marc's swivel chair was empty but spinning, like he'd just gotten up. I left to go to the funeral, which, as expected, was unduly dominated by golf jokes. The family put her favorite driver in the casket, making me wish I'd thought of that for Mom.

That night, Marc finally responded to my FB message. The kids were at Marty's. Surrounded by the cats lolling about in the evening sun, I was in my PJs, savoring a bowl of coffee ice cream on the back deck with the crickets and the fireflies.

Leslie, what would you do if I showed up at your door with a bottle of wine and a movie one night? he wrote.

Hmmm. Not the time to tell him I had two kids and was wearing purple PJs with cartoon cats on them.

I'd open the door, I wrote back instead.

You should wear that dress every time you come to the studio, he wrote. *And those legs.*

What the hell did a forty-nine-year-old write back to a twenty-nine-year-old—excuse me, thirty-year-old—after that kind of compliment?

I stared at his message for a few moments, at a loss for words.

Another message flashed on my screen.

Hey, babe, I'm a little drunk. Sorry if I made you uncomfortable.

Again with the *babe?* I loved it.

Would it be rude not to write back? The mom in me was concerned about his feelings. I had to respond.

Not at all, Marc. I appreciate the compliment.

I figured that could be interpreted as professional, right?

End of story. No more drunken Facebook messages that evening.

It seemed the lesson here was that men of all ages were confusing. Best to ignore their conflicting messages. However, I found that impossible.

I waited another week before texting Damon about meeting up at power hour.

I didn't hear back.

Strange. But whatever. He was busy, too. Probably making up for the work he missed.

After a few more days of silence, I called him and left a rambling message on his voice mail.

No word from him.

Two weeks passed. I started to feel hurt and confused. Maybe he'd met someone new. Maybe he'd had a special someone all along. Maybe he regretted opening up to me about prison and his heart surgery.

As we'd gotten to know each other over the past few weeks, I'd worried that he was going to cut things off, because I was too white and too "Rittenhouse Squarey." Perhaps I was. Maybe Damon was more realistic about our differences than I was. But it wasn't right for him to disappear on me like that. Didn't I deserve better?

Two days before, I'd heard a segment on the radio about "ghosting." In case, like me, you don't know, ghosting is when someone ends a romantic entanglement or even a marriage by disappearing, never answering texts or phone calls, sometimes moving everything

out in a few hours when their supposed loved one is at work. A
woman called in who'd been engaged *for five years* to a man who
ghosted her. She'd finally hired a private investigator. Her fiancé
had been married with kids the whole time. His youngest child
had been born while they were supposedly planning their wedding.

Was Damon giving me my first taste of ghosting? Like in so
much of modern "dating," anything seemed possible.

At yoga one evening, missing having him in my sweaty corner,
I realized I'd gotten something valuable from Damon: the feeling
he embodied, that scars could be beautiful, that it was okay to reveal that life had beaten us up. I felt like writing him a note that
said, *Screw you for ghosting me, but thanks for showing me that I
want a man with scars, and one who appreciates mine, even if I never
see you again.*

Walking back home from yoga in the summer night, the lyrics
from one of my favorite Leonard Cohen songs came to me:

There is a crack in everything
That's how the light gets in

The security of married life was gone, my life cracked apart. I
had another chance at happiness, no matter what shape it took, or
how briefly it lasted. Maybe the answer, for me, was to find a new
kind of happiness by learning something from each man who came
into, and out of, my life, complete with cracks, imperfections, scars,
and all.

———————

Hi Chris. This is Leslie. You know, the crazy socks lady from the
Philly airport.

I'm surprised I haven't heard from you. I figure it's one of three
reasons:

—You don't like meeting nice women in airports.

—You're married.

—Aliens abducted you.

So, which is it?

I had heard exactly zero from Chris Bailey, the Marine from the Philadelphia Airport. So I sent that text to the cell phone number he'd handwritten on his card. In my phone, I had named him Crazy Boy, so that my kids couldn't rummage through my contacts and then tease me about him. An hour later, Chris wrote back.

> Sorry, I was laughing too hard to answer you. Wrong about all three. What happened instead was my friends Googled you. They told me you are famous and also that your Wikipedia entry says YOU are married. I was intimidated, although I'm embarrassed to admit it. I didn't know what to do.

Fuck. KC had told me to fix that Wikipedia line. I'd blown it off. I replied:

> Don't believe everything you read online! I'm not that famous. The Wikipedia site is outdated; I'm very divorced. Guess what? My agent booked me to speak at an event in North Carolina. So I'm going to cash in one of those dinners you offered. What do you say?

I could practically hear his soft southern drawl as I read his response.

> Leslie, I'd be honored. Do you like motorcycles? I have a very nice one. I'll pick you up at your hotel and take you to the best barbecue in Carolina and a long country ride through the backroad hills. What do you say?

I texted away: I say you are the sexiest man alive.

The dots on my phone rippled as he wrote back.

No, ma'am. But I will try when you come to town. I certainly look forward to seeing you.

When did I get so ballsy? I didn't recognize myself. That felt like a good sign.

———————

CNN sent a town car to pick me up at the studio after my next local segment, in order to whisk me across town to *their* studio for a live interview about a football player who'd cold-cocked his wife during an argument in preseason. She was now recanting and claiming it was *her* fault. Normal behavior for victims caught in the psychological abuse web, and one of the many complex emotional dynamics I wanted to explain to CNN's ten million viewers.

I had on gobs of TV makeup and an aqua leather jacket from Saks (thank you, American Express Reward Dollars) ideal for harsh TV lights. The camera zoomed tight on my face and upper torso for the live feed, so I'd learned that only my top mattered; the studio desk hid my pants or skirt or whatever. So under the jacket, I'd worn my oldest black Capezio ballet leggings, my favorite. I will cry the day the fabric gives out and I can no longer wear them.

The CNN interview went so well, and I felt so jazzed from the car and the makeup, I felt like Ted Turner was going to call to offer me my own show. My media booker posted the clip on the front page of the company's website, which felt like getting an A+ from your first-grade teacher.

When I was home that night making an early dinner for the kids so they could get to their important social media responsibilities, I saw another FB message from Marc pop up on my iPad, charging at a kitchen outlet. Before I could read it, Bella stopped chewing a bite of pasta.

"Mom, why are you paying so much attention to Facebook?" she asked with teenaged laser suspicion, the conviction that every single thing her mom did was (A) embarrassing and (B) her moral obligation to correct.

"Uh, work stuff, honey. A client," I told her. I ruffled her hair and she pulled away. I turned back to the screen and Marc.

You should frame those goddamn pants you wore today.

A cold thrill snaked up my body as I stood in the middle of my kitchen, surrounded by kids, rigatoni, and splattered red sauce. The idea of lionizing my favorite old stretch pants did get my attention. I'd been in the studio for only ten minutes, yet Marc had noticed me. I felt the same adrenaline rush I'd experienced as a ten-year-old tearing across my elementary school playground, when I realized the boy behind me was chasing me because he liked me, because I was special and worth chasing, and as soon as I had the guts I'd turn around and let him catch me.

What on earth was I supposed to write back to let Marc know I wanted him to catch me, without embarrassing myself? Forty years later, I still had no idea how to flirt without sweating and hyperventilating. Especially with a man twenty years younger. Especially via social media. So I wrote nothing back to Marc.

I served the kids seconds, then took my iPad into the powder room to check whether Marc had left another message. Before I could unlock the screen, Timmy called to me.

"Mom, can I have a glass of milk?"

It was like the kids had ESP. I sighed and put down the iPad. "Sure, honey."

I headed to the fridge. The truth was, I loved these increasingly rare moments when the kids pretended to need me. Even if it was only for a cold beverage.

After they'd scooted upstairs, each clutching their phone like a slice of semiprecious metal, I turned on the kitchen TV to watch the news and finish my salad. A minute later, my iPad lit up. I guess it didn't matter that I'd never responded to Marc.

Hey, can I text you instead? he asked. I don't use FB much, except for work.

I typed in OK and my number. I only had to wait a few seconds.

Can I say something private?

Private? My curiosity won out. I wrote back: Sure.

The three blinking lights lit up the screen as Marc typed away.

I want to taste you, Leslie.

I spit out a bite of lettuce, launching it over the kitchen island onto Marty's antique blue and red Heriz dining room rug. Thank goodness the kids were safely in their rooms.

I read the rest of Marc's message.

I need to be inside you, Leslie.

I had to reread the texts three times to be sure they meant what I thought they did. Is this how people flirted today? With sexually explicit messages? What was next—a picture of his johnson?

I kind of hoped so. At fifteen or even twenty-five, I would have found it gross, or even traumatic, to receive a text like that. But now, the power dynamic had shifted. I had no reason to be appalled or frightened. This man-boy, twenty years behind me on the path of life, had no power over me. He couldn't deny me a promotion or pressure me into sex before I was ready. And he wanted me. *Me.* Was Marc going to be the second man I made love to in my new postdivorce life?

Once more, I hadn't a clue how to reply. So I didn't do anything except blush.

Dylan Smyth. The two words at the top of my computer screen stood out like an electronic billboard in Times Square, practically paralyzing me. It had been over a month since I'd said good-bye to Dylan. What did he want?

I bashed my fingers on the keyboard to open the email. I was working late in my office off my bedroom, the small room that had once been the kids' baby room, the crib long replaced by a white-washed farm desk. From the French doors leading out to the Juliet balcony, I could see the blue lights in the hot tub and hear my mermaid fountain gurgling in the dark.

It was after midnight, and I had taken a break from writing an essay for the *Star* about the similarities between childhood bullying and adult relationship abuse to check email. I gasped, out loud, into the still night.

I read the email from Dylan against the soundtrack of my heart thudding in my ears.

Leslie,

Sorry I didn't give you a heads-up but I am in Philadelphia tomorrow night by chance, unplanned. I don't expect you to respond but just saying . . . Don't forget about me.

Dylan

My first thought was, *Yes, I want to see you, Dylan.* My second thought was, *I'll never forget about you.* I picked up my phone to call him. But it was too late. So I wrote back, **Of course. Tell me where and when to meet you. I miss you.** It took me an hour to fall asleep.

After I dropped the kids off the next morning, I called his cell phone. Dylan didn't pick up. I think he blocked my number or turned off his phone because when I tried calling again, his phone started making a funny clicking sound. His voice mail had been disabled, so I couldn't leave a message. I refreshed my email queue and checked my text messages obsessively all day and into the night. He never replied.

It felt like chasing a receipt dropped on the sidewalk on a windy day. Awkward and desperate, I was reaching for a crumbled piece of paper almost in reach, then always out of my grasp. I started to question why he'd sent the email. Was it some kind of weird joke or a hallucination? But it was there, in my email queue, flagged so I could find it easily. Which of course I did a few times a day, even though eventually, I tried not to read it anymore, because it made me too angry.

How could I still want Dylan? When I left my first husband, I'd promised myself I'd never let a man abuse me again. I left Marty because neglect and deceit are another kind of abuse. And what Dylan was doing—saying no, then yes, then no again, on his terms only, even writing *Don't forget about me*—was yet another kind of manipulation, a form of saying *Your needs don't matter to me*.

But they did matter. I mattered. I only wanted men in my life who got that. It took me until the end of the day, but around ten o'clock that night I deleted that email and all his voice mail messages, except for the one he'd left after getting my first letter. I promised myself that neither Dylan, nor any man, would get the chance to yank me around emotionally like that, ever again. If Dylan emailed me or called me, I wouldn't jump. Well, maybe I would. I still had my list of sexual experiments I wanted to know if he liked. But if I saw Dylan Smyth again, I'd jump on my terms, not his.

———————

Still wet from the shower the next morning, my hair wrapped in a towel, I riffled through the shirts in my closet. Did I have the guts to do it? I had to give Marc some kind of visual sign, an answer to his dirty texts. Plus, I had to do something, anything, to stop feeling haunted by Dylan's email.

I felt like calling KC, but some things you have to decide yourself. Squaring my shoulders for courage, I took a pale blue blouse off its hanger and pulled on the Capezio pants. Then, for the first time in my adult life, I walked out my door braless. Thank God my mother was dead.

At the station, I didn't say hi to Marc or make eye contact. I can't tell you what he was wearing or if he'd shaved that morning. I stood in front of his desk, as I usually did, with my back (and the ballet leggings, and what was inside them) a few inches from him. I pretended to read my notes, when I was actually trying not to flush fire engine red.

After counting to fifteen in my head, I unbuttoned one more button on my blouse, and turned and leaned in front of Marc's desk, pretending to pick up a pencil from the floor. To everyone else, I'm sure I looked totally normal. Maybe.

Marc froze. Pretending to read my flash cards, I watched him out of the corner of my eye. After a moment, he went back to staring at his computer. He said nothing.

I got a text as soon as I'd left the studio after my segment.

I need to see you. Alone. Tonight.

So he had noticed.

I texted back. I can't. Kids will be home.

He replied right away, as if he'd been holding his phone and counting the seconds until I responded.

Then now. I have to fucking see you right away.

Laughing, I texted him again. Cleaning lady is here.

This was fun.

I don't care. I'll cover your mouth when I make you come, so she won't hear you scream.

God, he was bold.

Ok, I texted back. Then I typed my home address into the phone. And pressed send.

The doorbell rang. So little time had passed since I'd texted Marc my address, it was as if he'd run all the red lights and parked sideways in front of my house like a character in a Batman comic. I opened the door, and there he was, adorable, his hands jammed into his jean jacket pockets. His hair was ruffled and his face unshaven. As soon as I let him into the foyer, he slammed the door shut with his foot and pushed me up against the mirror in my hallway and started kissing me.

"Jesus, I could hardly drive, my cock was so hard."

He closed his eyes and started kissing me again, his mouth open, his tongue adamant. My back was pressed up against the gold lacquered mirror frame. He slipped his hands up my blue shirt and cupped a breast in each hand.

"Your breasts are gorgeous," he said, palming them. "Nice trick, showing them to me like that. Ahh, they feel good, too. I knew they would."

Before I could do more than kiss him back, he slipped his right palm down the front of my yoga pants, cupping his warm hand over my crotch.

"I'm keeping these pants," he said. "So no one else can see you wear them."

Then he slipped two fingers inside me. I was soaked. My knees buckled. He let out a groan.

The basement door squeaked. I whirled around, holding his wet hand behind me.

"Kiki!" I said quickly. "This is my friend Marc."

Marc flushed pink to his temples. He stepped beside me and folded his hands over the zipper of his jeans. I wiped his saliva off my lips with the back of my hand. Our housekeeper, Kiki, had taken care of the kids, the cats, our house, and me for over ten years. During which time she'd read all my rough drafts, tweaked my TV makeup, seen me cry a dozen times, heard me yell at the kids, checked on me while I was vomiting from food poisoning, and clucked over the weight I lost while worrying about my divorce. She'd probably seen Marty twice during that entire time.

"Nice to meet you." She greeted Marc in her Japanese accent, with a small, formal bow, as if he were a visiting diplomat. "Can I get you both something to drink, Miss Leslie?"

Kiki always pronounced my name *Resrie*. Which seemed fair, because the kids had altered her name from Keiko to Kiki when they were little. She made all of us keep calling her that, even after Tim and Bell learned better pronunciation skills. "Sexier name," she had deadpanned to me one day when we were home alone together.

"Ah, no, that's okay, Kiki. I'm going to show Marc the house. We'll have a drink later."

"I go back to the laundry," Kiki said, trying to keep her face expressionless. Her jaw twitched slightly and her black eyes sparkled in amusement. As I ushered Marc up the curving mahogany staircase to my bedroom, I looked over my shoulder. Kiki simpered at me, and made the universal finger shake with her free hand that meant "smoking-hot handsome," snickering as she retreated down the basement steps.

As soon as we were upstairs in my bedroom, I started taking off Marc's clothes. Unlike with Dylan, I wasn't on edge with Marc. It was as if I'd saved up my sexual desire for years and it all came out in bed with him. True to his promise, he made me scream. Twice. He couldn't cover my mouth, though, because at the time he was using both hands to spread my legs as far apart as he could, his unlined, unshaven cheeks rough on my thighs as I squirmed. He was into nipple biting, which I'm not in general, but at the time, it turned me on. Everything he did turned me on. Luckily, we'd turned his favorite country playlist to the highest volume on my bedroom stereo. Forget about alarming the cats and freaking out

Kiki; I was worried about my neighbors and strangers on the side-walk calling the po-po.

Afterward, exhausted, I lay in his arms with the afternoon sunlight streaming through the French doors to the balcony. Marc reached over to turn down the volume on the music, my sea-green sheets wrapped around his waist. I watched him in wonder. He had dark brown chest hair, muscular pecs despite his skinniness, and forearms sprinkled with the same dark hair. We talked—well, he talked, and I listened—about his problems and ambitions, much in the same way my kids and their friends talked to me about where they wanted to go to college.

He began reciting, starting in 1970, the Country Music Associ-ation's annual Song of the Year.

"You show-off," I teased, laughing. He was showing off. How-ever, the real reason for my giddiness was awe that I had just had sex with a handsome thirty-year-old sexpot who was naked in my bed. I felt like taking a video to prove it to KC and Winnie.

"What year were you born?" Marc asked, oblivious to my de-light. "I'll tell you your song."

"Ha, nice try, Marc," I retorted. "NFW. I'm not telling you how old I am."

"Nineteen seventy-three?" he guessed, smiling, looking like a country music star himself.

He was off by almost ten years. "Not telling," I insisted. I formed the words that would explain how complicated age is for women. Then I hesitated. Sharing about myself felt inappropriate, as if I were the teacher or therapist here, and shouldn't divulge per-sonal details about myself, even as I encouraged Marc to open up himself.

I had to change the subject to something more preferable than my age.

"So . . . what do you think of anal? I tried it a few times in high school." I rolled over and sat up on one elbow. "I had a crazy adven-turous older boyfriend. We didn't fully understand the importance of lubrication. It wasn't a terribly successful experiment. Ouch."

Marc bolted up on the pillow next to me. He shook his head in the afternoon sun. He examined me in wonder, with a melting cookie-dough glow in his eyes.

"You are fucking kidding me. Are you *perfect*? It's the one thing I've never done. Can we please do it *right this minute*?"

His dick grew hard under the sheet, almost like a *Playboy* cartoon drawing.

He started kissing my lips like they were edible fruit. He turned me over and cupped the sides of my naked butt in his hands. Above my bed I'd installed a large rectangular mirror right after Marty moved out, to bring the light into the bedroom. In the glass, I could see Marc looking at my ass like he was afraid it might vaporize if he didn't get cracking. I reached over for an industrial bottle of lube from my bedside drawer.

"Use a ton," I said, meaning it.

I watched him in the mirror as he entered me from behind. He was gentle, taking it slow. He had his eyes closed almost the whole time, his lashes forming half-moons. The expression on his face, reflected in the mirror above my head, was like a child tasting his first ice cream cone.

I asked him how it felt.

"*Amazing*," he managed to gush, his eyes still shut.

In all my years, I'd never knowingly been a man's "first" in anything. It felt like one of the most intimate things I'd ever done with another human being. Life as a forty-nine-year-old MILF was as confusing, and electrifying, as being a teenager in the 1970s.

Later, as we soaped each other up with green Vitabath in the shower, he leaned over to kiss me again, water pouring down over us. I could feel him getting hard against my thigh. He groaned and pressed me against the shower wall tile.

I suddenly remembered the rest of my life—specifically, the daughter I needed to deliver to the summer camp play. I pushed his chest away and grabbed a towel. I lunged for my phone, which I'd managed to throw in the sink at some point, to check the time. I had to pick Bella up in seven minutes.

"Oh my God, Marc! You have to go."

After a hasty good-bye, I jumped in the TT, rushed to pick up Bella from Marty's babysitter, and we sped to the summer camp amphitheater. When I checked my phone at intermission, I got Marc's first text.

You're not going to be able to walk tomorrow, he wrote, adding a devil-head emoji.

I could barely walk now, so he was probably right.

Then, an hour after Marc's smiling-devil emoji, another text arrived. It was right after the final curtain call. The cast of ninth graders had finished bowing amidst thunderous parental applause. The mom next to me was so close, I could smell the mint gum on her breath and see the chips in her pink nail polish. I knew she'd think less of me, that she'd judge any woman, especially an older mom like me, for having a sex life that included a wild daytime frolic with a man twenty years younger. I didn't care what she thought, but I also didn't want her bad-mouthing me to other moms, and I certainly did not want my kids to hear any nasty rumors about me. So I angled my phone away from her, so she couldn't read my screen.

Babe, that was incredible. Totally mind-blowing. I had to do that. You are unforgettable. But . . . I have a girlfriend. I don't want to ruin it with her. So, I think this has to be a one-time thing. Are you okay with that?

On what etiquette planet is it okay to tell me *now* that he has a girlfriend?

Goddamn younger men. They (according to my data set of two) want . . . everything. Adorable, direct, lighthearted, and ridiculously talented between the sheets, maybe because they came of age with 24/7 access to Internet porn . . . and then, poof! They're *done?*

Having sex with twentysomethings was like using crack. Once.

I could still taste Marc on my lips, and he couldn't see me again? Ironically, Marc made me feel terrific—valued—*because* I was older and wiser. Maybe someone would say Marc was using me for sex, or that I was using him. Maybe both were true. However, the absence of long-term intention, coupled with our intense desire for each other, felt simple and refreshing, like gulping cold water after a long run in the desert. I wanted to see him again, soon. And he wanted to see me again *never*?

I wasn't sure whether to laugh, cry, or both. Sitting in the theater, clutching my phone, watching children I'd known since kindergarten hug their parents on the varnished wood stage, I felt delirious. And, as I crossed my legs, very sore. This was not, in any of its physical or psychological details, how I imagined my life would be the day Marty moved out and I vowed never to have sex again. How was it possible that Marc could make me feel so sought-after, and so rejected, at the same time? Was this yet another chapter in the art of masculine manipulation, a man telling me again, *I decide how, and when, you matter to me*? Had I fallen yet again for a man's pursuit and abandonment?

I didn't know. I sat back, exhausted by the mental gymnastics. The bottom line: despite the flimflam of Marc and Dylan and Damon, or maybe because of it, my old married life didn't hold a tiny Bic lighter to my new single one. This adventure, no matter where it led, was better than the slow death of being with a man who didn't love me, or even like me. But obviously, I had more to learn about men, and what I wanted from them.

I smiled to myself and slipped the phone in my purse without replying.

———————

"Did you hear Mishka's back?" Bill asked, holding a yellow measuring tape larger than the Crazy Cat Lady mug the kids had given me for Mother's Day. Bill was the owner of the construction company Marty and I had used for our kitchen renovation a few years back. I'd asked him to stop by to give me an estimate to repaint the walls after years of scuff marks and scratches caused by Timmy using the hallway as a pitcher's bullpen.

Mishka was the project manager from Texas who'd overseen the remodel. He'd practically lived in our house for six months, six in the morning to four in the afternoon, five days a week. I saw him about a hundred times more than I saw Marty.

I remembered something eleven-year-old Bella had said at the time.

"Mom, why does Mishka stare at you like that? His face gets all loose."

I'd thought I was the one who had a crush on Mishka. He was one of those quiet men, always pausing before he answered a question. He was clean-shaven, with biceps large enough to pouf out the sleeves of his work shirts, like he'd stashed two blueberry muffins under the fabric. On his breaks, he liked to ask me about the national parks I'd hiked. Big Bend in Texas was the top of both our bucket lists.

It had not occurred to me that Mishka had a crush on me, too. He was ten years younger, which made me feel like a pedophile. (This was before I knew about younger guys and MILFs.) I started sneaking longer looks at him. Bella was right. He did stare at me for a few beats longer than normal, and his eyes lost focus when talking about wall studs and retractable screen doors. And we think children don't notice these things. However, I'd never let on to anyone, even myself, that there was chemistry between us. Part of the unwritten good-wife contract was that I had to erase men as sexual beings, and just as important, to block it out when men, like Mishka, looked at me, even though I'd craved that kind of attention. Being a wife got complicated.

"Glad to hear that," I said to Bill. "Last I knew, he was somewhere in Hawaii. On Oahu's north shore. Working as a lifeguard? Engaged to marry a local girl."

"Yep," Bill explained. "He's back to being single and he's done being a beach bum. Starting his own subcontracting business. Drywall, painting, that kind of thing. You could hire him instead if you want. Help him get started. We're probably too busy for this small a job, anyway."

Hmmm.

After Bill left, I texted the number he'd given me for Mishka. He wrote back a few hours later.

Great to hear from you!!!!!!!

There were almost as many exclamation points as there were actual letters.

I asked if he could stop by to give me an estimate. Friday at two o'clock, the doorbell rang, echoing up two flights of stairs to my office. I was lost in my computer like it was another galaxy.

"Fuck," I yelled. I hated when this happened, when I was writing furiously and found myself jolted back to reality by mundane life events like mail delivery. Half of what I paid Kiki for during the two days a week she worked was to open the door.

I thought it was probably UPS, or neighborhood kids selling candy bars. I thundered down the stairs before whoever was ringing the bell abandoned ship and decided to come back to interrupt me on another day. I threw open the door, breathless. There stood Mishka, his light brown hair streaked blond and falling to his shoulders now, like the Hawaiian surfer he'd become. A slight tan still colored his cheeks under the stubble. He wore faded jeans, and had his hands folded under his armpits like a nine-year-old boy.

He grinned at me impishly, like he'd been waiting all week to smile.

I had completely forgotten he was coming.

I gave him a hug, groaning over his shoulder to myself. Why hadn't I put on lipstick or brushed my hair? My leggings were covered with white cat fur. I had coffee breath.

I'd blown it again.

We walked around the first floor, looking at the white scrapes on the molding and gouges on the walls that made it seem, inexplicably, as if miniature medieval soldiers had used my house to practice sword fighting. Mishka and I had spent hours alone together every day when he was working on the house and I was home writing, so even after not seeing him for a few years, it felt natural for us to be alone now. He walked a few steps in front of me, hair spilling down his back, his thighs muscular in his Levi's, gently assessing my walls with his calloused hands. He stopped to pencil a few notes onto his clipboard. His yellow number 3 pencil looked tiny between his fingers.

He *radiated* sexy.

"I'll be right back," I said, ducking into the bathroom as he stopped in the hallway to run his fingers over a few dents in the cream-colored walls.

Once inside, I turned on the fan and faucet. I grabbed the lint roller under the sink and got the worst of the cat hair off my pants. I rinsed my mouth. I put on champagne lipstick and fluffed my hair as quickly as I could, so I wouldn't give away that I'd been primping.

As soon as I came out, he turned to me, holding his clipboard expectantly. He stopped mid-thought.

"Did you put on lip gloss?"

I forgot how up-front he was. Sometimes that was great. Now it caught me up so short, all I could do was blink. "Ah, yeah, my, ah, my lips were . . . chapped." I had to change the subject before my face turned as pink as my mouth.

"So, how was Hawaii?"

"Beautiful. Expensive. Unbelievable surfing. You'd have loved hiking Mount Tantalus." He ran his thumb over a two-inch pockmark outside the bathroom door. "But it was oddly . . . lonely."

He was still eloquent, and open, with only a few words.

"I heard you were getting married?"

"Engaged. Briefly. I couldn't go through with it. She was a great lady, totally amazing. But she wanted kids. To settle down. To live in Hawaii forever. That's not me. Don't get me wrong. I loved Hawaii and I'm crazy about kids. I saw how happy you were with yours. It was one of the best parts of this job. But I'm really a kid myself. I'm happy that way."

Now, this kind of blunt I loved. I leaned back against the dining room wall.

"Dating anyone?"

"Not really." He let the clipboard hang at his side. "God, it's good to talk about this with you, Leslie. My married friends and my mom don't get it. Do you mind?"

I shook my head. "No, Mishka, I like hearing all this."

He turned to examine a gouge in the wall above an electrical outlet.

"It's hard to date at my age. At this stage. Every woman seems to be hunting for *the one*. Since Lisa and I called it off, I decided to be frank on the first date that I don't want marriage or kids. Women like that I'm honest. But they're clearly disappointed, 'cause 'just dating' is not their agenda. I don't go on a lot of second dates."

He turned red and looked down at his boots. Wow. Once again, I wished I'd thought more about dating from a man's perspective. Maybe it was as hard for them as it was for us.

"How's . . . um . . . your husband?" It seemed obvious that he wanted to change the subject. "The Phantom?"

"Marty?" I blinked. Is that what the construction workers had all called him? Were our problems so obvious?

Mishka nodded, his smile at once all-knowing and mysterious, like the Chesire cat in *Alice in Wonderland*.

"We got divorced about a year ago." I scrunched my face, inadvertently, because it felt dishonest to try to capture our complicated dead end flippantly. Plus, I was embarrassed. Divorce seems like such a public failure, even though it feels more complex to me privately. Finding the right words isn't merely difficult, it's a fool's errand. The only people who can fathom the gory details of a failed marriage are people trapped in unhappy unions themselves. Friends who had never gotten hitched seem to accept divorce the most blithely.

Mishka was one of those. He looked at me and shrugged.

"It never seemed like you were really married, anyway."

No kidding, I felt like saying. But I didn't.

"That made it easier to nurse that crush I had on you forever."

I wanted to hide my head like a self-conscious kid.

"You didn't know?"

"What?" I pretended. "I had no idea."

Mishka looked at me like he knew I was fudging but didn't care. He kept talking.

"The first time I knew I was crazy about you was one Sunday afternoon. Probably four years ago. You were all here watching some football game. Marty was heading out on a business trip or something, going straight to the airport. I stopped by to take some measurements for that new basement door we were installing. You had on black yoga pants, kinda like the ones you have on now. God, those pants!"

Moms should *buy stock* in Athleta and lululemon.

He paused. He looked around for another gash to examine. There weren't any.

"You're such a MILF. I probably shouldn't be telling you any of this. But what the hell. I saw you hugging him good-bye at the front door. Something about that hug—you held him so long— made me think I wanted someone to hug me like that. Exactly like that. Then I figured out it wasn't someone I wanted. It was you I wanted. To hug me like that, like you really meant it."

My body heated up with that glow you feel in front of a bonfire. Mishka envied Marty, the man I loved, the father of my children, the man who didn't even like the way I hugged him anymore? Mishka *wanted* that same hug. *That* woman. *That* wife. Me. I stood in the hallway now, stunned by Mishka's transparency, more emotion than Marty shared with me during our entire last decade together.

"Can I take you out to dinner?" Mishka continued. "To talk more? I'd love that."

I nodded inanely, like a tourist confronting Al Roker's mic outside the *Today* show. Was this actually happening?

"Sure. But, Mishka, do you date moms you work for? What if someone sees us?"

Mishka paused and looked down at his hands in his jean pockets. His hair fell into his face.

"Yeah, you're right." He looked back at me, holding my gaze. "If Bill and the guys find out, they'll tease me for weeks. Not good for business to date moms who hire me. Well, actually—"

The smile lines took over his face. His eyes almost disappeared, turning into half-moons above his cheeks.

"I've got a better idea. Leslie, how about I cook you dinner? I learned some great Hawaiian recipes. I'm actually a good cook, for a single guy, especially a bachelor surfer from Tyler, Texas, with a weird Russian name."

"Um, sure." The kids would be with Marty next week. "How about Thursday?"

He wrote down his home address on the back of his new business card.

It was a date.

———

But first, I had to fly to North Carolina for a domestic violence awareness police officer training course. And to have one of my two Chris Bailey dinners. I fell asleep on the plane and awoke as if from a fever dream. What was it going to be like to see him again?

I'd invited him to my luncheon keynote, and he showed up just before my speech, handsome and formal in his Marine uniform, sitting quietly and very still at the head table next to me. His eyes were as blue as I remembered. He watched me during my speech, listening to me explain the complex psychological reasons victims stay in abusive relationships. I was busy for thirty minutes after the luncheon, answering questions one-on-one. Chris slipped out, texting me afterward. Leslie—I'm honored you invited me. I enjoyed it very much. Pick you up at your hotel at 5?

Excited but not knowing what to expect, I came out of the air-conditioned Holiday Inn lobby into the Carolina twilight. I'd changed into jeans and cowboy boots. Wearing a blue shirt that made his eyes stand out, Chris stood under the portico holding two helmets. Next to him leaned a gleaming red and black Harley-Davidson Road King.

"Evening," he said. He paused, as if about to add *ma'am*.

"Nice bike," I answered. "And thanks for coming today, Chris. I'm looking forward to the ride. And dinner."

I climbed onto the bike behind him and laced my arms around his waist. His abs were hard as molded plastic. His back muscles felt as thick as a horse's. His neck smelled of Dial soap. Chris revved the motor, and the Harley made the pavement feel like glass as we glided out of the parking lot onto a winding Carolina blacktop. For thirty minutes, Chris steered the bike past farmland. The road dipped and rose on gentle hills as the grassy fields changed into thick Carolina pines. The air cooled as the sun set and night fell. I breathed in the smell of fresh-cut grass and Chris's shoulder blades.

Chris slowed the bike at a low-slung roadside restaurant with swinging wooden-slat doors. We sat at a booth inside, near the doors. Conversation came easily. We talked of his family in Augusta. His efforts to teach his teenaged daughter to shoot squirrels. His days training in Hawaii and Fort Benning. The road trip to Niagara Falls he wanted to take on the Harley.

"You can stop for a night in Philly," I said, smiling. Chris smiled back at me, his eyes lighting up. "Or two."

For the ride home, he played a country mix on the Harley's stereo. Outside the hotel entrance, I handed him back his helmet. I shook my hair. We stood looking at each other, not saying a word. It felt like a scene in a romantic movie.

"Can I kiss you, Leslie?" Chris asked. Again, I felt like he had to stop himself from saying *ma'am*. I laughed.

"Of course."

His lips were warm and soft, like his hand had felt when he shook mine back in the Philadelphia Airport. He put his hand on the back of my head and stroked my hair. We kissed twice in the warm night, standing outside the Holiday Inn, the heat radiating off the asphalt and the Harley engine. And because Chris Bailey was a southern gentleman, that was it.

I stood outside the front door to Mishka's building, peering up at the windows, wondering which were his. The address was in South Philly, kitty-corner to Creperie Beau Monde, one of my favorite restaurants, in an old brick apartment complex of lofts carved out of a former lightbulb factory. It was five minutes after seven. I hadn't heard from him since last Friday afternoon at my house. I wasn't entirely sure we were still on for dinner. Which didn't matter, since I was too excited to register something as banal as hunger.

I rang the buzzer in the arched brick entryway.

"Yes?" I heard his scratchy voice coming out of the rectangular black slot by the door.

"It's . . . ah . . . me," I half shouted into the intercom. For some reason, I was afraid to say my name.

"Leslie? All right! I'll buzz you in."

I rode a creaky freight elevator up to the top floor.

Mishka stood waiting in front of the elevator, which opened directly into his loft. He smiled when I stepped out.

"Thanks for coming, Leslie. Come on in."

He had on faded jeans and a soft white button-down shirt. His long hair was still damp, brushing his shoulders. I caught a whiff of him as I walked into his foyer. He smelled like shampoo, and his apartment smelled like paint and sawdust.

His apartment was a breezy one-bedroom with a galley kitchen lined in exposed brick. There were power tools and paint cans everywhere. Windows everywhere, too. You could see the Ben Franklin Bridge from an open living room window. Two cats strode possessively toward me as I was taking off my jean jacket. Underneath I had on jeans, a sleeveless black silk blouse, and short black suede mules. Wearing yoga pants seemed too obvious.

His two cats sniffed me suspiciously, circling me like passport security inspectors deciding whether to let me into their country.

"Don't mind them," Mishka said. "My mom lent them to me so I wouldn't be lonely."

"Is it working?"

"Kinda," Mishka retorted. "But it's better now that you're here. I hope you like risotto with grilled pineapple."

He pointed to a large spiky pineapple on the butcher block counter by the fridge.

"Does anyone not like risotto?" I asked, trying to sound breezy.

I looked around, wondering where to sit. We regarded each other awkwardly. I'd never seen Mishka anywhere except in my own house. Being alone with him here felt like entering a secret tower to which I had the only key.

"Can I get you a glass of water? That's all you drink, right?"

"Good memory. Sure. Thanks."

I stood there like a doofus. I put my hands in my pockets.

Mishka came back into the small living room holding a glass of water tinkling with ice cubes. I took a big sip and then smiled crookedly at him, uncertain what to do next.

"How's work?" I asked.

"How are the kids?" he asked at the same time.

We both laughed clumsily. Then came a long moment of even more tongue-tied silence. He looked out of place in his own kitchen doorway. He glanced out the window. The cat at his feet meowed.

Damn it, I said to myself. *You didn't come here to stand around making shallow conversation.*

I put down the glass on a desk littered with bills and loose stamps. I went up to him. Before he could stop me, or I could stop myself, I laced my hands around the back of his neck. I looked into his eyes and pushed my hips against his. He put his hands on my waist. I felt small in his arms.

"I've wanted to do this for a long time," I said, leaning back into his hands so I could see his face. He didn't move. I wasn't quite sure what to do, so I moved closer to him and buried my face in his chest. God, he smelled great. I could feel his heart beating, slow and steady.

I took a deep breath and looked up at him. He seemed immobilized. I kissed him softly, letting my mouth fall slightly open. He kissed me back and then let out a full-body sigh. "Oh my God, Leslie. Me too."

We kissed. His lips were soft, like a nectarine, his cheeks rough with stubble. A good combination. Pressed against him, my body felt like pavement softening in the hot sun. We moved to the couch. Briefly. Soon we were on the floor on his striped wool Navajo rug. He lay on me gently, kissing me, his forearms cradling my head. I loved having his weight on me. It felt like there was a baseball bat under his jeans.

"Do you want to go into the bedroom, Leslie?" he asked quietly, shaking his brown hair out of his face, as if he was afraid I might say no.

I whispered yes.

Mishka held my hand as I followed him down a short hallway into his darkened room. I sat on his bed and he took off my mules as if he'd spent a summer working in the Nordstrom women's shoe department. He stopped undressing me to massage each of my feet, cracking my toes with his strong fingers, and slowly pressing his thumbs deep into the center of each sole. I didn't know a foot massage could be erotic. I wanted those fingers everywhere on my body.

I wasn't paying much attention to the bedroom decor, trust me. But I couldn't help noticing an entire wall covered with pictures of individual Dallas Cowboys and their iconic gray and blue starred helmets. There were at least twenty-five framed pictures, stretching from a few feet off the floor to the ceiling.

"The Cowboys?" I asked.

"Love them. I put the pictures up so women see stars in here."

Such a dumb joke, I couldn't help but laugh. He laughed, too, a joyous sound, as if he couldn't believe I was there in his bedroom, letting him undress me.

He slowly undid the buttons on my blouse. He slipped his hands up my back and undid my bra. He slipped the shirt off my shoulders and pulled the bra clasps toward me, loosening the shoulder straps, so that everything fell to his wooden floor in one smooth movement.

"Ahhh," was all he said, looking at my breasts. It was more of a groan than a word.

He undid the button on my jeans. He unzipped them and cupped his palm over the front of my pussy. He slipped the jeans off my hips more easily than I could have myself. Construction workers really know how to use their hands, obviously. He left on my white lace thong, which was already soaked through.

He pulled two pillows to the edge of his bed. Then he gently turned me over and slid the pillows under my belly, so that my ass was in the air and my thighs were spread on his bed. He did all of this excruciatingly slowly, intentionally, sliding his hands over my bare skin.

I felt like begging him to hurry.

"I want you inside me," I implored, looking over my bare shoulder at him. I hoped the words sounded slightly more genteel than *Fuck me now*.

He ran his palms over the soft skin of my hips.

"First, I need to do what I've been dreaming about for years," he said, pulling aside the thong with his warm, calloused hand. A jolt of desire ripped through me as his thumb touched the delicate outer lips of my pussy. "You have no idea how long I've wanted to do this." He bent his head between my legs. His tongue was soft and warm.

It was worth the wait.

——————

Wow, that happened fast. Loved every minute. But I don't want you to think I was expecting ALL THAT when I asked you to dinner . . . :)

I drove home from my date with Mishka—although little about this qualified as the kind of formal "date" I'd been on in my twenties—after we finally devoured the grilled pineapple risotto at midnight. I got his text while stopped for the light at a deserted intersection. I wrote him back as I sat in my driveway, still stunned and blissed out. Actually, I'd been waiting five years for that to happen. I loved it too.

The following Monday, I hired Mishka to patch and paint the downstairs walls, and then, to turn my basement, which had been a massive kids' rec room with a separate street entrance, into an apartment I could rent out for extra income. Keeping our home physically intact felt like the one source of stability I could provide my kids postdivorce. But on a writer's salary, shelling out for the house's upkeep would be hard. The maintenance and taxes alone outstripped my income. Rental payments would cover most of that.

"Forget about tenants," Mishka teased the day he started the project, sweaty and covered in paint flecks, sawdust like pieces of yellow confetti stuck in the ends of his long dark blond hair. "I'm gonna marry you and move in."

It didn't sound like he was joking.

"No other basement in Rittenhouse Square comes with these kinds of benefits," he said, smoothing his hands over my hips and pulling me close to him.

Almost every day at my house, he came upstairs to my bedroom during his lunch break.

"I've been masturbating to you for years," he confessed the second time he came up. "In Hawaii. Back home. Everywhere I went."

"Are you serious?" I asked, unable to hide my delight.

"Oh, you have no idea. Everything you do is erotic to me."

Mishka couldn't take his eyes off me when we were together, which made me feel like I had a one-hundred-dollar bill in my pocket. When I was with him, that is. I rarely heard from him in between. It was true, what he said: despite our lights-out sexual connection, he had no interest in any sort of commitment. After he finished the basement, I didn't hear from him for two, almost three weeks.

To my surprise, that felt perfectly okay to me, too.

———————

Back in Southampton, washing breakfast dishes one morning after ferrying my kids to the beach parking lot, I nearly dropped the dish soap on my big toe. I'd been randomly remembering how my ninth-grade boyfriend, Lyon Nash, used to kiss me and surreptitiously slip his hand up my shirt at school when no one was looking. Although I'd been boy crazy since first grade, Lyon had been my first true boyfriend. He'd driven me nuts. First with lust. Then with rage.

Out of nowhere, I suddenly understood Lyon as I never had before. With a clarity that made the backsplash tile seem a more vivid blue, I knew why I needed not one but all my "boyfriends" now.

We met in pre-K. Lyon was a six-year-old with floppy blond bangs. We used to sit in an old Buick that was part of the playground equipment, giggling together and pretending to know how to drive.

I didn't recognize him at first when he showed up again, ten years later, at my high school. Our two-hundred-student school was such a fishbowl, everyone tracked the new tenth-grade boy's movements as if an invisible camera man had a klieg light trained on him throughout the school day. Lyon was over six feet now, large-boned, with dirty-blond hair that fell below his ears. He looked like a Viking, impossible to miss or ignore.

Lyon was one year ahead of me, but an entirely alien species of boy compared to my classmates in their neat polo shirts. He landed with us after getting kicked out of a hippie New England boarding school. Not that Lyon told me any of this. I picked it all up, like candy wrappers that had missed the trash can, as he talked to tenth-grade girls between classes and before football practice. I stood at the edge of the huddle, figuring no one would notice me, a psychotically shy ninth grader who loved to write.

So it was a shock when the phone rang one Saturday afternoon.

From behind the study door, I heard Mom answer in the patrician Manhattan coo she saved for strangers on an elevator. I lay across the couch, reading *The Grapes of Wrath* for the second time.

There was a pause from the kitchen. I stopped reading mid-sentence.

The hairs on the back of my neck stiffened as I heard Mom say, with the hint of a fake British accent, "Well then . . . I'll get her."

Mom called through the door for me.

"Les? There's a boy on the phone for you." Her tone implied *believe it or not*. "His name is Lyon Nash."

Asking to speak to me. And then it got even better—he asked me out.

Our first date was filled with awkward silences, but I was thrilled the whole time. *I'm on a date!* I kept whispering to myself. We went bowling, and then out for ice cream sundaes. I told no one. I didn't think any of my ninth-grade bookworm friends would believe that I had a sixteen-year-old boyfriend whom all the senior girls flirted with. On our second date, my mother dropped me at a pizza place, and then afterward Lyon walked me to the bus stop. On our third date, Lyon took me home after school. I had told my mother I was teaching a gymnastics class to second graders.

I had never lied to my mother before.

Lyon's house was empty.

I was taken aback by my audacity, the way I had felt as a kid at camp, about to grab the rope swing that dropped you twenty feet above the swimming hole.

Holding my hand, he led me down a set of rickety wooden stairs to his basement bedroom. I tried as hard as I could not to look at Lyon. Or, wait for it—his *waterbed*. The scent of the bed—Lyon's oceany, chlorine-laced, plasticky smell I'd first noticed during my days sniffing him in the school hallways—filled the room and made me feel almost high. Sitting on the edge of the waterbed, Lyon lifted me up and around so that I was facing him, sitting on his lap, one knee on either side of his. He put each of my arms around his neck, like I was a doll. I let him kiss me over and over again. If I'd read that someone else's saliva could taste good, I'd have puked. But with Lyon, it was true.

I felt like I'd gotten a part in a play I'd never auditioned for. I was fourteen. I weighed a hundred pounds. I owned one bra, which I almost never bothered to wear, because I had little to fill it with. I focused on kissing him, because I didn't know what else to do. I felt the soft patch between my legs warming like chocolate melting, a feeling I'd never had before. I wanted to crawl inside Lyon's T-shirt like a kitten, and I craved his hands on me. Yet I couldn't bear for him to unbutton my shirt and look at, much less touch, my uncovered breasts. It felt like my body was pleading with Lyon to do what most petrified my mind. At the same time, I was equal parts terrified of making a mistake myself, and abjectly terrified of touching his penis, which had to be somewhere inside his pants, right?

After an hour making out in his dark basement, my hands accidentally brushed the front of Lyon's jeans. The denim felt warm and soft, the jeans so loose the folds formed vertical hills and valleys. I let my palms press around his hips, pulling our bodies together. Then my hands brushed his zipper, which felt cold compared to the blue jean material, and I let them rest on his penis. I was taken aback by how hard it felt, like he had a skateboard stashed sideways between his legs.

"Oh. My. God," Lyon groaned, startling me. Then his body shuddered and he collapsed against me. Holding me heavily, he didn't move for a few long seconds. Then he buried his lips in my neck.

I waited a moment. "What . . . happened?" I whispered tentatively in the basement gloom.

"I . . . ahh . . . I came," Lyon whispered huskily. Was it wrong to make a boy come in his pants? Was that gross? Weird? My neck and chest flushed hot with shame. Then, to my surprise, Lyon said something I'd never envisioned any boy saying about me. Ever.

"Damn, you're sexy."

Me? Sexy? I had tangled blonde hair. Goofy no-name jeans. A cheap blue and yellow winter jacket handed down from my cousin. Zero makeup. Braces on my front teeth. I was most definitely the "before" picture in a *Seventeen* makeover.

"I've never come like that before," Lyon whispered, like he'd scored the winning touchdown in the homecoming game. He sighed and wrapped his arms around me as if I were a cone of crumpled paper. His body was huge, his arms like oblong cushions, warm like the basement. His embrace filled me with relief and a new kind of inspiration, hope for my future as a woman.

Eventually, after I'd lost my virginity with him on that waterbed one chilly Valentine's Day weekend, I learned that I wasn't the only girl Lyon made feel special. We got back together after the first time he cheated on me. His mom had left his family and moved back to Boston, by herself. This made other girls feel sorry for him, which translated into Lyon getting into the basement waterbed with them, as he had with me. He couldn't say no to any of us, as if he needed a never-ending parade of high school girls to make up for his mother's abandonment. Each Monday morning, the school buzzed about another girl Lyon had taken into a back room at a party over the weekend. Did he also tell every one of them *Jesus, you're sexy*? It was humiliating and infuriating, because his cheating didn't make me any less crazy about him.

Three decades later, standing at my kitchen sink, I saw Lyon for who he was. Who he'd been at sixteen, anyway. Lyon had turned to me and other women for comfort, for self-esteem, for affirmation that he was lovable in the wake of his mother's baffling exit. He'd eventually righted himself, marrying and fathering two daughters. Thirty-three years after we'd broken up, dealing with a different kind of disappointment, I was doing the same thing. I was crazy about men now the way Lyon had loved each of his high school hookups. Including me. Each of the men in my life was a chip of self-worth, helping me rebuild myself.

Why had it taken me almost fifty years to validate my sexuality and the psychological gifts men gave me? Fulfilling my desire to connect with men, sexually and emotionally, following my and Marty's breakup was possibly the healthiest thing I'd ever done for myself. Dozens of male friends and colleagues had turned to women in the wake of divorce, without any long-term plans or commitment. Why was this response less socially acceptable for a woman? Men and women are built no differently when it comes to the rewards of sexual connection. Yet in nearly every culture, sexually active single women are disproportionately targeted by society's judgment. Was divorce at forty-nine making a man out of me? Absolving me from caring what the village thought of my sexuality? Or was I learning what it truly means to be human? Maybe all of the above.

———

Tonight?

Every two weeks or so, Mishka would text me, or I'd text him, this one word. If I was free from kids and work obligations, I'd drive to South Philly, park the TT, and sneak up to his loft. He'd make me dinner and then we'd take our time making love. Then I'd sneak out and slip back home under the cover of darkness, feeling like I was a teenaged girl again.

There were many joys of a minimalist boyfriend who wasn't really a boyfriend. Mishka and I did not go out to dinner, or a movie, or stop by the grocery store together. I didn't know what kind of car he drove. We didn't fight over how to load the dishwasher or hang the toilet paper. Our relationship was unadulterated: we ate, we talked, we made love. Not always in that order.

Plus, he cooked for me, and everything he made was delectable.

Sara said I was getting slivers of intimacy from Mishka, trying out vulnerability in doses I could handle. Her take was that I'd never had true intimacy with Marty, even in the good days, because he'd used condescension as a wedge from the beginning.

"Over time, you'll want more, and you'll be ready for more," she told me, with confidence I didn't feel myself. "Doesn't uncomplicated closeness with a man feel good to you?"

It did.

"Those eyes," Mishka told me once, kissing me as he cradled my face in his hands. "And this body," he said, running his palms down my hips. Even that momentary connection made me feel like a flower about to bloom.

One night, when it had been over two weeks since I'd gotten one of those Tonight? messages from Mishka, I texted him I miss you so badly my stomach aches.

Why? he asked back, fishing. I knew he was smiling at his phone.

Because you're sexy and funny and I love to hear what you think about life.

He sent back a smiley face, followed by And you're gorgeous and laid-back and smart.

I saved that text for the next time I missed him. Was this the ideal relationship? At least at this moment in my life, it was.

Mishka and I usually made love slowly, drawing it out as long as he could last. He always looked in my eyes when he came, finding them no matter what position we were in. Once he stayed inside me for an hour of bliss before reaching orgasm. Another night, when the kids were at Marty's, I fell asleep and woke up at three in the morning, the lights still on. Mishka was snoring and had his arm thrown casually around my back as if I slept there every night. It felt like we'd created a secret, and completely safe, world together.

"It's going to be hard to get married if no one knows about us," Mishka said when he woke up next to me. He ran his hand over his hair and cupped my hips to pull me in for a full-body kiss.

This marriage thing again. He'd been joking about it for the entire time we'd been seeing each other. He was teasing, right?

"You told me you never want to get married," I kidded him back, pulling his hair.

"Ouch," he said, holding my hands in his. "I'm beginning to change my mind." He smelled like wood chips and safety, strength. It elated me to hear him say that—and it alarmed me. This wasn't a relationship that could survive the harsh light of kids and fights about money and who should take the wheel on long car trips, even though it was probably the sweetest connection with a man I'd ever experienced.

We made love again before I had to leave. He lay on top of me, inside me, looking at my face as if he couldn't get enough.

"I love you," he whispered, his brown eyes meeting mine. I whispered the same three words back to him. To my amazement, I meant it. What was happening between us?

The early-morning breeze rippled the curtains by his bedside windows.

"Do you ever want more, Mishka? To see me more often?"
He leaned down to kiss me.

"Leslie, the truth is . . . no," he said, affection making his eyes go soft. "You know how much I like you. I love this."

He ran his hand over my bare lower belly like he was smoothing sand on the beach. It was where I had the most cellulite. Mishka never seemed to notice my body's flaws.

"But I don't actually like being with people too much."

Did Mishka deliberately limit our relationship? Did I? Was that so bad? I couldn't come up with any reason why it was. Between his work and my travel and my weeks with my children, it would have been a strain for both of us to find more time for each other. But every time I left Mishka's bed, I wondered: was that the last time? Despite what he'd said, that morning when his loft door banged shut I felt as I always did: I didn't know for sure when, or even if, I'd see him again.

"I'm taking you guys to Mexico!" a man's voice boomed from my speakerphone. The kids and I were playing cards and watching a rerun of *Almost Famous* one rainy Sunday afternoon. It was my little brother Mac, who had been six inches taller than me for thirty years. Mac sold beer at Candlestick Park and his voice had gotten permanently three decibels louder as a result.

"What?" The kids and I looked at one another.

"You heard right. I have a buddy in Ixtapa. And I got a big bonus. I'm spending it on you nutbags. Mexico is cheap now."

Timmy had a travel baseball tournament that weekend. So my brother, Bella, and I met in Ixtapa. We snorkeled. We parasailed. We kiteboarded. We got sunburnt.

It was heaven.

The last day of our vacation, Mac had booked our flights so that instead of flying straight home, we went through Mexico City so we could spend a day sightseeing there. Scarfing down fresh mango in the open-air lobby of the Nikko Hotel, Bella heard from other American guests that Popocatépetl was erupting. She came to me holding a scrap of paper with several numbers and dollar signs scribbled on it.

"Mom, I know this is crazy. But Paradiso Pilots will take us on a helicopter ride to see the lava and the eruption. The website says they use American pilots. Please? I know you're scared of heights. I know it's a lot of money. But I really think it's worth it."

Mac smiled at me, his salt-and-pepper bedhead hair sticking up, saluting with his guava juice and nodding *yes, yes, yes.*

"Come on, *mamacita,*" he cajoled, like he was in the baseball stands hawking five-dollar cold ones. "It's the goddess of the inner earth calling. We all need a little molten Mexican lava in our lives."

Three hours later, after charging hundreds of dollars to my credit card, we were all strapped in a glass-enclosed flying machine with four strangers hovering over acres of volcanic rock. We had been assigned seats based on weight distribution. My gigantic brother was behind me, flanked by Bella, who was overjoyed to have a window seat, best situated to take pictures to immediately upload to Instagram, plus two strangers. Thank God I was seated up front next to Captain Jeff, who introduced himself in Spanish as Jefe Jeff. His navy blue uniform and gold buttons somewhat allayed my fear of heights and helicopters. I took a couple of deep breaths as I strapped on my harness. It helped that if I breathed deeply, I could get a reassuring waft of Jefe Jeff's aftershave. It smelled like Old Spice Fiji. I snuck a better look.

Ay, caramba. Jefe Jeff looked to be in his midthirties, with spiky blond crew-cut hair. I looked at the control panel. He had gnarled thumbs, built up from years of tweaking the helicopter buttons and joystick. What else could he do with those thumbs?

Jefe Jeff narrated the flight over an earpiece and microphone. He had a melodic, slightly raspy, extremely seductive voice.

"Molten lava is fourteen hundred degrees, folks. That's not smoke over there, it's hot steam . . ." Jeff pointed out a former twelve-acre gated community, now covered in volcanic rock that looked like asphalt. Fascinating. All of it. Especially because even though the entire helicopter-load of passengers hung on every word he spoke into the headset, my name cropped up in almost every sentence.

"Leslie, look at the lava against the snow over there. Leslie, I hiked that trail up Popo last July . . . Leslie, that's the top of my apartment building . . ."

I doubted he was sincerely flirting with me. He was too young and too cute and Jesus, he was a helicopter pilot, one entire level of hotness above firemen and country music singers. He was probably looking for a big tip. He'd pegged me as the Money Bag, naturally. I'm sure flirting with older moms carrying designer handbags usually paid off quite nicely. No offense taken.

After a spectacular hour swooping into the steam above the lava, we climbed out of the helicopter, stiff from sitting, stunned by the natural beauty we'd seen. Bella immediately sprinted to my side. She looped her arm through mine and whispered conspiratorially, "So, found your soul mate, Mom?"

"He's a sycophant," I whispered so he couldn't hear.

"Mom, no," Bella said right away, her eyes wide and deep blue. "He's got a crush on you. Go get his number."

She gave my hip a shove with her butt.

I could have walked away. Most people would have been content with a cute story about a flirty pilot. I wanted more. After all, this year was about taking risks with men. So I whirled around without thinking and headed back to the copter. Jeff stood outside, smiling at us, like he'd been watching us. He still had on his headset.

"Hey . . . Jeff?" I said, buying time for my brain to think of something. I crossed my ankles as awkwardly as a girl waiting for a boy to ask her to dance at prom. What to say?

"Ummm . . . If you give me your email, I can send you the photos we took of the volcano. They're pretty good . . ."

I dug in, physically willing my body to stay put despite the fight-or-flight adrenaline coursing through me.

Fortunately, Jefe Jeff smiled. "Paradiso doesn't let pilots give out our info to clients," he said, shaking his head as if the policy was idiotic. But I wasn't sure. Maybe he thought I was idiotic or at the very least, a misguided cougar.

"It's actually in my contract. But tell you what. Leave a comment postcard with your email and phone. Put my name on it. I'll be in touch."

So I did. Bella shrieked like a banshee as soon as he was out of sight.

After the lushness of Mexico, daily life on the East Coast was a shock. No more volcanoes. No more fresh mango. No more helicopter pilots.

Two days after I got off the plane, an email arrived. The header got my attention pretty quickly.

Re: Red Hot Lava!

Hi Leslie! I got your email address and cannot wait to get your fantastic pictures! We've been doing training the last couple of weeks so it makes for really long days of flying and then ground school:(

Popo is still great. I can't believe you left;) I got to swim with this guy last weekend near Cancun.

He had attached three pictures of sea turtles.

Let me know when you're back in town;) or I'll let you know when I make it back to Philly to visit my old Peace Corps friend.

Jeff

The next night, I showed KC his email over sushi at our favorite place a block away from Penn. I was kind of embarrassed that there were so many typos. What was up with all the semicolons?

KC started snickering after reading Jeff's email.

"Those are not typos!" KC said, shaking my phone in my face. "They are winky faces."

"What are winky faces?"

KC grinned at me with the pity-face older sisters reserve for their hopelessly clueless younger siblings, even though, in this case, I was chronologically older.

"Leslie, if you'd date online like I've told you to, you'd know what a winky face is," she said, shaking her head at my pathetic cluelessness, miming *How does my dear friend survive in the world?* "It means he wants to have sex with you."

"What? Okay, smarty pants. Explain this entire email to me. Translate."

"See that thing—the ;)? After the 'I can't believe you left' and 'Let me know when you're back in town'? Those are winky faces. Like emoticons. A secret message. You only send those when you want to hook up with someone. Basically, he thinks you're hot."

She insisted on helping me write a reply, squeezing in my own winky face.

Hey Jeff! Thanks for your great email. I was reminiscing about how amazing the ride with you was ;). How's the lava? Been missing Mexico every day since I left. When you get stir crazy for the good ole mainland USA come visit me in Philly!

Leslie

I blushed as I hit send.

———————

Hello, love. I woke up to Mishka's text. I hope you enjoyed Mexico.

I texted him back. Yes. Dreaming of you.

I didn't hear back from him, which was typical. I decided to surprise him at the office space he rented in South Philly, something

I'd never done before. I parked behind his building and crept inside past a half dozen other leased office spaces. I stood in the doorway of his small, cluttered, square room, one hand on each side of the door frame. Tools and papers were strewn everywhere. He had finished lunch and was about to sip his Coke when he looked up and noticed me.

He smiled mid-sip. "Nice of you to stop by," he said after swallowing. He looked me up and down in frank assessment. He put down the Coke and dried his hands on a crumpled brown napkin.

"God, you look hot," he said softly. He stood and cupped my face in his hands. "Prettier and prettier every time I see you." His words made me feel as if the Mexican sun were still shining on me.

He stood up, went over to the door, locked it, and turned off the lights. I watched him, unable to figure out what he was doing.

"Come over here," he whispered, standing in the empty space between some large boxes of tile and the locked door. "No one can see us."

I went to him.

"Stand in front of me. Jesus, I missed you."

He put his fingers on my hips to turn me around so my back was facing him. He pulled down my yoga pants and he entered me from behind. He held me tight and bit the back of my neck as he pounded my pussy, going as hard as he could standing up, until he let loose inside me. He held me for a minute, breathing heavily. Then we both burst out laughing. He pulled my pants up, and I smoothed my hair and sat on a refrigerator box next to his swivel chair as if nothing had happened. He drained his soda.

Did a quickie in Mishka's office make me feel like he was using me? No. The reality that a man I liked and trusted could not be alone with me for more than a few minutes without wanting to be inside me made me feel valued and sensual. And I craved Mishka with the same desire. I couldn't think of a reason to feel badly about either.

I had a conference call at one thirty, so I had to go. When I stood up, there was a small oval wet spot on the box where I'd been sitting. We caught each other's gaze and laughed out loud again.

———————

Nice visit, Mishka. When do I get to see you again? Tonight?

My text that afternoon was a joke, considering Mishka and I rarely saw each other more often than every three weeks. So I was surprised when he wrote, If only. I have to work tonight. This week is pretty busy. But Saturday is all yours. Can you stay over?

Whoa. A Saturday-night sleepover, like a real girlfriend? I was honored. And scared and confused. I didn't want to be anyone's girlfriend. Or did I?

I texted back one word: Yes.

All week, my palms tingled every time I replayed the breathless way he'd said "I love you" as he moved inside me the last time I'd gone to his loft. I hoped he would say it again Saturday. Multiple times.

He called me on his way home from a job one evening a few days later. It was the first time he'd ever called me rather than texting.

"Leslie? It's me."

"Hi!" I was cleaning up cat vomit from the stairs, a pyramid the size of a small portion of caviar in a nouvelle cuisine restaurant. I sat down on the stairs and put the paper towels next to me. "How are you?"

"I'm good. Hey, look, I'm wondering about something. I don't get it. Why you like to see me."

Where was this coming from?

"Um, well, it's obvious that I like you, right, Mishka?"

He laughed.

"Yeah, but is it just the sex?"

"Well, yes, of course. I love making love with you. But you know I really like *you*. Not just the sex with you. Why are you asking all of a sudden?"

"I can't figure you out. You're not . . . needy the way other women usually are."

What was this really about?

"Mishka, you've always made it clear that you don't ever want to get married, to me or anyone. The other day you said you don't even like people that much. It's sweet when you tease me about marriage, but I assume you don't mean it. I'd be setting myself up if I tried to get something from you that you don't want to give. And also, I'm not ready for any kind of commitment myself. What's going on?"

"It throws me off. That you don't need me. I guess it's okay, but maybe I like to be needed. Even when I don't want more."

That made no sense. Why was it okay for Mishka to say he didn't want a commitment, and not okay for me to feel the same way?

"Well, okay, Mishka. Thanks for telling me this."

I paused, thinking this over. I decided to be bold.

"Why don't we admit we're falling in love with each other and that it frightens us both and talk more about it this weekend?"

"Well, okay," he mumbled. An unexpected lump rose in my throat. We both hung up. I finished cleaning up the cat puke. Were women supposed to be needy, even when men made it clear they weren't going to meet that neediness? How was that double standard fair? What woman would fall for it? Mishka never struck me as that kind of sexist guy. But he was a man, after all, and I still had much to learn about them.

Winnie heard through the high school grapevine that Lyon was in Philly for the weekend, visiting his dad. She knew I was trying to reach him. She looked up his father's landline and sent me the number.

His dad sounded far more delighted to hear from me than he ever had back in the day, when gliding into Lyon's childhood house through the kitchen door at midnight like a moccasined Cherokee was one of my superpowers. While he took the phone to Lyon, I shut my bedroom door and lay on my bed, as I had as a teenager talking to him late into the night.

"Leslie? Is that you?"

Even after a thirty-year silence, we knew each other well enough that I didn't chitchat.

"Hi, Lyon, look, I hope you're well. I'm going to jump right in. First, I love you, I always loved you, and you will always have a special place in my heart."

Silence on the other end. Of course. After three decades of me being angry with him, what could he say in response?

"Second, I finally get it. Why you cheated. Why you couldn't say no to those girls. You loved me. I know you did. But you loved all of us, right? That's why you couldn't say no."

Lyon made a sound like a dog choking.

"Yes. Yes, Leslie. That's exactly what it was. I'm not defending myself—it was wrong for me to cheat on you. But you and the other girls were all amazing. Nice. Beautiful. You made me feel so special. I never meant to hurt you, Leslie. I know I hurt you more than the others, because you came first. But I couldn't stop myself. I needed every one of you."

He sounded so relieved, I knew he was smiling. I wished I could see his face.

"I'd love to see you again, Lyon. Next time you're in town, let's go for a walk or have coffee. I'm not making a play for you. I promise. But . . . all this came to me, finally. And I wanted you to know. I didn't understand before. I couldn't. I wish I had. But I do now."

———————

On Saturday afternoon around four, as I was starting to think about what to pack for our sleepover, I got a text from Mishka. One of the cats is sick and i have to take her to the emergency vet. I don't think tonight is going to work.

A sick cat? I know what you're thinking: this is the oldest, lamest trick in the book. But I knew how much he loved that cat. I believed him.

I texted him back, with as much sympathy as I could cram into the phone. Oh my god. I'm so sorry. Is there anything I can do?

No I'll keep you posted.

He didn't keep me posted.

In fact, I didn't hear from him for hours and then days. He didn't even text me to let me know if the cat was still alive.

I waited until the next Friday. I asked him if he wanted a makeup sleepover that Saturday. Because sweet Jesus, I did.

He texted that he wasn't feeling well. A bad cold. The second-oldest excuse in the book. I fell for that, too, even though a quiet part of me whispered: *You know how you always feel you might not see him again? This might be it.*

I waited another week. I sent him a teasing text: It's gonna be hard to get married if we only see each other once a month.

I didn't hear back from him for forty-eight hours. Then this:

Well, I'm actually thinking of leaving Philly. My business sucks. I'm thinking Dallas would be better.

I finally got the message. I stopped texting him and was met with radio silence in response.

I found a new handyman to finish the basement. He was seventy-five, bald, and openly gay.

Maybe I should have been angry. I wasn't. Instead, I felt sad for both of us. We'd had such a sweet, private connection. But he'd gotten spooked, and maybe I had, too. It was over.

Or was it? With Mishka, I never knew for sure.

———————

Jefe Jeff sent two pictures of himself hiking naked, in addition to the winky-face, emoticon-laced, flirty emails I got almost every day. He was too modest to send a full frontal, so they were only of his butt, the skin pale until the tan line started halfway to his knees. I found his approach charmingly old-fashioned in its reserve. Through our emails, we got to know each other a bit, because it's hard to flirt all the time via email; you need some filler. He'd moved to Mexico only three months before, after living for ten years in Boston. He loved traveling and had flown a helicopter all the way across the United States. I could tell he'd never dated an older woman. His shyness came through, as if emoticons and naked butt photos were the only way he could channel brashness.

One weekday afternoon I was sitting in yet another postdivorce mediation session as we continued to finalize details about the kids' vacation schedules and who got which Persian rug, trying not to scream *When will this torture end?* The windowless law firm conference room felt like a jail cell. I surreptitiously snuck a peek at my phone under the table, while Marty was droning on about how his "effective tax rate" affected the "net present value" of his child support payments.

Desperate for a distraction, I read an email.

Hi Leslie,

Thank you for the lava pictures. Jeff shared them with me a few weeks ago. They truly are beautiful. Your recent emails have become inappropriate. Please tone it down and remain friends or do not write again.

Annabelle
Jeff's girlfriend of 7 years

Oh my God! Jefe Jeff never mentioned a *girlfriend* amid all the ;) ;) ;)!

What adult man lets his girlfriend read his emails? And what about the "inappropriate" emails *he* sent *me*? She'd signed her name as "Jeff's girlfriend of 7 years" as if it were an official job title.

But I wanted to take the high road here and treat her as part of the sisterhood, rather than start a catfight over email. Plus, she had been civilized, mostly. So I decided to be polite, too.

I did not send a snarky reply to Annabelle, or forward her message to Jeff with a note saying, "Did you know your girlfriend reads your emails? ;)" I do not condone cheating, or snooping in someone else's computer. But love is messy, and boy do I know firsthand how it brings out everyone's strange and sometimes terrible insecurities.

When I looked back up from my phone, Marty was still waving his HP 12c calculator with one hand and stabbing his pointer finger at me. I blinked to discover myself back in an airless law firm conference room in Philly, rather than sitting next to a hot helicopter pilot pointing out a waterfall in Mexico. I nearly burst out laughing. Instead, I bit my cheek in order to keep a straight face.

Marc smiled as I walked passed his desk in the newsroom on my way to the on-air studio. It was simultaneously erotic, and unnerving, to see him. Sometimes I stopped to say hi after my segments. Sometimes I walked by. How did we pretend, in a public workplace, that we had not been naked together in broad daylight a month before? That this boy-man twenty years younger than me had never gushed, "God, baby, your cunt feels incredible," when he first moved inside me?

After I got home, he sent me a text.

Good to see you today, babe. You looked like you really want to get fucked.

Which turned me on. God, had I always been this dirty? If a man had sent me a text like that when I was a single twenty-six-year-old, or a married forty-year-old, I would have bolted my doors and contemplated legal action. Today, my response to Marc was simple: Yes. I did.

His next text elaborated.

I broke up with my girlfriend this weekend. Well, she broke up with me, actually. I can't stop thinking about you and I want to see you again.

I texted back. I'm so sorry. About your girlfriend. What did you have in mind?

Many many things :)

Whoa. That made me smile.

Tonight?

The three dots on my phone rippled.

Yep. Or sooner. I'm dying to see you.

And, shazam! Marc was back.

———————

An hour after he left the fun and games of my bed, an hour after he held the back of my neck and kissed me good-bye, fiercely, at my front door, Marc sent me a text that read, That was just a one-time thing again, right?

———————

On the way back from my next business trip, this one to Houston, I got to spend an entire day in airports. A year before, I would have seen it as a day wasted. Now, it felt like research.

I changed planes in Charlotte and sat in a plastic seat near the gate for my Philly flight. Layovers had once meant frantic diaper changes and snack restocking; now, I leisurely found an outlet for my phone and surveyed the men waiting for the flight. Even though I'd done it a few times, I wasn't sure I had the guts to talk to anyone, but it felt like therapy to evaluate random men as if they were *Bachelorette* contestants.

One man walked toward the ticket counter, which made it seem as if he was walking toward me. He was tall, with thick, dark hair. He wasn't looking at me or anyone else. Instead he looked down at the airport carpeting. He gave off a shy vibe, which I liked far more than masters of the universe, with their expensive shoes and multiple cell phones. He had on a striped gray and white rugby shirt and faded Nantucket red cloth shorts, the kind Timmy liked from J.Crew. He was carrying a matching red and white duffel bag. Definitely not a businessman, given he was wearing red shorts in an airport.

The flight was called and I boarded early. I got settled in my window seat, climbing over a clean-cut, attractive, gray-haired man in the aisle seat. The middle seat was empty. I was already feeling sleepy. I usually passed out before a plane even took off. A few weeks earlier, I had slept for an entire flight from Boston to San Francisco, drooling on a strange man's shoulder. (We went out on a date afterward.)

The dark-haired man was walking toward me again.

No way does he have the seat next to me, I thought.

He did.

God, he was attractive. And polite—barely able to squeeze out "Excuse me" to the gray-haired passenger in the aisle seat. He slipped carefully into the middle seat, as if, conscious of his size, he was afraid to be rude. His legs and forearms were strong and muscular, with a sprinkling of soft, straight black hairs.

Suddenly, I wasn't sleepy.

I read and worked on my iPad until we were about thirty minutes into the flight. I kept looking surreptitiously at his thigh muscles. They were very nice. I was wearing yet another pair of black leggings, my travel uniform. I felt uncomfortable in the cramped window seat, so I kept crossing and uncrossing my legs.

Tall Shy and Handsome leaned back in his seat and sighed the first time I crossed my legs. As a test, I crossed my legs again.

He closed his eyes and sank back, like he was in pain, gripping the armrest, exhaling as if he couldn't take it any longer.

What was going on? Was I turning this man on by moving my legs? I had to find out. I put my iPad in the mesh pocket in front of my seat.

"So, are you from Philly?"

So easy, these travel pickup lines. He looked grateful that I had initiated a conversation, his brown eyes liquid, like a puppy waiting for a treat.

"I was visiting family in Charlotte, but I live in Philadelphia," he said, meeting my gaze for a minute before looking away. His thick, dark lashes fluttered against his pale skin.

"Me too," I offered. "Been there long?"

"A year." He smiled. Gloriously white straight teeth. One slightly crooked front tooth. "I'm a soccer player."

Whoa. Another athlete? When had Philly gotten a professional soccer team? I could hear Timmy saying *Mom, you are so clueless.* But I did know, from my microscopic inspection of Dylan's physique, that elite players had, naturally, elite bodies of hard muscle. This seemed like the more relevant data than the official list of Philly's sports teams.

I crossed my legs—again—and he let out another big sigh, looking at the circular air vents on the plane ceiling. It was like he was pantomiming *Help me, God!*

It was clearly up to me to keep the conversation going.

"So, how was your family?"

"Oh, great. Nice to see everyone. Nice to be home. I actually went back to celebrate my . . . um . . . my birthday."

Such a sweet smile! How did I get so lucky? This was fun.

"Was it a big birthday?"

I was trying not to be too obvious. But the more personal information I could get, the better chance I had of connecting with him, of making it seem natural to give him my card and suggest coffee sometime as we were getting off the plane. Maybe I could offer him a ride home from the airport in the TT.

"Yes," Mr. Hot Thighs Soccer Player said. "Kind of a big one."

I smiled. He had nice knees, too. Would they taste good if I licked them?

"Sounds fun."

He smiled back. This was getting good.

I imagined kissing him. It wasn't hard to do. Go girl. KC would be proud.

"My twentieth."

His twentieth *what*? His twentieth *birthday*?

Gulp. That meant that two days ago, he was *nineteen*. My facial muscles felt like a river in the act of freezing. This "man" was practically a teenager, three years older than my own son.

I managed to survive the rest of the flight, chitchatting a bit about sports and college. Philadelphia did not, in fact, have a professional soccer team. He was a sophomore at Temple University, playing on an athletic scholarship, majoring in econ, starting to look for a summer internship in finance. Trying to recover from my shock, I blabbered about a few people I knew who might be able to help him network. In my own defense, I promise you, he looked more like thirty than twenty. But still.

I did not give him my card. I did not tell him my name. I did not cross and uncross my legs again. Dylan being drawn to me, I understood. Sexually frustrated, married too young, a country boy curious about, and attracted to, an older city girl (who looked like she was from Manhattan despite being a Philadelphia matron). Marc had an established thing for older women. And he had no idea how old I really was.

But a twenty-year-old? Attracted to me? Unable to breathe normally when I crossed my legs? And vice versa? *Me* attracted to a twenty-year-old?

This was getting weird.

––––––––––

Girls' Night Out. KC and Winnie met me at Monk's Cafe, a Belgium brewpub around the corner with a shiny red door and a colorful chalkboard listing over twenty-five craft beers. Blind Pig? Pliny the Elder? I was hopelessly out of touch with artisanal brews and their funky monikers.

We grabbed an empty couch by the jukebox, better for talking than the narrow, noisy bar or one of the tables on the sidewalk, which I did point out would be ideal for man watching. The girls were sampling a reddish beer called Damnation and a pale golden ale called Chimay, while I devoured salty *pomme frites* dipped in dijon mustard dressing.

"By the way," Winnie told me, her new aviator bifocal glasses—a fiftieth birthday gift from her husband—perched above her snub nose, which was still as cute as the day we met in fourth grade. "I ran into Jake Bryant at that alumni lunch in New York last week. He asked about you. He wanted to know if you were still living on Rittenhouse Square."

I shrugged, feeling sorry for Jake stuck with that petty girlfriend. Winnie popped one of my fries into her mouth as she went on talking. "So how many boyfriends are you up to now, Les? Five? Got any new pictures?"

"As you know, I went without sex for three years. I've rediscovered that I actually like men. I *like* being treated as a sex object."

We all laughed.

"I'm just jealous," Winnie explained, although I knew she didn't really mean it. Married women were always the most curious about my dating escapades, but it wasn't that they wanted what I had. It was more that they couldn't imagine what my life was like compared to theirs. Every one asked the same question, almost whispering the words: "What's it like to be naked in front of someone new?" I told every one it was more fun than they could imagine.

My phone hummed with a text. Winnie grabbed it off the low table in front of us. "Ooooh, Crazy Boy . . . that's Chris Bailey, right? Wants to know if you're watching hockey preseason—in China—with him tonight. Doesn't he live in . . . North Carolina?"

"Yeah, so we watch together and text the whole time."

"You know nothing about hockey," Winnie pointed out. Winnie had a mustache of beer foam above her lips. She licked it off.

KC cracked up. In honor of Girls' Night Out, she'd thrown a leather jacket over her silk work shift.

"Leave her alone. She's gonna write a book about this and then start a franchise called MILF Boot Camp and we're all going to be working for her. So you better be nice."

Winnie couldn't stop teasing. "Is Chris the helicopter pilot, or the one who's riding his motorcycle to Philly to visit you? These are the sexiest men I've ever heard of. A construction worker? A football player you met in fucking yoga class? A hot single thirty-year-old Marine on a bike in your backyard? You could sell tickets."

"Didn't your mom always say it was important to have a few boyfriends you couldn't explain?" I shot back. I told them about the email from the helicopter pilot's girlfriend, and KC laughed so hard I could see her fillings.

Winnie kept asking questions like she was writing a research paper on me. "Do they ever wonder about your kids? Do they even know you have them?"

"Hmm." I thought about this. "No. I don't think anyone except Damon and Mishka ever asked about my kids. Marc is a kid himself, so it wouldn't occur to him. And Dylan, well, the whole subject of kids made him squirm since he felt so guilty."

"Do you ever feel like you're using them? Or they're using you?"

"Maybe. But not in a negative way." I paused to figure out how to explain it. "What's most astonishing is that there are so many men out there. I'm getting more sex at forty-nine than at nineteen. So that's good. But sometimes I think men have studied how to torture us, and that the older men get, or really, the older we women get, the more they think it's okay to treat us terribly. It's not as easy as it looks, guys."

KC and Winnie looked at me with zero sympathy.

"Some days, it seems like your life is like *Sex and the City: Pushing Fifty*," Winnie said. "When I'm driving carpool in my sweats

I picture you walking down the street in ripped jeans, accompanied by a cheerful acoustic soundtrack warbling in the background, smoking-hot men of all ages falling at your feet."

I chomped on an ice shard before responding.

"No one is more surprised by how many men are out there. I feel like a kid in a candy store. Actually, what I feel like is one of those men I used to make fun of, men who face divorce by buying a sports car, dressing younger, and dating people half their age. It's actually a smart strategy. I feel much better about myself now. But it isn't as if I waved a magic wand and every man likes me now. All that's changed: I'm finally seeing the men who were there all along."

"And what's your hit rate?" Winnie inquired. "Asking for a friend."

"Worse than you think," I answered. "You know when I was in Alaska and I saw the double rainbows? On the hike down I met this amazing guy, Rob. Funny, handsome, from Portland. I gave him my number. We hugged good-bye. And trust me, it was a good hug. He never called.

"Last month, I met a professor from Swarthmore on a flight home from California. He moved up to the empty seat next to me. We spent four hours talking. Cute, shy, no wedding ring. He bikes and runs and has two cats and a dog and he lives twenty-two miles from here. His mother's name was Leslie! I was half in love by the time we said good-bye. Never heard from him, either."

"That's ghosting, right?" Winnie asked, like she knew.

"Sort of. It was technically too soon to be ghosted, because we weren't actually dating, but it's no fun to be rejected or ignored like that, and it happens all the time to me. Marty did it, too, in far worse ways, telling me I was unattractive and unlovable and emotional and insecure. There's a lot of value in not giving a crap what a man thinks about you. Rejection is, actually, meaningless. Especially at the early stages, before you've let someone in."

"How many texts do you get from the ones who like you?" KC asked. "The only people who text me are you all and my boys and the CFO at work. I wish I got a few messages from hot twenty-nine-year-old men."

I did the math in my head.

"Probably four or five texts from each one every day. So, twenty-five texts?"

They both looked blankly at me.

"A day?" Winnie asked. "How do you get anything done? How do you keep them all straight?"

"Well, yeah. It's easy—they're all different. But you know, it doesn't feel like enough," I confessed with chagrin. "It's like I'm dating several guys and no one at the same time. I wish I heard from them even more. I'd like to get at least one mushy text from each one every hour. Maybe every fifteen minutes."

Winnie looked into her beer. KC eyed me curiously. Had I said something offensive?

"These guys are like Twinkies and Diet Coke, Les." KC knew more details than Winnie did about the men in my life. She also knew that I'd spent Labor Day weekend alone, crying, because the kids were with Marty and all of my so-called boyfriends were with other women or their families. "Ever think you are overcorrecting here? How much can you down without feeling sick? Don't you want to hold out for something a little more . . . nutritious?"

She didn't give me time to protest.

"Ever ask yourself what you are really looking for, honey? Sometimes it seems like you're willing to pay an awfully steep price in order to feel loved. That's what you always say about your first marriage—that the definition of an abuse victim is someone who pays too high a ransom in exchange for love. With all these men, why are you still feeling lonely? What do you think would feel like 'enough,' Leslie?" she asked.

Her words gave me pause.

"I don't know. Fifty messages? All of them madly in love with me at the same time?"

She raised her eyebrows. "Girl," she muttered. "You ever think that's too much?"

Had I gone too far? I was getting exactly what KC and I had envisioned. But once again, maybe KC was right. The question now was simple: was I getting what I needed from my approach to men? My life today was far superior to being stuck in a dead marriage. But it was a crash diet, not a sustainable way to live. Whenever I checked my phone and there wasn't a text from one of my "boyfriends," I felt hollow inside. Maybe it was time to move on and stop this manic dating frenzy. But I had no clue what would come next. I blurted out what was running through my mind.

"It's not that it's too much, KC. The problem is, it's not enough."

Winnie and KC looked at me again, their eyes like marbles.

"And I have no idea what to do next."

We all knew I was speaking the truth.

THE
NAKED
TRUTH

Mid-September. The kids woke up each morning to alarm clocks instead of ocean waves, complaining about life's injustice over cereal. Pumpkins appeared on our neighbor's stoops. The leaves on the oaks and maples in Rittenhouse Square turned the park red and golden yellow. Soon they'd flutter down to fill the fountain, the city would drain it, and winter would officially arrive.

No more Coopers Beach until Thanksgiving. By then, the sand would be cold, the waves cobalt and choppy with whitecaps. The kids and I would have the beach to ourselves, along with the seals, an off-season oasis that felt exclusively ours.

It had been one year since Marty moved out. The kids seemed okay so far. As for me, I was closing a chapter and opening a new one, but I didn't know what the future held or even what I wanted from it. All I knew was I'd proved what I set out to: I still liked men, men still liked me, and there were plenty of them out there. Had women all drunk the same Kool-Aid, the patriarchal message that we must cling to whichever man we had, because we all thought there were no good men who wanted women my age? It was as if an unconscious conspiracy pressured us to stay in miserable relationships, even if our husbands were cheating on us and making us feel worthless and sexually repulsive. We should feel lucky! We should feel grateful! To have nailed down one man through matrimony, no matter how awfully that man treated us, because he was our only chance.

What the hell were we thinking? The subliminal beliefs I'd held for years about men and women, especially older women, were entirely, blatantly, obscenely incorrect. But Winnie and KC had raised a question I couldn't ignore: What did I want from men over time? What could they teach me? As nice as it was to have men spinning around me like cotton candy, I was hungering for more than spun sugar. How to get more protein in my diet, I had no idea.

───────────

If the reminder hadn't popped up on the calendar on my phone, I would have missed Jake's documentary screening. I'd gotten the paperless invitation before Damon, Mishka, Chris, and Marc—a lifetime ago. Now the screening was finally happening and I was going to be late. I dropped Bella at seven o'clock volleyball practice in Marion, then turned the TT straight back toward our high school friends' Jim and Penny's luxe condo overlooking the Schuylkill River. The apartment door was half-cracked and I tiptoed in. Fortunately, the beige wall-to-wall carpeting was about three inches thick, so no one witnessed my surreptitious arrival.

The rooms buzzed with men's and women's party voices, amped laughter, and the clink of wineglasses. I stopped for a moment inside the front door next to a squat Diptyque Roses candle flickering on the antique hall table. I took a deep sniff and smoothed my blouse, my favorite black silk camisole with three silver opals sewn along the scoop neck. My pantyhose already felt like a corset around my waist. Going to a high-profile party where I knew so few people always felt like marching onto a battlefield.

Through a frosted-glass doorway leading to the crowded living room, the only man I recognized was an elegantly dressed thirtyish photographer from the *Star*'s style section, bending over to snap his camera at shutter speed, his navy bow tie crooked, moving frantically from socialite to socialite as if he was afraid the A-list couples would leave before he got enough pictures to appease the gossip column editor. I greeted Jim and Penny, secured a club soda with lime from the tuxedoed bartender, and dodged clusters of couples to make my way to a small knot of high school alumni in a corner.

I didn't know anyone else. Every person looked like a New York celebrity sent down via town car for the night. Maybe Jake's publicist had invited Katie Couric, too. The overall effect was that I felt like the hometown hick, itchy with paranoid suspicion that half the guests were talking about the fact that I'd been invited only because I knew Jake from high school, and the other half were whispering *Those wrinkles on her forehead make her look older than fifty and that skirt is awfully short.* There was nothing I could do about my wrinkles or my fiftieth birthday next month, but fortunately, the skirt was cute and black, with a sassy vertical leather stripe across the tush. Of course, no one was actually talking about me. But still.

Jake stood holding a beer, looming half a foot taller than the small mob asking film questions. It had been two years since I'd seen him anywhere but on Facebook. If anything, he looked younger today, scruffily handsome and happy, albeit frazzled by being the night's star attraction. I went over and touched his forearm. He smiled fleetingly, his gray-blue eyes bright, and leaned down to kiss my cheek. He squeezed my hand, then turned back to his fans. I stood there for a minute, before stepping toward the bar for another club soda. More awkwardness.

Chairs and a screen had been set up in the large dining room for the preview. The film was wry, wise, and irreverent, like Jake had been even at sixteen. During the Q&A, I snuck out to pick up Bella and drop her at Marty's. With any luck, I'd be out of my pantyhose and naked between my sheets by ten.

Instead, around nine thirty, I was listening to Bella chatter in the TT's backseat as I drove down Walnut Street when my phone lit up with a text message.

Stopped at the next light (no texting and driving!), I checked the screen. The message was from an area code I didn't recognize. It read, simply, Do you want to have a drink?

I had no idea whom the invitation was from. I wasn't sure if it was a man or a woman. Maybe someone I'd given my card to at the party?

If this person had my cell phone, surely a drink with them would be fun. Why not? I still had on my (now wrinkled) black skirt, cutout heels, and camisole. I didn't even have to change.

I played along.

Sure. Where are you?

Rittenhouse Square. A few blocks from your house.

Who could it be? If mystery texter knew where I lived, it had to be someone I liked and actually would want to serve a drink to.

Idling in the driveway as Bella walked to Marty's brownstone door, I texted back: Why don't you come by in 30 minutes? I purposefully did not give my address. You know, safety first.

My anonymous date, who apparently already knew my address, texted back a simple See you then.

———————

The doorbell rang a few minutes before ten, the chime echoing deep into the house. I'd lit a half dozen fat white candles in front of the fireplace. A bottle of chilled, sweating Perrier and another of white wine sat on the glass coffee table.

I took a breath before opening the door. I couldn't wait to see who it was.

On my brick doorstep stood Jake, grinning in the lamplight, towering over me, his spiky hair *GQ* messy, looking almost exactly as he did at sixteen when picking me up at my parents' house. His eyes, ice blue under the light of my chandelier, met mine. His eyes always reminded me of an Alaskan husky, radiating intelligence and the drive you need to pull a sled across the arctic tundra.

"Hey!" I tried to hide my surprise. "Wow. So nice you could come by." That much was true.

"Glad it worked out," he said, sidestepping into my foyer, his hands deep in the pockets of a scuffed chocolate-brown suede jacket, slightly distressed to the edge of hipness.

"Come on in." I put my hands out for his blazer. I was tempted to sniff it, to see if he still smelled like Eau Sauvage, the cologne he used in high school.

We went into the living room and sat next to each other on the red, gold, and blue silk couch Marty and I had shipped back from a tiny Italian furniture shop we'd found in Lake Como on our honeymoon. I made sure to sit a few inches from Jake, which was hard on the slippery tufted love seat, especially because ex–basketball players have legs like ladders. I was afraid if my pantyhose slid up against his jeans, he might think I was hitting on him. I didn't want to be that girl from high school, drooling over her old boyfriend long after he'd moved on to New York women with stick-straight hair and thinner thighs.

"Wine?" I asked, gesturing to the bottle.

"Sure," he said, leaning forward to get it himself, since he knew I didn't drink.

We talked for two hours, the conversation zipping from topic to topic. Mostly about the new movie, his mom, film parties, life in New York, my kids, his dog Jennie, and random friends from high school. When I asked about his girlfriend, he looked away.

"That ended a few months ago. I'm pretty sure she cheated on me a bunch of times. Not a happy subject," he said, by way of opaque dismissal. I didn't press, even though I was thinking, *Who the hell would be stupid enough to cheat on a guy like Jake?*

The painted French clock on my fireplace mantel showed it was almost midnight. We'd run out of questions to ask each other. Jake stirred, as if he was about to get up and ask for his jacket. I started craving my sheets again.

Jake wiped his palms on his jeans. Then, instead of getting up and saying good-bye, he put his left hand over my right one on the couch. I stared at the dark hairs above his knuckles. His palm was warm and rough, and covered my hand completely.

He met my surprised gaze and said, "I don't know whether to say good night, or to kiss you."

I wasn't sure I'd heard him right. Jake wanted to kiss me? After all this time?

"Oh, Jake, that's easy," I answered without taking a breath. "You should definitely kiss me."

"Leslie, I've wanted to do this for the past thirty years," he told me, taking my face in his palms.

His words, and his eyes like gray-blue granite, made me melt inside.

With my own eyes closed, I waited for him to follow through.

———————

So, first, I have to tell you about the sex. The sex with Jake. Prepare yourself.

Back when we'd dated in high school, Jake had been a sixteen-year-old, 145-pound virgin, as inexperienced as he was tall and skinny. By contrast, I was a seventeen-year-old sex aficionado who'd been sneaking out of my parents' house for three years to drink, smoke weed, and explore my nascent sexuality with an assortment of older boyfriends. I never thought of my behavior as slutty. I liked boys and I liked sex and I liked the two together. And I used birth control every single time, dammit.

But despite his tentativeness, Jake had been inherently, undeniably talented sexually, driven by intuition rather than experience. One night he stole the key to his father's law firm office and we snuck in after hours to have a place to get naked. I undid my shirt slowly after he got flustered with the buttons. He slipped his hands around my waist, buried his head in the V of my bra, and let out a sigh so deep and drawn out, it sounded like he'd been holding his breath for sixteen years.

Surrounded by yellow legal pads and maroon tax code binders, he put his soft lips on my breasts with a kind of reverence my more experienced boyfriends lacked. I remember the feeling like it was yesterday. His lips were warm and soft, and he circled my areola with his tongue over and over. The way his tongue moved made me cry out in his dad's office, and the memory of it drove me crazy. I'm sure it drove him crazier. But as I said before, I was reluctant to be his first lover, because I knew, from losing my own virginity, how intense an experience it was. I wasn't ready to lead someone else through that jungle. I broke up with him after about eight weeks of dating and unforgettable kissing.

So, that night in my living room, it felt like we'd been waiting three decades to come together physically. It was sex unlike any other in my life. But I'm ahead of myself.

First, we kissed for a bit on the couch, sloppy, crazy kissing, like we were trying to devour each other's faces. For a few minutes, I thought that's all we were going to do. Then Jake slipped his hand inside my bra. He gently tweaked my nipple as if he knew exactly how to touch me, even after all these years. An erotic jolt blasted through me. So much for stopping at kissing.

A few minutes later, I stood up. I slipped out of my skirt, panty-hose, camisole, and bra. I faced Jake, naked.

"Hi," I said.

He looked me up and down. I hoped the candlelight hid the cellulite on my thighs and the fact that my breasts hung at least three inches lower than the last time he'd seen them.

"Wow." The word came out of his mouth as a low sigh, almost as if he were in pain.

He stood up and kissed me again with a ceremonious air, putting a hand on each of my shoulders. Then Jake slowly bent down, unlaced his boots, and slipped them off. He unbuttoned his shirt and let it fall open. The lighting was dim, but I caught a glimpse of the ripples of his strong abs and the dark brown hairs encircling his belly button. Next, he unbuckled his leather belt and undid his jeans snap. He slipped his pants and boxers off, and left them in a pyramid on the floor, stepping out toward me, barefoot and naked. I was afraid to look up. His feet were tan from summer, with a few dark hairs on each toe. His calves were still enormous, bulging out from behind his shinbones. Each thigh had a large X carved by the muscles above his knee. I looked away; was it really okay to look north of his thighs? He let his shirt fall on top of his jeans. He stood up to face me, as naked as I was.

"Hi," he said. He put his large, cool hands on my waist.

I'd never seen him without clothes on.

"Wow," I whispered back to him, finally looking up and taking in the sight of his huge erect cock. I reached out both my hands and slipped them over the velvety head of his dick. He leaned back and groaned. I dropped to my knees and put my mouth over him, and sucked gently. His cock throbbed in response. I could feel the skin stretching taut as he stiffened between my lips. Looking up at his face, I sucked harder.

The candles flickered and burned down as we made love for over three hours. At first, the aura between us felt as if I were finally initiating him into sex, at long last taking his virginity. But to my surprise, it also felt like he was doing the same to me. As if neither of us had ever truly experienced the magic of sexual intimacy before. We tried every position and combination of activities I knew already, plus a few I didn't. Consent was a new addition to lovemaking since we'd been in high school. Jake whispered, "Do you want me inside you, Leslie?" *Yes.* We used the ottoman by the fire. "Do you want me to make love to you like this?" *Yes.* He bent me over a narrow embroidered couch. *Yes.* He lay me down on my back on the Bijar carpet. *Yes.* We abused tasteful furnishings that, for nearly two decades of elegant cocktail parties for 150 in that house, I'd never once imagined serving as props for wild, hard-core sex.

The net effect was as if Jake had spent the years since high school studying the way women's anatomy worked, in anticipation of applying every lesson to me. And as if I'd spent thirty years getting wet, waiting for him to knock on my door to show me what he'd learned. Plus, because we already knew each other so well, there was none of that first-fuck awkwardness to slow us down.

At all.

When we were finally spent, we walked slowly through the

backyard holding hands, past the mermaid statue by the hot tub, and I drove him home in the TT. We kissed good-bye in front of Penny and Jim's building in the 3:00 a.m. stillness. All I could think was: *I want more of this.* Despite our hours making love, I felt like the audience at a Rolling Stones concert, standing and clapping for one more encore. Even at that moment, I believe I knew I'd never get enough of the sweet sensation of being twisted open by Jake Bryant's hands on me and his cock inside me.

The next morning, only about four hours after I dropped Jake off in the middle of the night, I was up, bleary-eyed but blissed out, scrambling eggs and getting the kids ready for school. Marty had dropped them off at seven, still in their pajamas, because he had an early flight to Chicago for work. I had scratchy Persian-rug burns on my knees and upper back. My hair was mussed by sex and sleep. I waved good-bye to Timmy and Bella at the front door and crawled back into bed. Thank goodness I was a writer with a flexible schedule.

When Jake called around noon, I was still asleep. He left a message. I listened to it in bed, thinking how much I wanted him there next to me, right then.

"Hey, it's me."

His voice sounded as husky and sweet as it had long ago, when we saw each other at school every day and talked on the phone every night.

"I'm calling you like a gentleman, to thank you for a wonderful night," Jake said on my voice mail. "I was kept awake all night with visions of your perfect body and your awesome beautiful blonde hair and . . . how great it felt." His voice dropped an octave. "How great it felt to be with you. Finally. It was . . . amazing. So . . . I'll talk to you soon, I hope."

I listened to the message three times, my stomach unzipping each time I heard his voice.

I picked Bella up from school and told her I'd meet her inside the house after I parked. I sat in the TT in the back alley with the windows rolled up. I slipped off my clogs and put my stocking feet on the dashboard. My fingers were cold and stiff, like I'd been holding ice cubes. I took a bunch of deep breaths and dialed Jake's number.

Jake answered after one ring. His voice sounded scratchy, like he was clearing his throat.

"Hi, it's me," I said, as eager and nervy as a kid on the day the neighborhood pool opened for the summer. "I got your message."

There was no point in holding back. Honesty still came easily to us. He'd cracked me open, and it felt safe to be transparent about how I felt.

"I had a great time last night, too, Jake. One of the best nights of my life."

"Oh, Leslie, you have no idea."

His voice made the tension drain out of me, like water swirling down the bathtub plug. I had been afraid he'd pull back, saying once was enough, that despite our passionate sexual connection and history, this was just another one-time thing. God, I craved being wanted for more than one night, especially by this handsome, intelligent, kind man I'd known since I was seventeen. This, of course, scared the hell out of me. It felt like way too much to hope for.

"So when do you head back to New York?" I asked as casually as I could, ignoring the catch in my gut. Last night, Jake had said he had a train that afternoon.

"Not until tomorrow," he answered, taking me by surprise.

My heart felt as if I'd tripped and caught myself before falling.

"Well, why don't you come over again tonight?" I spat out, before Mom's voice stopped me, chastising that a lady never chases a man.

"Um, well, um, I actually have plans."

I prayed he was being honest and not evasive.

I held my breath. *One . . . two . . . three . . . four . . . five . . . six.* I counted in my head, forcing myself to let the silence talk for me. *Please please please.*

"Ah, I'll cancel. Of course I'll cancel. Jeez, what was I thinking. What time are you free?"

I fell back into the driver's seat, my armpits sweaty. I didn't feel cold anymore.

———

That night, I met him at the door.

"Sorry about my outfit," I said, gesturing to my mom uniform of black stretchy V-neck and yoga pants. "Bella's at the movies. I have to pick her up in three hours."

"I forgive you," Jake said. "Because you're not going to have those clothes on very long."

He put his hands around my waist and pulled me toward him, kissing me hard.

"Upstairs," I said, pulling back and pointing. He put his palms on my butt as I walked up the steps in front of him. Since he was so tall, he practically had to bend in half to reach my butt cheeks. We both started laughing at how funny we surely looked.

We spent the next two hours under the soft blue comforter in my bed. First, we stripped naked in less than five seconds with zero formality. Jake was gentle, like he was afraid to hurt me, like he couldn't believe he was touching my body. He turned me on my stomach, facing the oversized mirror that doubled as a headboard. I spread my thighs and pressed my ass against his hard abs and thighs.

"Am I too deep?" he asked, a question mark in his voice, as if other women had harangued him for hurting them.

I looked at his face in the mirror.

"Jake, there is no such thing as too deep."

I meant that on so many levels.

———

Jake called me every day after he left Philadelphia. Sometimes two or three times a day. I leapt every time my phone rang.

A letter arrived three days after he went back to New York. His

chicken-scratch writing, the bane of our high school English teachers, had, if anything, gotten more indecipherable over the years.
Holding the crisp, cream-colored card with his name engraved on
it, I eagerly read, and reread, every word written in his signature
blue cartridge pen ink.

> *Leslie—I feel a maelstrom of conflicting emotions, ranging
> from the pathetic to the sublime. You're a really important
> person in my life, the first person I ever felt I was in love with.
> Anyway, what I'm trying to say is that reuniting with you has
> stirred up a lot of powerful stuff in me, like silt that's been set-
> tled at the bottom of a lake for years. Decades. A lot of time has
> gone by. You are a beautiful and amazing woman. I admire
> you, and desire you, so much. But life is complicated. The true
> path is not clear yet, at least to me. All I know is that I feel
> deeply touched, and so alive. To be continued . . .*
>
> *Love, Jake*
> *PS—Have fun with my handwriting. XO*

There was so much wonder in my chest as I read these words, I
no longer wanted ten text messages a day from five different lovers.
I wanted letters on card stock from this one.

Jake left a voice mail on my phone the next afternoon.

"Leslie. I have to see you again." His voice was breathless.
Taxis honked in the background. "Soon."

The words, and the insistent way he said them, made my heart
rev unexpectedly.

"There's an indie film festival I have to go to in Atlantic City
this Thursday. The festival will be over by nine. Do you want to
meet me there and spend the night?"

As a matter of fact, I did.

Timmy's team had a baseball banquet that afternoon, so I

couldn't leave for New Jersey until after the awards were handed out and I'd gone home to change out of my mom clothes into something sexier. I felt like a postmodern princess, the kind where I was my own fairy godmother and the TT my carriage. I made the drive in less than ninety minutes, pushing the accelerator, trusting Waze to avoid the Jersey state troopers stationed strategically along the Atlantic City Expressway.

I wore a dress I expected Jake would love, the clingy white lace number I'd originally bought with Dylan in mind. It was shorter than any dress I'd dared to wear when I was his high school girl-friend. I could barely walk in my shiny silver T-strap sandals. When Jake came down to meet me around nine thirty, he had to pull me out of the TT with both forearms. His hands were strong and warm.

He led me into the boutique hotel, with a postage-stamp lobby made to look larger with ornate, frameless stepped mirrors every-where, torchiere art deco lamps giving off soft, golden light. As we walked along the crimson carpet to the elevator, his slipped his palm down the small of my back, looking over his shoulder and grinning at me, as if he couldn't quite believe I had come. The doorman and bellhop stared at us. Jake's hand traveled down toward my ass as he laughed at the tiny steps I had to take in the strappy heels.

Once we were in the elevator, Jake slipped his hand up my thigh and thrust two fingers inside me, as if he couldn't wait an-other second to make love to me. He took his fingers out and put them in his mouth. Weak with wanting him, I had trouble making my way down the hallway to his room. We were kissing before the hotel door clanged shut behind us. He picked me up and carried me to the bed. It was a fancy brass queen covered with a dozen pil-lows in crazy shapes—cubes, rolls, squares—piled up at the head-board. He pulled up my dress, spread my legs, and started licking my inner thighs as I writhed and moaned. He made his way up to my pussy with small licks. I started whimpering. I'd only been out of the TT for five minutes before he was inside me. My four-inch heels stayed on, as Jake moved my legs up over my head. He ran his hands along my calves as he made love to me, hard.

As he moved in me, I looked at his face, reading the feelings written there. I couldn't look away for a second. His long eyelashes brushed his cheekbones. His chest was lean but muscular, with a few silver-black hairs sprinkled across it. His arms made a diamond shape around my head as he looked in my eyes. I saw and felt something new in his face, a sensation totally different from what I'd felt before with any man. *He's making love to me*, I told myself. Was Jake falling in love with me? Or had he always been in love with me? Could I be the reason he'd had decades of unfulfilling relationships with women, and never married or had children?

The sex was hot as hell. But it was more than that. It was . . . deep, in all the profound ways I ached for. With words and his eyes, Jake made sure I liked every thing he did to me. His body shook with pleasure, he was so blissed out by the ways I touched, kissed, and sucked him.

Afterward, I lay cradled in his arms. We were both slightly sweaty, spent, relieved of hours of sexual anticipation, almost but not quite ready for more. He disentangled himself carefully and leaned up on his forearms to look at me.

"I love you, Leslie. I always have. I always wanted this with you."

I answered by meeting his eyes with mine. I didn't trust my voice.

I had never imagined Jake still felt so strongly about me. But I could feel love in his body, and in mine, validating our connection. Love was the only explanation for the way our bodies came together. The way I'd dreamed about, but failed to achieve, with Marty. How could this be unfolding so quickly? But since I'd known Jake for most of my life, this didn't feel reckless or crazy. It felt like a key turning in a lock.

I never wanted to let him go. Ever.

But I had to. There was a concert at school that morning, the a cappella student-run club. Bella was singing a solo from *Rent*, the sweet, wise love song "Seasons of Love."

So, in the dark of night, Jake walked me outside the hotel to the TT. The street was shadowy and empty. The cool sea air made me quiver in my lace dress. The Atlantic crashed in the background. He guided me into the TT in my ridiculous shoes. My pussy felt swollen and sore. I realized I'd never taken off my heels, a princess so brazen she kept her slippers on.

As we kissed good-bye one final time, me sitting in the driver's seat, Jake bent over me, I put my arms around his neck. He smelled like Eau Sauvage and *me*.

My phone lit up on the passenger seat with the frosted white light of a new text. I didn't even glance at it. I kissed Jake's soft lips long and hard enough to leave a bruise.

As I zoomed west in the TT, the painted white stripes on the highway's edge rolled by silently in the night as I headed back to Rittenhouse Square. The seventies Jefferson Starship song "Miracles" came on. I pushed repeat song on my iPhone car dock. *If only you believe in miracles, so would I* . . . Listening to Grace Slick's throaty background vocals, I relived how it felt to be under Jake's strong, warm body, with him inside me, on the hotel bed's velvety sheets. I believed in miracles. Did Jake, too?

This was mind-blowing sex, and so much more. It felt like the first taste of everything I'd ever wanted in a relationship. On the heels of that buzz, a rush of fear scared the hell out of me. Could this feeling vanish at any moment?

Sara had warned me to be careful. She cautioned that the first serious relationship following a divorce can be more intense than the marriage itself, because after a divorce, you are raw and broken and filled with hope that the next time, you're going to find lasting love to make up for the love you lost. She was right. This is what I'd been starving for with Marty for two decades. Less than a week had passed since my first night with Jake, but it felt like life had gone from a black-and-white TV show to Technicolor. The look on Jake's face as he held me, the way his blue eyes turned gray as he looked into mine, kept me warm for the whole ride home. I could feel my heart opening to Jake. By any measure, this was happening too fast for my own good. But I knew Jake. I trusted him. He'd loved me since I was seventeen. And—this matters—I was starved

for love and intimacy, as well as the delectable feeling of being de-
sired. I was Cinderella, and my prince had tracked me down.

———————

Three days later, the postman dropped off another chicken-scratch
note. I opened it immediately and took it into the kitchen. I sat on
my stool, drinking black coffee, eager for Jake's romantic recap of
our night in Atlantic City. But that's not what I got.

> *Leslie, it's funny, my life is pretty much an open book to you,
> and so are my feelings. We've both been really open with each
> other about our emotions, which has been great. Like now.*
>
> *But I don't actually know much of anything about the
> rest of your private life. I try to tell myself it's none of my
> business. But when your phone lights up and there's a message
> from someone you call "Crazy Boy" or some such name that I
> can't help seeing, my mind goes to funny places.*
>
> *Like, I start to wonder if it's worth upending my entire
> life for you, if I'm just going to be another Gorgeous White
> Boy. I know that I won't, hopefully. Obviously you're a free
> woman. We're still figuring things out between us, and I'm
> probably being an incredible hypocrite because I spend time
> with other women, and you've been very clear about your feel-
> ings, which is all that should matter, but these are some of the
> thoughts that go through my male brain.*
>
> *I think I'm falling in love with you. It's gut-wrenching.
> I've started down the road that leads from here to you to We,
> the first steps, but it's a complicated one. We'll get there. And
> beyond.*
>
> *All my love, forever—*
> *Jake*

I stared at his note, stunned. Although I hadn't looked at the
text that night as Jake helped me into the TT, apparently he had.

There was a sharpness to his words that made me recoil. Falling in love with me was . . . gut-wrenching? His note was simultaneously, and paradoxically, jealous, passionate, suspicious, and loving.

I put the letter down on the kitchen counter, puzzled. Jake seemed so confident, so experienced with women. So what if I got a text from another man? I'd kissed Crazy Boy, my phone nickname for Chris Bailey, once during my trip to North Carolina a month before. Okay, twice. But it was before I'd started seeing Jake. Why would he ruin our night in Atlantic City, and question my loyalty, especially when he was dating other women, and it was too soon to talk about seeing each other exclusively? And how on earth did Jake know to name himself Gorgeous White Boy, a moniker so similar to Gorgeous Yoga Man, the name that was still in my phone for Damon? I'd left my purse open when I went to the powder room before the drive home. Had Jake looked at my contacts while I was peeing?

The truth was, Jake had nothing to worry about. My five-boyfriend cupboard was bare. Mishka, Dylan, and Damon were gone. Marc was occasional at most. Chris, the one who'd sent me the text, was about to deploy to Afghanistan for twelve months, and could hardly be considered a threat. Jake and I had not made any kind of commitment to each other; we hadn't even *discussed* it yet. We weren't there, although I could feel us getting close. I was scared, and cautious, after what I'd been through in both marriages. If I rushed this, I'd ruin it, and lose a piece of my self-esteem and independence.

Cinderella never dealt with *this*.

Beneath the undercurrents of fear in his letter, I knew Jake was still that sweet boy I'd let undress me at seventeen. I trusted him. That's all that mattered. Life is messy, right? Everyone has scars and vulnerabilities. Especially after almost fifty years on the planet. I could feel how much Jake cared for me, how much he craved the connection we'd reignited. Jake and I had been in each other's lives for three decades. I had to believe that we'd be okay for three more.

I didn't ask Jake to explain the contradictions in his letter. It felt rude, and somehow disloyal, to train a microscope on his raw emotions right then. A few days later, he mentioned on the phone that he was flying to his family's house on Sanibel Island in Florida for three days. The ramshackle beach house had been in Jake's family for over a century. We'd spent a dreamlike spring break there together my senior year. This time, Jake was going with his mom, sister, and two nieces. I thought he was about to invite me.

Then he said that another woman he was dating was going with him instead.

There was a long silence on the phone as I tried to absorb this news.

"Leslie, it's nothing. Hannah means nothing to me compared to you. But she'd already bought her plane ticket and my family is expecting her. And you have those other men who send you texts. I can't cancel at this late date . . ."

I put the phone down on my desk while I took a breath. I looked around my airy office and out the French doors to the mermaid by the hot tub. I felt like crawling through the phone to strangle him. Was he doing this on purpose because he thought I was still dating other men? Did he rationalize that somehow my getting a text from Crazy Boy justified his taking another woman on a trip with his family? To a place we'd been together? It wasn't the same, at all.

My head hurt. My heart did, too. Was he *trying* to ruin our transcendent beginning? Was I overlooking warning signs because I'd known him for so long?

I stared into my gray computer screen. My distorted reflection stared back at me, my nose furrowed in confusion like a rabbit munching grass.

"Okay, Jake, okay." That was all I felt safe saying. "I've gotta go now. Talk later."

I hung up the phone and threw it onto my bed.

I put my head in my hands. We were in no-man's-land. Was I ready to stop dating and make a commitment? Was he? I didn't know how to figure this out when we lived in different cities, had compelling lives separate from each other, and when we both felt so naked and vulnerable. This was all unfolding awfully quickly, distorted by intensely strong emotions and white-hot sex. Part of me longed for the distraction of a few crazy but shallow texts from Mishka or Marc. Later that night, I turned to words to untangle myself and all the powerful feelings inside. I sent my letter via email to be sure he got it before he left for Florida.

Dear Jake—

I'm sorry that seeing that text hurt or unnerved you. I would never hurt you on purpose or lie to you. Ever.

You are not one among many. You are incredibly special to me.

However, if I didn't have a few other fans, like Crazy Boy (who I've seen twice in the past two months, btw), I might be eating myself alive with insecurities. And I might be eating you alive too. Neither of which would be pretty.

Ironically, dabbling with a few other men who've told me all the wonderful things I didn't hear in my marriage has helped me be available to you. Those experiences rebuilt my self-esteem. But none of these fans mean anything close to what you do.

At the right time, I'm happy to tell them all that they missed their chance. Permanently. But you have to be ready to commit to me too. Fair is fair, right?

I'm falling in love with you too. But only you can decide if you are ready.

Given all this, I think it's best for you not to call or email me until you figure out whether you want to make a commitment to me, to be only with me, and to stop seeing your other girlfriends. Take your time. I'm not in a rush.

xoxo Leslie

Jake called and texted me every day he was in Sanibel. I refused to answer. I couldn't stop imagining Jake and this woman, whom I imagined as a cross between Isabelle Adjani and Beyoncé, lounging in bed listening to the Sanibel waves, making French toast with his mom, or spilling her cleavage out of a string bikini while playing jacks with his nieces on the wide mahogany porch overlooking the banyan trees. Jake sent me a postcard of a pink dolphin, which I got two days into his trip; he must have snuck out to the ramshackle Sanibel post office the day he arrived. In his messy scrawl, which despite my hurt and anger made my heart flip over a few times, he'd written one of my favorite quotes, widely (and mistakenly) attributed to Joan Didion, but originally penned by the French philosopher and historian Philippe Ariès:

"A single person is missing for you, and the whole world is empty."

That was all that was written on the postcard besides my address. He didn't sign his name. He didn't need to.

———————

The day he got home, Jake sent me a one-line text.

I want you and me to be a We.

I read, and reread, his words, my heart rocking in my chest. I knew what it meant. I was scared of merging into a "we." I wasn't ready to say good-bye to my solo life. But in relationships, you don't order perfect timing like a Domino's Pizza. Falling in love felt different this time, because I felt so differently, because I was in a relationship with someone kind and open like myself. This was Jake, a man I respected and knew inside and out. We'd take it slow, because we lived in separate cities. Saying yes terrified me, but saying no would have broken me.

A few months before, if Damon or Mishka or Dylan had suggested such a thing, I'd have been close to retching. I'd thought the last thing I wanted was to be vulnerable to a man again. But Jake's words made me feel like I had warm honey in my veins instead of blood.

This time, I called Jake back.

———————

Birthdays rock. My fiftieth? Not so much.

I sat in my office, scrolling through Facebook as a writing break. I had several acquaintances, mostly college friends, whose birthdays were clustered around mine. One after another had posted photos about their huge fiftieth bash, sometimes accompanied by wise reflections on their "first half century." All of these celebrants had been married for decades, as I had been. As I had thought I always would be. My friends seemed to look back on their lives with deathbed pride, as if most of the journey's highlights were now in the rearview mirror. My focus on the future felt wholly alien compared with their perspective. I wasn't going to ignore this milestone, but my instinct was to keep it low-key. When they trumpeted their age across social media, I couldn't help but cringe, thinking, *What twenty-nine-year-olds are going to date you if they know you're fifty?* Instead I liked their posts and kept my opinions to myself.

My internal birthday pep talk came easily: I was lucky to have my health, my kids, work I loved, and a floor of economic security. I didn't feel old. I felt younger and more excited about life than I had in at least a decade. However, fifty was undeniably older than I'd ever been, no matter how many "boyfriends" I'd screwed in the prior six months, and no matter how young *they* were. The only thing worse than openly celebrating five decades of life etched across my face, and body, was every single birthday coming after this one. Sixty? Good grief. Thank God I had a decade to get used to the idea.

I couldn't deny that part of my optimism stemmed from the fact that Jake and I had been together since he'd come back from

Florida. He came to see me the day after we finally spoke. He told me it was over with that girlfriend, Hannah. Forever. He wanted me and only me. I believed him. I told my kids we were dating, tense about their reaction, since I'd never introduced a boyfriend to them before, but neither one even shrugged the first morning he came down for breakfast, obviously having spent the night. He trusted me enough to leave his dog, Jennie, with me for a night while he went on a research trip to Canada. She was so arthritic that she couldn't walk up and down stairs, and it took her five to six minutes to turn in a circle and lie down on her bed. Watching her struggle, I wondered if Jake was being selfish, even heartless, to keep her alive given the amount of pain she was enduring. Plus her habit of pooping in the house, all over my Persian rugs, alarmed me. She'd defecated on my grandmother's hundred-year-old runner in the master bedroom, while Jake and I were making love two feet away. It was hilarious and entirely disgusting.

"Isn't sixteen old enough to be housebroken?" I'd asked Jake afterward.

"Are you kidding?" he'd answered. "She used to be so much worse."

What could possibly be more appalling than lovemaking interrupted by a pile of steaming doo-doo on an antique hand-knotted Kashan?

A week before my birthday, he sent me another card written in his uh . . . *unique* handwriting.

Dear Leslie,

I could tell at 16 what an amazing woman you would turn out to be at almost "L" (as the Romans would write it), and I fell in love with you almost immediately—and now I'm wondering why I didn't pursue you all my life.

Never doubt for a second that you are one kick-ass babe: incredible mind, deep wisdom, magnificent beauty (those eyes!), and a rockin' body. You are kind, generous, and so erotic. I'm so happy to have reconnected with you like this, right now. It's perfect.

Love, Jake

Jake, Timmy, and I stayed in the hot tub one cool Indian summer night until our fingers shriveled. We sat crunching salty blue chips on the deck by the fire table. Jake leaned up against the brick wall on one side of the grill, drinking a beer. The slate was still warm from the afternoon sun.

Bella burst onto the deck, flushed and sweaty from volleyball practice.

She popped open a coconut water and took a sip.

"Jake, you know my mom's birthday is next week, right? She's turning fifty."

Bella looked at me and smiled sweetly as she drew out the word "fifty," knowing I couldn't get mad at her in front of Jake. I felt like grabbing the grill fork and stabbing it in her ass. Instead I blinked and tried to show no reaction, the only rational way to deal with a vexing teenager.

"Yeah, I know," Jake said, wiping a palm on his orange bathing suit. "Everyone knows that. She's the best-looking almost-fifty-year-old in Philly."

Bella had miscalculated by assuming he didn't know my age. I wanted to grab Jake's face and give him a smooch in gratitude for burning her teenaged sass.

"I'm taking her skydiving to celebrate," he proffered casually, looking at the lights glowing in the backyard, holding his green Rolling Rock bottle.

I spat my water onto the sweet potato vine sprouting out of my terra-cotta pots. Timmy and Bella stood up from their deck chairs like synchronized swimmers. *Skydiving?* Everyone knew I was terrified of heights. Including Jake. I gagged on the drops of water in my throat.

The kids had all witnessed me freaking out atop the Empire

State Building, on various chairlifts, and hiking down the south rim of the Grand Canyon, which is why Bella had been so delighted I'd agreed to the helicopter ride in Mexico. My usual reaction was to sob while both kids tried to reassure me ("The gondola cable is *not* broken, Mom!"). The challenge for the kids was to avoid laughing, which would have only made me mad. We all collapsed hysterically as soon as these fits passed; even I found my fears absurd *afterward*. But in the moment, I was sure I was about to die. The hilarity reached new heights after the kids got cameras on their phones. We have a collection of my face atop high spots in exotic locales. I look like a squirrel monkey being pursued by a cheetah, eyes as big as fists, curled-back lips.

But Jesus H. Christ, it felt nice to have Jake remember my birthday. And to treat me as someone special in front of my kids. Under my cover-up, my heart grew a few sizes, and not from the fear of jumping out into the sky.

"Awww," I said. "You are so sweet."

I leaned into Jake and kissed him, hard. Damn the kids. He reached around and grabbed my butt in my bikini bottom.

"Stop it!" Bella shouted, hands on the hips of her green volleyball shorts, irritated she'd failed to embarrass me. "Mom!"

Bella then looked at Jake with blue eyes that matched her cobalt volleyball jersey, a little girl again.

"She'll never go," she said in a half-whisper.

Timmy had already sat back down. His hands were open on his knees, his Gatorade cradled in the lap of his flowered board shorts. He grinned at me, and then turned to Jake.

"Are you taking us, too?" Timmy asked.

"Sure," Jake said, letting me go and taking a sip of beer. "We're all going to celebrate how great your mom is. I've already booked the plane."

Of course, I called KC the next morning, to tell her about being taken skydiving, more or less against my will, on my fiftieth birthday.

"I love this man!" she said. "Rekindling a high school flame is like eating an entire Key lime pie by yourself. Only a real gentleman takes a girl *skydiving* for her birthday." I could hear her office printer whirring in the background. She was always working. "And the kids, too! Woohoo. He's bringing his kids, right?"

"Noooo . . . He never had kids, KC. Never married. No ex-wives! Isn't that great?"

How had I not mentioned this before? There was a long silence. I thought maybe she was distracted by a spreadsheet or something. Her office was never this quiet.

"Honey, I hate to tell you this. You cannot date anyone without kids."

Huh? KC was always so logical.

"What are you talking about?" I countered in a swirl of crestfallen defensiveness. "It's *fantastic* that Jake doesn't have any baggage. He does have a dog. She's sixteen. She's like his kid. A complete pain in the ass, by the way."

"A dog? Not even close, honey, and you know it. You trust him because you dated at seventeen. But what you've got together is not true intimacy, even though it feels like it. There's so much you can't know about him. And Leslie, moms cannot date—seriously date, screwing is fine—men without children. A man without kids is like a Porsche with a dead battery. You can drool over 'em, but they're useless. They don't know how to put someone else first, or to accept that sometimes, kids come first. Most men without kids are not grown-ups."

"But KC, Marty had kids. He was an utter narcissist. Jake is great, KC. You'll see. And I love that there are no . . . complications with his past. Everyone has baggage. His baggage is that he doesn't have any baggage."

"Leslie Morgan," she said sternly. She saved my whole name for times when she was truly serious. "No baggage equals no empathy. You need empathy. No relationship lasts without it. We're not teenagers. We're grown-ups. That's who you need. I'd personally never, ever date a man without children."

I had never known this. I understood what KC meant, though. Having children had turned me inside out and upside down; it was like being reborn myself, in the best possible way. KC and I agreed to disagree, and we both pushed the red circle on our phones. Mulling it over, I went back to my computer.

For a long time, I had no occasion to reconsider what KC said.

The day before my birthday, another card arrived from Jake. Demonstrating the self-restraint of a twenty-year-old frat boy, I opened it right away, standing barefoot on the black-and-white art deco floor of the Rittenhouse foyer. The envelope fluttered to the ground.

The cover was a watercolor painting of two white horses running together on a blue-green background. Inside, the quote read, "You were made for amazing things." I felt a pop of joy beneath my rib cage.

Below the "Love, Jake," he'd handwritten a P.S. almost as short, and exhilarating, as the quote.

Prepare yourself for an all-star pussy-licking session on your birthday.

Well, I could certainly use that, too.

"*Mom's fifty, Mom's fifty, Mom's fifty . . .*" Bella and Timmy sang as the wind whipped through the car windows and blew their hair around their faces. Piled into the TT the morning of my fiftieth birthday, the kids and I drove through rolling hills covered in red and orange fall foliage. Black-and-white Holstein cows dotted the small family farms we whizzed by. The air smelled like the piles of leaves I used to jump in as a kid. When we pulled up to a golden field in the middle of Pennsylvania Amish country, Jake was already there, leaning up against the hood of his Jeep, arms folded, an adorable smirk on his face.

However, we did not go skydiving. As the date approached, I had gotten more and more hesitant. Some in my family would use the technical term *hysterical*. Plus, as the kids were under eighteen, I needed Marty's written permission. My lawyer urged me not to ask for it. So instead of a skydiving field, that morning we parked in the grassy lot outside Hershey Park. It was the last weekend before the amusement park closed for the season. I promised the kids I would usher in my fiftieth by riding any roller coaster they strapped me into.

The first ride was called Fahrenheit, which I rode once and will never ride again. In case you've never been, Hershey Park's Fahrenheit is a yellow and red steel torture device with six horrifying "inversions," plus one of the steepest drops in the world (ninety-seven degrees). Then we rode Great Bear six times; that was only a teeny bit terrifying. Finally, we went on a ride called Skyrush, which Bella promised was "a mini Fahrenheit, Mom." It went two hundred feet up into the sky at seventy-five miles per hour. Nothing "mini" about it. In a picture taken by the automatic camera, I'm bolted into Skyrush next to Jake, Bella, and Timmy. They have looks of crazed glee on their faces while I appear to belong to a separate species, some alien, terror-stricken tribe. I recall a brief, spectacular view before the initial two-hundred-foot plunge, then teeth-gritting terror when our car dipped straight down, a violent feeling that I was insane, and the surety that I was about to be flung off Skyrush at seventy-five miles per hour to face my maker. In the moment, I tried to calm my jumpy stomach with the reassuring thought that at least I was with my kids and Jake at the end of my life. And thankfully, because my life was over, I'd never turn sixty.

We had to take a break afterward, because I threw up in a blue recycling trash can next to sooperdooperLooper. Which struck me as an appropriate response to turning fifty. Jake and the kids all loved it, even my vomiting. It made a supercool story whenever people asked what I'd done for my birthday.

Even if I'm never, ever doing that again.

———————

Before we left Hershey, Jake invited me to New York for the week-end before Halloween. He'd lived there for ten years, but I had no idea what his home was like. In the days after I said yes, he inexplicably tried to cancel.

"Ah, it turns out it's really not the best weekend for you to come," he announced one night over the phone. I said nothing in response.

"Unless, of course, you really want to."

I stayed quiet, letting the silence speak for me.

"You have such an adult house. Rittenhouse Square and all. My place is an apartment. It's small and not so fancy."

Like I cared? He was a documentary filmmaker, not an investment banker. His father, despite wealth that included a Central Park West penthouse, never gave Jake handouts. I wanted to see Jake's life. I wanted to belong there.

"Jake, I'm coming. And I'm really, really excited."

"Okay, okay." He sounded as overjoyed as Pooh's friend Eeyore.

I spent one Starbucks sessions with KC, and half a phone therapy appointment, dissecting the possible reasons behind Jake's ambivalence. Were there other New York women cluttering his life? Why did he seem so eager to come into my world, and yet so reluctant to invite me into his?

"He's intimidated by you," KC said. Really, intimidated by me?

"He's afraid of commitment," my therapist, Sara, thought. "Any man that age who hasn't married or had kids has a phobia about being vulnerable."

Neither explanation fit the Jake I'd known for thirty years.

So, early on Saturday morning, Jake waited for me at Penn Station, his head and shoulders sticking above the crowd under the blinking Amtrak arrivals board like a scruffy rocker. I slipped my arms around his back, and buried my face in his chest. He smelled so damn good, even at nine in the morning. I pressed my body against his warmth.

He leaned back and held me at arm's length. He chuckled at my effusiveness, checking to see if a nearby grandmother in a fake leopard coat holding a six-year-old's hand was watching our PDA.

A few feet away a homeless man stood clutching a long-empty Dunkin' Donuts Styrofoam coffee cup.

"Whoa, girl," Jake said, in his soft, easy way, pushing me back but holding on to both my hands. "You don't want to frighten the horses."

Then he picked up my scuffed black suitcase and said we'd drop it at his lobby and go for a bike ride in Central Park. I agreed that sounded lovely. What I really wanted was to take him home, check out his apartment, and fuck his brains out.

"It's such a good day, so crazy warm, we want to get out early before the park gets mobbed," he said, looking over his shoulder as we crossed Seventh Avenue. Was he still trying to back out of having me over?

"Okay, Jakey. Your turf, your rules."

He led me down a narrow, curved Village side street, overhung with Callery pear trees that arched into a yellow tunnel above us. Little black wrought iron gates guarded each sidewalk box from dogs looking for a picturesque place to pee. It felt as if Robert De Niro or Christy Turlington were going to walk toward us at any second. Jake stopped in front of a tall, stately redbrick building with arched stone cornices above the doorway and each window.

"Ta-da," he said, waving his free arm toward the entrance. We walked inside a lobby, lined with cracked and faded elegant marble walls, formerly white, now gray, and a defunct stone fountain carved into a corner. But instead of walking to the elevator with its polished brass buttons, Jake took me through a swinging painted gray door and down the utility steps to the basement. In a poorly lit bike room off the hallway, he unlocked two street bikes.

Once helmeted up, I followed him as he weaved like a bike messenger through the streets, dodging New York taxis and blowing through red lights. Central Park was cool and relatively empty, the hundred-year-old elms bright orange and red. After we cycled two loops up to Harlem and back, Central Park got crowded with families out for Saturday strolls, increasing the likelihood we would squash a runaway toddler. Around two o'clock, we abandoned the park and biked down Broadway, heading home amid yellow cabs. Back in the Village, we locked Jake's bikes near his front door. Jake took my hand and announced another delay, a long, sunshiney walk along the High Line. Was I ever going to see the inside of his building?

When I finally walked into his prewar apartment in Greenwich Village late that afternoon, as the sky outside was purpling with dusk, I understood immediately, viscerally, why he hadn't wanted me to see it. We crossed the black mahogany threshold, and I could tell right away the apartment itself was spectacular: spacious, with soaring nine-foot ceilings, vintage crown dentil molding, a coveted extra half bathroom with black and white subway tile immediately off the front entry hall, all pouring into a large dining room. I caught a glimpse of a galley kitchen and a living room beyond the dining room. On the far side of the apartment, there was a massive arched doorway leading into a bedroom with floor-to-ceiling windows overlooking the pear trees.

The problem? First, there were books piled everywhere. Of course you'd expect that, plus hundreds, or even thousands, of DVDs. As you'd imagine in the apartment of a filmmaker and screenwriter.

But the volume of clutter went beyond the mad-genius-poor-housekeeper bachelor mess. I counted three bicycles in the dining room alone. On the table, there wasn't room for a single place setting. Instead, there were stacks of old, wrinkled magazines, small mountains of what looked to be forgotten mail, empty envelopes with cellophane windows, loose unfiled bills, crumpled parking tickets, and old water-stained letters in precarious towers. On one corner of the dining room table, Jake proudly pointed out a sloppy two-foot pyramid of cards and posters he was planning to frame to give to his mom, his sister, his nieces, his favorite documentary narrators. The detritus repeated itself like mold on the living room coffee table, mushrooming along the floors, inching up the walls, covering the windowsills, even lining the hallway leading back to the front door. I counted six deflated basketballs and what looked like at least four dozen plastic water bottles with various sports logos littered throughout the place.

My sweet boyfriend was about a year away from being the star of an episode of the A&E show *Hoarders*.

There was no way Katie Couric's Manolo Blahnik heels had ever touched down on these floors. I remembered, abruptly, Jake telling me once that a girlfriend had broken up with him the day after she first saw his apartment. Looking around, I knew why.

"Wanna see my bedroom?" Jake said, tilting his head to a doorway framed by elaborate stringcourse square tooth molding.

I nodded, unable to speak, but not from sexual anticipation.

In the bedroom, there was a cherry sleigh bed loosely covered with a faded navy blue comforter thick with dog hair. There was a lumpy pile on the far side of the bed. That turned out to be his dog, Jennie, who was asleep under the covers, her head on the pillow. It was simultaneously sweet, and confusing, because wasn't I supposed to sleep there? A pair of snowshoes were leaned up against Jennie's side of the bed. Piles of Jake's messily folded T-shirts, jeans, and flannel pajamas blocked the bedroom windows, going up at least three feet high. There were two sleeping bags on top of the radiator.

There wasn't room for me in the bed, in the bedroom, or anywhere in the apartment.

Jake stood in the doorway, framed by the intricate white trim, looking somewhat dazed, but also very sexy. Was he oblivious to the way his place looked to others? Embarrassed? Afraid I'd be Girlfriend No. 2 who broke up with him after seeing his hoarding proclivities? I turned sideways to carry in my suitcase. I stumbled over an empty Amazon box. Jennie raised her head from the pillow to look at me suspiciously, like one of the three bears catching Goldilocks tiptoeing by. She gave me a hairy eyeball, like, *Huh? Who's this in my bedroom?*

After I caught my balance, I looked around.

"Jake, is there a good spot for me to put my stuff?" I asked, trying to clue him in.

"Yeah, sure, right here," he said, inching over to the foot of his bed, his tone suggesting a luggage rack or open space I'd missed. Instead, he perched my bag precariously on top of a stack of unfolded orange and red beach towels. He patted the suitcase to secure it onto the towels.

I picked my way carefully to the main bathroom to shower. There were so many bottles of ibuprofen and shaving cream and Bengay and Bumble hair gel, boxes of Band-Aids and Epsom salts and even more water-wrinkled magazines, there wasn't room for my toothbrush. I hung my purple toiletry bag on the back of the door and didn't unpack anything. I used a towel that I thought—hoped—was fairly clean. He hadn't put one out for me. I felt like I was visiting a spoiled frat boy, not a man in his late forties.

We had less than an hour in his apartment before our dinner reservation, which made it easier for me to avoid commenting on his piles of stuff. Or the food-encrusted dishes stacked in the sink. Or Jennie's six food bowls on the floor. He had not cleaned up. He had not made any room for me. Although he, obviously, knew I was coming.

I tried to let that sink in.

Jake obviously had no idea how his jammed, claustrophobic nest looked to outsiders—or maybe he did. The psychologist on the one segment of *Hoarders* I'd watched (it was excruciating, so I never watched a second show) explained that hoarders used material items as a barricade to prevent intimacy, and to fill unmet childhood emotional needs. "Possessions that seem useless serve essential purposes for hoarders," she explained sympathetically. "What looks like junk to others can be both a substitute for intimacy and a way to drive people away." I could see how it worked. An old, crotchety dog who pooped while we were having sex and slept under the covers between us was an added bonus.

Did Jake want me in his life? Looking around his apartment, I struggled to believe so. But it was a free country, wasn't it? Jake was a grown-up. He could live however he wanted. I couldn't wait to get out of the place.

In the bathroom, I changed into a snug black knit dress with exposed shoulders, and over-the-knee black suede boots. Jake whistled when he saw me, which picked up my spirits considerably, making me feel like a black swan emerging from a muddy fishpond. Coming out of his building into the cool evening and his idyllic Greenwich Village side street, we hailed a cab to his favorite Spanish restaurant, where he knew the chef from his last trip to Madrid. For dessert, we ordered every item on the menu—mini ice cream sandwiches, brownies fit for an American Girl doll, and bracing Spanish espresso.

And then, of course, we went back to his apartment to make love. I'd been waiting all day to feel his hands on my body, and as proof, my black lace underwear was soaked. Once I was kissing him, the mess in his apartment seemed utterly irrelevant.

With only one hurricane lamp in Jake's bedroom, and Jennie on her dog bed out in the hallway, it was easier to ignore the stacks of T-shirts, piles of unmatched socks, neon-yellow racing skis, and one set of crutches in his bedroom I hadn't noticed on my first pass through. And when Jake held my hand under the cover all night long, I felt like I'd been a fool to question my feelings for him.

───────────

Sunday morning, Jake got up early to make coffee. I heard him whistling in the kitchen, grinding beans, and teasing Jennie about what a pain she was for refusing to eat broccoli for breakfast. (Eew!) He tiptoed back into the bedroom. Jennie tottered behind him, with a toothy dog smile.

"Do you want some of the best coffee in the world?" he asked when he saw my eyes were open. He reached across the bed to hand me my very own blue Wonder Woman coffee mug, a token to keep in his apartment, making me feel as if I were his Wonder Woman.

I drank that first sip of coffee, black and delicious, with both eyes closed. There was no place to put down my mug, so I cradled it in my lap. We didn't get dressed until dinner. We made love throughout his apartment, despite the clutter, taking breaks to read the *New York Times* Sunday paper. I came twice, once lying on my back in his bed and once on the living room floor, the only clear spaces available. He came four times, twice in my mouth, as I knelt between his legs at the dining room table and in the shower, water streaming over both of us. "That's a personal record," he told me after his final orgasm. "I don't think there's a single sperm cell left in my body." Even then, I wanted more, as if my body still needed to make up for years of underemployment.

As we both lay naked across his bed in the late afternoon, totally worn out, Jake curled away from me. The bed started to shake. I looked at his back. His shoulders were trembling. I edged closer to him. He was crying, but like someone who didn't know how to cry. His body heaved, but without tears. He hid his face between his arms. I wrapped my arms around him from behind.

"What is it, Jake?" I whispered into the hollow between his shoulder blades.

"This feels too good with you," he choked out. "I can't take it. You don't criticize me or tell me to be different. You don't get angry at me for anything. You want to bike with me and visit my place and know me. It feels so right that it hurts."

A sob ripped through him. I felt like crying myself. I held him until he stopped trembling.

Later, when he got out of bed, he turned away, like he couldn't bear to face me. Pulling on his T-shirt and boxers, his bare back looked like a boy's, like the boy he once had been, and something splintered inside me, too.

That evening, Jake's biggest film donor, the hedge fund investor who'd contributed to Jake's movies since he'd graduated from Princeton, hosted a Halloween costume party. I was elated to be Jake's girlfriend in New York, to meet his work friends, to take our relationship public. My mama bear came out when Jake, who'd turned back into his normal jocular self, confessed that one of his ex-girlfriends, Hannah of Sanibel fame, would be there with her new boyfriend, a Calvin Klein underwear model whose three-story

Times Square billboard was causing traffic accidents. He was reportedly coming to the costume party wearing nothing but Calvin Klein underwear. Where did Jake find these women?

"I can't wait for you to meet everyone," he said. "And to protect me from Hannah."

Jake had picked up a Wonder Woman costume for me at the same nutty Manhattan adult costume shop where he'd bought my coffee mug. Jake went as an Andy Warhol Campbell's Tomato Soup can, with gel in his hair to make it stand up crazily, as Andy's once did. The costumed guests blurred together, except for Hannah. Fortunately I saw her only from across the double living room. She was dressed as an Indian princess with a beaded suede headband, although the turquoise gem above her forehead had fallen out. She smiled at me warmly, like she knew a secret I didn't. I turned away, confused.

I had to leave the party early to get home to the kids. My custody started at eight o'clock. Tim and Bella would be fine alone for a few hours, but not overnight. So I made my exit at ten, wiped off my eye makeup with a Kleenex in the taxi to Penn Station, and caught the last Amtrak back to Philadelphia.

I didn't hear from Jake for the rest of the night. I texted from the train. Send me pictures! And How late did you stay? I kept on my coat so no strange men would get any ideas about picking up Wonder Woman.

When I finally snuck into my house around one in the morning, and checked on the kids in their beds (nothing more adorable than a sleeping child, especially teenagers temporarily unable to sass or snarl), I sent Jake another quick message. Home safe. Love you. And still I heard nothing back. Had he lost or misplaced his phone? Thank God I was exhausted enough to fall asleep without wondering when, where, or with whom he'd disappeared.

I got up at seven to make the kids avocado toast before school. Then I wrote for a few hours and went to noon power hour yoga.

I checked my phone every ten minutes. Nothing from Jake. In the five or six weeks we'd been seeing each other, we'd emailed or texted each other several times a day. In my email queue, I had over two hundred saved messages from him. His silence unnerved me. What had happened? Was it possible that he had gone home with another woman? Maybe with . . . Hannah? I didn't think so. Every time I looked at my blank phone screen, I took a deep breath, and tried to soothe my anxious inner child like a jockey trying to coax an unruly Thoroughbred into the starting gate at the Kentucky Derby.

Luckily, I had a phone session with Sara at one o'clock.

"Well, Leslie, have you two ever talked about commitment?" she asked. "Being monogamous? Making this official?"

"Well, I've been faithful to him. Even when he was seeing Hannah. I assume he is, too. But I guess it's more of a . . . guess than an explicit agreement."

"And Jake? Has he ever brought up the subject of sexual fidelity, yours or his?"

I explained about Jake's text that read, I want you and me to be a We. And what he whispered almost every time we made love: I want to be the only man who gets to fuck you.

Even to me, my pronouncements sounded as convincing as a six-year-old telling her parents she had not eaten the last brownie. There was a pause on the line.

"Hmph." Sara sounded perplexed by what I'd told her. "That's not the same as a conversation about fidelity and sexual exclusivity, Leslie. Most people fall into this trap, by making assumptions. That's risky. You have to talk about monogamy explicitly. There's no other way for a couple to approach commitment. It seems like Jake expects you to be loyal, to not even get texts from other men. He wants to be in your life. I'm not sure he wants to let you into his, or to make an unambiguous commitment. Maybe he's afraid to make himself vulnerable, and that's why he's never gotten married or had kids, and why his apartment is such a disaster. Careful,

Leslie. Nostalgia for a high school crush can create a powerful false intimacy. You've missed thirty years of Jake's life. I know it's hard to believe after Marty and Conor, but there are many far better men out there. You don't have to settle for this."

Shit.

I was behind the wheel of the TT, heading to school to get Bella, when Jake finally called. I pulled over to the side of Chestnut Street and put on my flashers to talk to him. Drowning out his voice, an institutional loudspeaker blared in the background.

"Hey you," he said, clearing his throat. His voice sounded as if he'd scraped it with steel wool. "I'm in the ER at Beth Israel. Don't worry. I'm okay."

"Oh my God." Clutching the steering wheel, my shoulders and chest stiffened with worry. I imagined a dented yellow taxi crashing into him or a tanklike Mercedes running a red light through the crosswalk as he biked up Broadway. "What's wrong?"

"Well, after you left, we broke out some mezcal. Not sure what I was thinking. We started doing shots. I don't remember exactly how I got home. But I spent the night throwing up. Kind of like you at Hershey Park. But, um, this morning . . . afternoon actually . . . I was throwing up blood. So I took a cab to the ER. I have some kind of esophageal tearing from 'excessive vomiting.' I promise, it's not as fun as it sounds."

He was joking, or trying to. I didn't laugh.

Once I was sure he didn't need me to come back to New York to take care of him, we said good-bye and I sped to get Bella before the school's late-pickup fees kicked in. I was relieved Jake was not lying in a New York morgue or in bed with another woman. Yet I felt emotionally singed—puzzled, surprised, disturbed. If Jake had torn his throat at eighteen, when we were kids thrashing out how to handle booze, maybe I'd have understood. But Jake had been drinking alcohol for thirty years. The feelings Jake elicited in me were like roller-coaster loops: empathy, confusion, frustration, worry, passion. For the first time since he'd gone to Sanibel with

Hannah, I didn't want to talk to Jake at all. Sara was right: I had no clue who Jake Bryant really was.

———————

Two weeks later, Jake left for South Africa to work on a film about Cape Town's citywide water crisis, a trip that fell over Thanksgiving. Which they don't celebrate in Africa, obviously.

"Can you come?" Jake had asked, once my irritation cooled and we were talking again after a two- or three-day hiatus. My detachment had backfired, because I'd missed Jake desperately during our time-out. Fear-driven questions, like chiggers under my skin, haunted me. *Who will hold me all night the way Jake does? How can I go back to starving for love and sex? What man will understand my writing the way he does?* Despite the esophageal vomit-fest, I wanted to go to Cape Town with Jake, to see the magnificent, faraway metropolis with him, at the height of South Africa's summer. Especially because he hadn't had anything to drink since Halloween. I hadn't asked him to stop; he'd voluntarily decided to dry out. His escapade seemed too ridiculous to be anything but a fluke that wouldn't, couldn't, happen again. Once we connected again, he told me he was going to take a month off from drinking. I felt giddy with relief, as if computer pixels were rearranging themselves in the shape of my heart, blissed out by sinking back into being in love with him.

With descriptions as vivid as if he were pitching a new documentary, he tempted me with images of a city on hills surrounded by shark-infested cerulean-blue ocean. Exotic food and artisanal wine. Friendly people. Complicated cultural history. Jake's images almost made me drool. I wanted to say yes, as much to be with him in an exotic new place as to witness Cape Town for myself.

However, if the Cape Town invitation had included a mind meld with Mandela, I still would have said no. Thanksgiving is my kids' favorite meal; in fact, it's one of the only meals I can cook. I would have felt guilt-ridden throwing them over for any man or any exotic trip on the homiest holiday of the year. Usually we went to Southampton, but Marty insisted we stay in Philly so he could see the kids after the meal, and it wasn't worth a fight.

Alone in my bedroom on Thanksgiving Eve, high above my sleeping kids, I poured out my feelings for Jake, two oceans away.

Jake—I'm missing you and thinking about how much I appreciate you and what we have together.

It's a bit intense, so prepare yourself.

Years ago, when I started to realize how dismal and deadly and completely cardboard everything in my marriage had become, I had an unbidden wish: to like sex again, of course, but even more, I wanted to have a sex life that was real, and close, not just exciting sexually but emotionally.

Even though I've always been an avid fan of sex itself, I felt like maybe I had never had a truly intimate connection. Or at least, it had been so long ago or so terribly fleeting that I'd forgotten what it was like.

I craved that closeness as much or more than the erotic component, which naturally I did also want again. But I wanted much, much more. It could have been with a man, a woman, myself—I didn't have a clear picture of what I wanted. I needed that kind of connection in addition to sexual pleasure.

Most amazing to me is feeling close to you. Sex is never "just sex." With you, it's simultaneously, exponentially, not only the best sex of my life but also the deepest, most satisfying, intense emotional connection as well. It means more to me than I ever could have imagined in my bleakest hours. Being with you makes me so very, very happy.

Love, Leslie

Thanksgiving morning, I slid the twenty-pound turkey in the oven. The kids were still asleep. I laid out the stuffing, washed the Brussels sprouts, soaked the rice, and wiped the dirt off the raw mushrooms. I checked the pumpkin pie in the fridge. I walked Jennie. Then I crawled back in bed and checked my phone to see if Jake had replied. He had.

Leslie, I was going to call you tonight but I think I'd better write this all out. I, too, have obviously felt our incredible more-than-sexual connection, from the beginning. I'll be very honest, it had always bummed me out that our first young love affair had never really gotten a chance to flourish, sexually and otherwise. Of course I desperately wanted to lose my virginity to you, but there was more to it, and it really made me sad when it ended.

So when we got together again, at first, it was kind of about healing the past in that sense. It wasn't just that, of course. I, too, had obviously been trapped in a series of listless relationships that left me unfulfilled in so many ways. You have to both like your partner, and lust for them, but love is something more than the sum of those parts. I frankly had neither. I wanted to be with someone who inspired my lust and who I more-than-liked.

For me it happened in Atlantic City. We ended up on the bed as if we couldn't wait, with your dress pulled up and my cock buried deep in your wonderful pussy, and it was erotic as hell but I had this incredible feeling that was so much more than sexual. It felt so emotionally fulfilling to be inside you that way. It was fantastic.

It had been a long, long time since I'd felt that way. It was deep. No pun intended. (OK, pun intended.) I was afraid to admit it but that was the first time that I Knew. That was what made me want to continue to pursue you. And it was also kind of terrifying, not only because it threatened my lame existing relationships and status quo, but because it represented very real emotional risk. Every time we got together, it wasn't only our bodies that were naked, it was like my heart had been pulled out of my chest. That's why I kept telling you that I was scared. It WAS scary. Also great. And so much better now that we're together forever.

I miss you so much. When I get home I want to spend hours in your bed, until we're both completely soaked and spent. I can't wait for that. You are the best girlfriend ever.

love, me

Two days later, I drove to the Philadelphia Airport in the TT and pulled into the one lone space hidden in a far corner of the hourly lot. Finally, Jake walked through the international security doors, disheveled, exhausted, mine. I held him long and hard. He felt warm under his pin-striped cotton shirt; I felt safe in his arms, surrounded by strangers and piles of overseas luggage. He ruffled my hair and kissed my forehead as I buried my face in his neck. He whispered in my ear, "Loved that sweet email. Good to be back, BGE." It took me a second to translate: Best Girlfriend Ever.

Sunday morning, I brought him black coffee in bed.

"Surprise," I said, handing him the steaming mug. "Today is Thanksgiving again."

Even his eyebrows looked jet-lagged. "What?"

"I've got another turkey already in the oven. Stuffing, Brussels sprouts, pumpkin pie. Everyone's coming."

"You're kidding," he said. "That may be the nicest thing anyone has ever done for me."

Later that day, sitting at the Kentucky black walnut dinner table my grandfather had made, as we were all saying our thankfuls, I took Jake's hand under the table.

"I love you," I whispered. His eyes got wet as he smiled back at me.

"Thank you so much," he whispered back, squeezing my hand.

I was the Best Girlfriend Ever. Jake was all mine. Nothing had ever felt this good.

"Do you want to come to the beach for a week?"

There was silence on the phone after I asked him. He knew what it meant.

No man except Marty had ever spent the night at our beach house, well, my house now. I'd never had sex with anyone there, not even with Marty. I wanted Jake to become part of my and the kids' oasis. I picked a week in mid-December when both kids were with their dad, so Jake could experience for himself how the beach in winter became an exclusive, uninhabited paradise.

I could almost see Jake's smile over the phone after I asked him.

"Yes, Leslie. I can't wait to come. I'll bring my bike. And Jennie."

I was so excited for him to see everything I loved there, I got up at seven the Monday he and Jennie were arriving. I mopped the floors and folded the sofa throws and fluffed all the pillows. I showered. I blow-dried my hair. I painted my toenails bright fuchsia. I went to Citarella for hamachi and fresh-squeezed orange juice. I built a fire in the living room and the library. I raked the gravel driveway. I made a bouquet of dried lavender cuttings for his bedside table.

Jake was going to be in my bed at the beach. The holiest of holies. We were going to be a *We*.

My cell rang around one.

"Hi," Jake said groggily, drawing out the *iiii*. He sounded like he had fog in his mouth.

"How . . . are you?" I asked, disquieted by sudden panic. He sounded like he had the flu. Was he canceling?

"Um, not so good." Long pause. He cleared his throat. Then he laughed.

"Dave and I went out last night. Drinking tequila."

My mind blanked. Who was Dave? Why would Jake stay up late drinking anything, much less a bottle of tequila, the night before he visited me at the beach for the first time? Especially so soon after the Halloween fiasco. A tiny alarm sounded in the back of my head.

"He made me do shots. I forget how many. There's only about an inch left in the bottle. I threw up. Twice."

I didn't know what to say. Vomiting, again? All of my adult puke stories involved pets, children with the flu, or food poisoning. I didn't know a single person over twenty-five who had thrown up after drinking too much booze. Why did Jake drink so much? How was I expected to react? I didn't want to be all uptight and bitchy, the school principal storming into the student lounge to bust weed smokers. Confusion trickled through my brain like syrup over pancakes as I clutched my cell phone, looking around my painstakingly vacuumed white living room rug. Because I'd tried to distance myself once already, and failed because I missed him so badly, I was afraid to try again. It felt kind of like not leaving my first husband after the first time he hit me, five days before our wedding. If you don't leave right away, it gets harder to leave the next time. But wait—this was ridiculous, comparing Jake's self-destructive behavior to physical violence. I knew Jake loved me, wanted to see me, was dying to see me and to come to my private retreat. To write next to me in my office. To make love to me all day long. Right?

"So, uh, okay, um, well . . ." I didn't know what to say. Was he still coming? I was afraid to ask. I blinked furiously. My throat swelled and tears wet my eyelashes.

It was as if he read my mind.

"I am actually about to get in the car, Leslie. I may have to stop at my sister's along the way to . . . uh . . . nap. Or throw up again. And the traffic will probably suck since I screwed this all up."

He said this with a mix of self-deprecation and wistfulness, asking for forgiveness although unable to say the words out loud.

"I should get there late tonight. Probably by eight or so."

The empty day stretched before me. I'd already been up for over five hours. Every hour waiting for him felt like a twelve-hour assembly line shift.

"I'm sorry to hear that, Jake." Trying to buff the disappointment out of my voice made my throat hurt. "I hope you feel better. Drive carefully."

As I hung up the phone, I looked around the house at the two roaring fires, the flowers, and the fluffed couch pillows. It came to me with a jolt. Although he'd sounded as if he regretted polishing off a bottle's worth of tequila shots, Jake had not actually said he was sorry, or that he understood that he'd disappointed me. Or at least inconvenienced me.

Not once.

Jake finally arrived, tired and sweaty from the drive, his shirt wrinkled, a queasy, drained look on his face. He held me in his arms like I was a life raft. Despite his exhaustion, his erection under his jeans grew against my right hipbone. We stumbled onto my bed. And stayed there for two hours.

Is there anything good sex can't make up for? The next day, using his hands and his mouth and his cock, he made me come twice before noon. His tequila-fest seemed like another aberration. Like it had nothing to do with me or us or the magical way our bodies connected. He had a single beer that night with dinner. Maybe I was out of touch with how much people actually drank these days; maybe he was normal and I was paranoid. We were two good people in love, deepening our relationship and working through problems, in a way Marty and I had never been able to.

We had a cozy, lazy week. I stole his gray cashmere sweater and wore it every day. Sometimes that was all I wore. We took slightly frostbitten bike rides and windy, sun-drenched beach walks with Jennie. We cooked fish on the grill every night and had sex twice a day in front of the fire, in my bed, on the couch, on the kitchen counter, on the steps leading to the second floor. Jake transformed my beach house into an oasis for making love, for new beginnings. I couldn't have felt more sensual.

Our last night together, lying naked in bed, two candles flickering and the rest of the lights out, I asked what he wanted from us.

He smiled.

"More of this," he said, leaning over to give me a drawn-out kiss. "That's my short answer."

———————

Twenty-four hours after he went back to the city, I got another email from Jake.

God I hated leaving you.

Especially after some of the hottest sex ever. Seriously.

You looked absolutely gorgeous all week. You're glowing, radiant. I'm insanely jealous of any man who even gets to look at you.

I love you, overwhelmingly.

You asked what I want, and I don't really have a checklist, but let's start with:

I want to be with you, lots
I want to screw you on the hood of the TT
I want to keep exploring sexually with you, trying new
    things and situations
I want to write electrifying erotic stories for you and text
    them to you in the TSA line
I want to cook delicious meals for you as a way to show
    my love
I want to read 2,000 books with you, side by side
I want to swim across Long Island Sound with you

I want to ski with your kids and do lots of other fun things
   with them
I want to take you skydiving, just one time
I want us to share our deepest emotions with each other
I want us to be "there" for each other, for anything that
   happens
I want to be the only one who gets to make love to you
I want to be your collaborator, your first reader, and your
   biggest fan
I want to be your partner, in everything.

I was tempted to frame it so I could read it to myself every day.

"I need one more power hour," I told the teacher checking me into hot yoga. "Before the Christmas insanity takes over my life."

She laughed, handing me my change and a bottle of cold water.

The studio was fifty degrees hotter than the air outside in Rittenhouse Square. In the middle of Warrior Pose, stretching out my hamstrings in the heat, I reread Jake's email in my mind, which was easy because I'd already read it so often, I'd practically had it memorized. *This is it. This is why I left Marty. To find love like this. True love. With Jake. He's been waiting for me for over thirty years. I was too blind to see it.* Reuniting with a man like Jake was the jackpot every woman who'd left a loveless marriage deserved. I should give lessons.

When I got home from yoga, there was a card with my name and address scrawled in Jake's handwriting amidst the Christmas cards in the pile of mail in my foyer. My heart filled as I slit the envelope open with my pointer finger as I stood by the newel post on the staircase.

Leslie—

Not even a psychic could have predicted that we'd be spending this Christmas together. I almost can't believe it myself. What a

strange, surprising, wonderful few months we've had together.
And still every day (and night) with you feels like a gift.

Love, Jake

———

December twenty-third. I held a messy heap of $19.99 wool sweaters outside the Forever 21 dressing room, surrounded by teenagers and their mothers toting credit cards. My friend Sig from high school stood next to me in his graying ponytail and plaid lumberjack shirt. Sig lived on a ranch in Montana and was visiting Philadelphia for the holidays. Starved for cheap fashion, his two teenaged daughters tried on clothes for themselves, their cousins, and Sig's wife. Sig and Shelly had gotten married the same year as Marty and I.

"Mom will love that one, girls," Sig told them through the slatted dressing room door. What a small but meaningful gesture, to encourage your children to buy a present for their mother. Marty had never taken the kids shopping for a present for me. It was fascinating, but in some ways terribly sad, to see evidence of why Sig and Shelly's imperfect but happy union had outlasted my own.

Jake was already in Philly to spend Christmas with me and the kids. Jennie's dog bed lay in front of the fireplace, next to the blue spruce Jake had helped me haul home. The kids had been with Marty for Hanukkah, but they were all mine until New Year's. My house was filled with presents, the cats, Jennie, Tigger, and Jake, on the verge of chaos in a way that made it feel like we were a blended, messy, happy modern family.

I had awoken next to Jake that morning, as the sugary, floury smell of Bella's Christmas cookies baking in the oven wafted up to the second floor. I asked Bella to join us for the shopping trip with Sig and the girls, but she had to make two more batches for friends. Jake didn't know Sig as well as I did, but they had played intramural basketball together.

"Jake, you're welcome to come. Do you want to?"

"Hmmm. Shopping with teenagers? I think I'll play pickup at Penn."

He'd kissed me and slid his palm slowly down my butt as I walked by.

After four hours spent exhausting all shopping possibilities in a six-block radius, I hugged Sig and his daughters good-bye at their rental car, and walked in through the alley toward my back gate.

To my astonishment, Jake's Jeep was pulling out of his parking spot. I stared at his red taillights and bumper receding down the cobbled alley. Where was he going when we were supposed to have dinner with the kids in an hour? Something was wrong. Jake put on the blinker on his Jeep and turned right, away from me.

I ran through the backyard, inside the house, up the stairs to my—our—bedroom. The room was neat and tidy and . . .

Empty.

His bags were gone. Jennie was gone. I looked for his tooth-brush. The Eau Sauvage cologne I loved. The brown tortoiseshell reading glasses he kept on the bedside table. All gone.

I frantically dialed his cell phone, already crying, shaky with adrenaline and fear. What had happened?

He picked up. "Hello?" His voice was steady but laced with anger.

I could barely choke out, "Jake, it's me. Did you . . . leave?"

"Yeah," he said, the wrath in his voice increasing. "Um, I de-cided to go say hi to Jim and Penny."

But he'd had coffee with Jim that morning.

"With your toothbrush? What happened, Jake? You can't leave like that."

"Well, Bella said you were out with Sig."

He snapped off each word, coming down especially viciously on Sig's name.

"Alone," he continued. "Not shopping with his kids like you said."

"Bella is fifteen, Jake. She was probably watching *Scandal* when you asked her where I was. Olivia Pope was probably out shopping by herself."

I was speaking too fast to get a breath. I couldn't slow myself down. Growing up with active alcoholism and a childhood filled with false accusations had seared my psyche. My volatile early marriage made me even more thin-skinned. And this allegation was most definitely false.

"You know where I was, Jake. I was with Sig and his daughters. Sig is *married*. We went to Forever 21 and had falafel. Did you think I was . . . sneaking off to fuck him? And now I'm lying to you about it?"

I could not believe those words were coming out of my mouth. To the man I loved and trusted. Two days before our first Christmas together.

It felt like the bedroom walls were spinning around me.

"Come back, Jake. Talk to me about this. You can't leave like that. This is . . . insane."

I felt small and surprised and broken. Not only that he'd accuse me of cheating, but that he'd left without even talking to me, without giving me a chance to explain or defend myself. It was as if he'd already decided I was guilty—as if he *wanted* me to be guilty.

I was still crying, hunched in a ball on my bedroom floor, when I heard Jake's boots methodically meeting the wood as he came back up the stairs. I felt like I didn't have enough skin to cover my body. He knelt down on the floor and hugged me hard, his whole body wrapped around me, until I stopped crying.

Jake didn't explain why he suspected me of cheating. He didn't apologize for scaring me. I couldn't discern whether he even *knew* he'd frightened me. But how could he not see how upset I was? I was alarmed by his possessiveness, his lack of maturity, his rush to judge me. But blocking out all those feelings was a flood of gratitude that he'd come back. I wanted—needed—to believe he had not abandoned me like that.

Still reeling, I splashed water on my face and squeezed a few allergy drops into each eye. The walking-on-eggshells dread that came from growing up with an alcoholic parent, and then living with my troubled, abusive first husband, had long ago wormed its way into my bones. I'd become perhaps too adept at swift recovery following a crisis. Oddly, it felt normal to walk downstairs with Jake to make dinner for the kids. Jake tackled the salad. I put the chicken in the oven. Quiet and shaking inside, I told myself, *Everyone has insecurities*. What matters is that he's facing them. With me.

Was he facing them? With me, or without me? I didn't know. How could Jake simultaneously be afraid of commitment *and* jealous? Why couldn't we talk about it?

I tried not to think about our fight over dinner. The kids jabbered and teased each other about what they were getting for Christmas. When Jake and I got into bed that night, we made love silently. I woke in the middle of the night, and he was still holding my hand under the covers. So forgetting how he'd made me feel wasn't as difficult as perhaps it should have been.

The mermaid sat proudly, to me at least, amidst the dead brown sticks of my midwinter backyard. It was Christmas Eve. Jake was carrying two Whole Foods bags heavy with roast beef and Yukon Gold potatoes for Christmas dinner. I had two CVS bags filled with stocking stuffers, M&M's and gum for Timmy, makeup and hair conditioner and eos lip balm for Bella.

"Hey," Jake said, putting the bags down on the brick walkway. He turned and smiled at me over his shoulder.

"Any chance I can have the mermaid for a Christmas present? I'll put her at the cabin."

I put my bags down and faced him. He loved her, too. Because she was me. At that moment, I felt like I'd give Jake anything he asked for.

"I'll consider an adoption," I said. I kissed him before he could react. "But if you ever break up with me, I get her back."

Our fight, or whatever it was, seemed like ancient history. I hadn't told Winnie or KC or Sara about the cheating accusations; I didn't want to embarrass Jake. It was a misunderstanding that would never happen again. This was what Sara called "relationship repair": a fight with hurt feelings, followed by apology, explanation, reconnection, and an agreement to avoid any such future misunderstandings. In other words, a normal bump in an emotionally healthy union, a concept with which I was still rather unfamiliar.

Jake wrapped his arms around my shoulders. "Deal," he said.

———————

New Year's Eve. Jake and I got home after eleven, sated with trout almandine and foie gras. I'd made dinner reservations five weeks before at a new French bistro we'd spotted on one of our city walks. The day after Christmas, the restaurant critic from the *Star* awarded it four bells, making me feel like a foodie psychic. Bella and her friend Izzy stayed home with Jennie, delirious and hyped to be unchaperoned on this epic night, getting excited to watch the ball drop in Times Square on TV.

I went upstairs and got our biking clothes from my closet. I came back down. Confused, Jake eyed the bike pants with a puzzled frown.

"Wanna go biking around the Liberty Bell and Independence Hall?" I asked. "To ring in the New Year?"

Jake's shoulders dropped and he smiled.

"Hell, yes. What a great idea."

It was fifty degrees out, warm for late December. The streets were dry, and we didn't get chilled, even when we were speeding on the bikes. We both had blinking lights on our front handlebars and helmets. Touring the historic square over the bumpy cobblestone streets, we had the world of 1776 all to ourselves.

After the midnight bell at Old St. Joseph's chimed, we stopped in front of Independence Hall. The 250-year-old brick building was lit from the inside, as if exclusively for us. Jake took off his helmet. His hair was plastered to his head, like a kid waking up in the morning.

"I'm so lucky," he said, leaning over the handlebars of his bike to kiss me. His nose was cold and running. Mine was, too.

"Can I be with you for the next fifty years?" he asked, his gray-blue eyes shiny and soft.

"Yes." I kissed him back. "But first, I better check to make sure the girls are okay."

I took my phone out from the bike pack under my seat.

"Holy shit." There were three text messages from Bella. Some-things wrong with Jennie, one read. The next elaborated: She cant walk right. Then, the slightly panicked I dont know what to do.

Jake checked his phone, too. Bella had left him two additional messages. His face turned white and streaky with worry. We hopped on our bikes and pedaled furiously up Walnut Street, sweating in the cool night air.

Jake let his bike fall on the sidewalk by the front steps of the brownstone. He tripped and hit his shin on one of the red sandstone stairs as he rushed to the door. He didn't even swear, he was so frightened. As soon as he hit the brass knocker, the girls swung the door open. I could see Jennie's brown body lying motionless on the black and white marble floor behind Bella.

"Jesus, Leslie, go get my car," Jake said, clutching his bloody leg. "I'll bring her out front."

I drove his Jeep, Jake cradling Jennie in his lap in the backseat, to the twenty-four-hour vet in South Philly. Jake had wrapped her in a makeshift sling made out of one of my white throw blankets. I helped him carry Jennie sideways up the stairs to the automatic emergency room doors, each of us clutching two edges of the blanket. Tears dripped down his face.

Jennie wasn't a pet to Jake. They'd been together for sixteen years. She was on par with a child to him.

"She's the only relationship I've ever had that's lasted," Jake said to me, as we sat on the green plastic waiting room chairs after we gingerly transferred the sling to two veterinary technicians. I searched for the right words. *She's lived a good life*, or *You can always get another dog*, didn't cut it. He buried his face in his hands. All I could think to do was wrap my arms around his shoulders.

Two hours later, the disheveled, overtired vet in dirty blue scrubs and orange Crocs came out. We both stood up simultaneously. I reached for Jake's hand and gave it a squeeze. It was cold and clammy and he didn't squeeze mine back.

"Jennie." The vet said her name like you would a human's, and then paused. "Is okay, for a sixteen-year-old large-breed. Her blood work shows she's developed an age-related balance issue called ataxia."

Jake's shoulders plummeted, like a comic book character exaggerating collapse.

"Oh God, she had that before, a year ago," he explained, his voice hoarse with relief. "But it only made her head tilt sideways a little bit."

"Well, she's older and weaker now. She's living on borrowed time. You've kept her alive with your . . ."

The vet looked down at her clipboard.

"Six hand-cooked meals and those fifteen vitamins and pills a day. Going forward, she'll have trouble coordinating her legs, and her bowels, but she'll get noticeably better once the antibiotics kick in."

The doctor's eyes softened when she looked at Jake, and she put her hand on his shoulder.

"You know, she may only have a few weeks left, no matter how beautifully you take care of her."

Jake nodded at her, and then looked away, squeezing his lips together tightly so he wouldn't cry again.

We got Jennie home around three in the morning. I was exhausted and cold. Jennie seemed drugged and slow moving. Jake was silent, distant, and overwhelmed. We were still in our bike clothes. The girls were asleep on the couch in their pajamas. Both of their mouths were open. The TV was blaring.

A not very happy New Year had indeed begun.

Jennie made a surprisingly quick recovery, given her age and over-all frailty. Jake was swamped with a deadline for a film festival sub-mission, so he headed back to New York with Jennie lying on a blanket in the back and my mermaid strapped into the passenger seat of his Jeep. His emails washed up in my inbox like perfect sand dollars on the beach.

Monday.

Taking a quick writing break to tell you how much I adore you. (A lot.)

Tuesday.

I'm so in love with you.

Wednesday.

Every time I see you, I want to make love to you, imme-diately, but the best part is that the whole magnificent, carnal package is part of YOU, in all your wonderful you-ness, with everything else about you that I love so much. I'm so glad you're in my life. I can't wait to see you again.

Thursday.

I love spending time with you. And the more time we spend together, the more I love you. Spending Christmas with you opened up my heart; after you gave me the mermaid, I staggered off to walk Jennie with tears running down my cheeks. I hope I deserve your love. Or is this all a dream?

Friday.

It's not a dream: It's crazy and wonderful, and real. And while I think we both recognized, pretty early, that this

was something special (Atlantic City, for me), you're the one who's kept it going, with your patience, your openness, your willingness to take a huge emotional risk. I love you so much.

Saturday.

Is it OK if I love you in some way for the rest of my life?

I read, and reread, Jake's words in my sunny office, the space heater humming at my feet as I wrote and paid bills and researched summer camps for the kids. I was too anxious to reveal to him, or even myself, that I was so moved by his vulnerability that my palms got sweaty reading them. This fairy tale was happening. Finally, I'd found a man I loved who treated me the way I deserved.

"A speaking engagement two days before Valentine's?" I complained over the phone a few nights later. "In Miami? On a Saturday night? It blows the weekend."

"Yeah, I feel so, so badly for you," Jake teased back. "You know what's great about Miami? It's only three hours from Tulum. I'll take you to my favorite beach for Valentine's Day. It'll be our practice honeymoon."

Practice honeymoon? The idea of getting married again still made me retch. But about one thing I was certain: I wanted, forever, the warm-cocoa feeling I got from knowing that Jake wanted and needed me. And the sex, so spectacular every single time.

"You're crazy, Jake." I avoided repeating the phrase *practice honeymoon* like newly planted grass, too tender to risk trampling. "Mexico sounds incredible. Let's do it."

The fund-raiser in Miami turned out to be worth the trip. The agency raised a half million to help Jewish victims of domestic violence with hotel rooms, groceries, childcare programs, therapy, and legal assistance—people from devout families whose communities still clung to the myth that relationship abuse was something shameful that didn't happen to "people like us." Mickey Silverstein, the chairman of the board of the agency, took me out to a South Beach bar for drinks to celebrate afterward. When he heard I was heading to Tulum, he told me that his family had a retreat—an actual tree house with six bedrooms—there.

"You have to go on a hike to my favorite secret cenote," he explained as he dipped a chip in guacamole. "It leads you through a purple bougainvillea tunnel, utter magic. Then you come to a private volcanic well, lined with black lava, where you can swim in spring-fed fresh water and stand under a waterfall. The most romantic place I've ever seen. No tourists ever go there."

I wrote down the top-secret directions, excited to tell Jake.

"Jake, guess what we're gonna do?" I said, taking his hand in mine as we reconnoitered the open-air Cancún airport on Sunday morning, after taking separate flights, mine from Miami, his from New York. We wandered under the hot sun, surrounded by milling tourists, all of us gringas wearing identical confused expressions, scanning the airport roadway for hotel shuttles like ship captains searching the horizon for shore.

"Doesn't that hike sound idyllic? I cannot wait."

Jake didn't respond as he lifted my duffel and his backpack onto the van, crowded with German tourists who were already drunk.

Once the bus deposited us outside our resort in Tulum, we carried our bags across the scalding sand to our private thatched-roof hut. Our villa was nestled in the dunes, only yards from the crashing blue waves. Jake had stayed at this boutique hotel before, probably with another girlfriend, but I was with him now. It felt right. I felt lucky. That's what mattered.

"Babe, about that hike. I don't want to go. I've been to cenotes before," Jake said as he put on his black sunglasses, surprising me. "I'm exhausted from the Silverdocs submissions. I want to be lazy on the beach. With you. All day and all night."

"Okay," I said, flattered. But also disappointed, a little thrown off by how spent he sounded. He was usually more adventurous. And willing to indulge me.

"I want you, now," he said, taking my duffel bag off the bed and putting it on the wooden slat floor. "Stop packing. Take off your clothes."

"Bathing suit?" I asked, slipping off my pants and pulling my shirt and bra over my head.

"No. Nothing."

He lay me out naked across the bleached linen bedspread, which was hot from the scorching Mexican sun. He ran his hands over my body and spread my legs open. He licked my pussy for twenty or thirty minutes. As the ocean wind whipped the white curtains at the front of our villa, he plunged his fingers inside me again and again, in the rhythm he knew drove me crazy. The sun and the bliss of his mouth and his hands on me warmed my bones.

"I can't live without this, Jake. I love you. I love you," I repeated over and over. A multiwave orgasm built until I screamed into the wind, not caring if anyone heard. Jake drew himself up to me and made love to my swollen pussy until he came deep inside me. Sweaty and exhausted, we lay on top of the bed, wrapped together in the sun and the fierce wind.

The next day, we drank black Mexican coffee and ate flaky churros dipped in powdered sugar for breakfast. We snorkeled in the pale aqua water until we were covered in salt from the sea. Late that afternoon, we took an outdoor shower together on the deck of our small villa. After all the salt water, the shower tasted sweet, like iced mint tea. As I soaped up his back, I told him I couldn't get the bougainvillea tunnel out of my head.

"Jakey, I may never come to Tulum again. I think I'm going to go on that hike anyway. I'll get up early one morning and let you rest. But I really want to see it."

He looked over his shoulder at me with a bemused expression, like I was a child stamping her foot, about to throw a tantrum.

"Okay," he said, shrugging, looking back at the ocean, picking up his towel to dry off and draping it over his shoulders. "Whatever. I'll catch up on emails while you're gone."

The second-to-last day we were there, I snuck out in the misty predawn shroud, tucking the covers over Jake's bare chest before I left. I caught a local *guagua* bus with Mexican maids heading to area hotels. After the van dropped me by a chain-link fence alongside the road, I didn't see a soul as I hiked barefoot along the dusty dirt path disappearing into the jungle. Emerald-green parrots flew around me and brown howler monkeys chattered in the bougainvillea. But after an hour of hiking, I felt lonely without Jake. I got to the cenote, looked in, marveled at the cobalt water, and turned around, eager to get back and to slip between his arms.

I found Jake wrapped in a blue and white striped towel on his beach chair in the blistering sun. I bent to kiss him and he laughed at my feet, dirty up to my shins from the hike. We lazed on the beach all afternoon and walked into town for our bittersweet last dinner. We finished the night with languid, relaxed sex in our bungalow as the waves crashed and the wind roared. We fell asleep with him on top of me and his cock inside me.

As we packed up early the next morning, Jake was quiet.

"Honey, anything wrong?" I asked. "You're not getting a bug from the water here, are you?"

He looked away. "No, just tired. I guess."

We had separate flights home to our separate houses in our separate cities. I kissed him long and hard at the Cancún airport security portal, where we said good-bye. Two Mexican guards in uniform stared at us. A crowd of oblivious Brits, hungover and sunburned lobster red, hovered nearby.

"This has been a great vacation." I almost said *practice honeymoon* out loud. I didn't, even though I'd repeated the words silently in my head so often they'd taken on a mythic ring. I was afraid that repeating his words would spook him, or me, and destroy their magic. Instead, I looked in his gray-blue eyes as the last hunk of loneliness that had been wedged behind my ribs for several decades dissolved. "The best vacation ever, Jake. Can't wait to see you in a few days. I hate being apart from you," I whispered in his ear as I hugged him good-bye before we went to our separate gates.

"Okay. See ya."

His words sounded off-key. I watched him hoist his backpack over his shoulder and walk away from me. Then, as I went in search of my gate, I decided something *was* wrong. I looked up his gate number and rushed to it, hauling my duffel. I waited as long as I could, for at least twenty minutes, scanning the crowd for him. Jake never showed. When my flight was about to board, I finally texted him. Where are you, babe?

The three dots on my phone blinked.

Stopped to get a gin and tonic. Sorry. See you back in the States.

It was eleven thirty in the morning. Early for a gin and tonic, right? I found my way to my assigned seat, puzzled.

The flight to Philly took four hours. When I turned my phone back on, there weren't any texts from Jake. None that night, either. Strange. He had two deadlines for work. Plus he liked to spend a lot of time with Jennie whenever he had left her alone, especially given the ataxia health scare. But surely he had time to shoot me a text? Two days later, he finally sent an email. It popped up on my phone as I sat on a stool in the kitchen watching the evening news and slicing cherry tomatoes for our dinner salad. There was no subject line. I clicked it open.

Leslie, I'm still really pissed you went on that hike without me. Tell me the truth: were you meeting some guy? The helicopter pilot?

Holding the knife midair, I momentarily stopped breathing. I stared at the words on my phone screen in disbelief.

The helicopter pilot? From Mexico City? *Six hours* from Tulum? I'd told Jake the whole story about Jefe Jeff and his crazy seven-year girlfriend, and Jake had thrown his head back with laughter. And now he thought I'd snuck out at five in the morning to have sex with that same stranger hundreds of miles away? During our Valentine's Day practice honeymoon? Me? The day before my cenote hike, with enthusiasm that's impossible to fake, I gave him two blow jobs in the space of eight hours. It's hard to argue with that fairly explicit declaration of passion and devotion. How could he believe I betrayed him?

Before I could type any kind of answer, or pick up the phone to call him, another email blinked through to my screen.

Leslie, I know it was wrong to send you that email or even think that. I'm crazy. Forget it. Please ignore that I sent you that. Please. Promise me. Ok?

How did Jake's jealousy, or his tequila and mezcal boondoggles, or the fact that we couldn't talk about any of these problems, fit with the Jake who loved me?

―――――――――――

I was busy with the kids in Philly. Jake was holed up in his New York apartment. It seemed best not to bring up his strange email over the phone; maybe he would talk about it more easily when we were in the same room―or, better yet, in the same bed. We spoke briefly a few days after we got back from Mexico. He sounded distracted. I figured he was deep in work zone, pressured by his deadlines. I called him again Sunday morning. I was lying in bed with the cats, feeling too sleepy to get up. I asked what he'd done the night before.

"Ah, went bowling in the Village. With some friends. Allan, Erica, and―" He paused. "Never mind."

He sounded evasive, frankly. But he'd told me so many stories about how prior girlfriends had been possessive, and suspicious, that I let it go, to give him some freedom and privacy. BGE, right?

On Monday, I told Sara about Jake's accusation that I had snuck away to see Jefe Jeff in Mexico. I also told her that he'd done the same thing with Sig before Christmas. This was starting to look like a pattern I couldn't deny.

"Leslie." She sounded calm and sure over the phone, in her breezy California way. "If Jake or any man threatens to leave you, or accuses you of cheating when you haven't, you cannot beg him to stay."

She made it sound so simple. I held my hand up to the phone, which of course she couldn't see, to signal to her to stop criticizing our relationship. When my first husband started abusing me, my reaction was similar: we were fine, I wanted to help him, to teach him what true love was, to fix what was broken in him through love and passion.

My pattern wasn't looking much prettier than Jake's. At least I could see that. It wasn't doing me much good, though.

Sara kept talking.

"Jake is almost fifty, Leslie. Not that sixteen-year-old boy you fell in love with when you were a teenager," she said.

"Well, okay. But no relationship is perfect. I don't want perfect. I want Jake. Jake wants me."

"Okay," Sara said. "Let's talk about what's not perfect. List a few things you wish Jake didn't do."

It felt disloyal to criticize him, but I tried to conjure up the times he made me feel less than, invisible.

"Well, um, he sometimes makes derogatory comments, and gives me funny looks, when I put on comfy PJs instead of lingerie. I mean, come on, I can't wear my four-inch heels to bed every night. When someone compliments me on my TED Talk about how difficult it is for domestic violence victims to leave, instead of backing me, he always makes a remark that it was unfortunate that I'd been twenty pounds heavier when the video was filmed. He complains that, like all women, I talk too much."

"Okay," Sara said. "Not nice. Is there more?"

"Umm, on the way to Bella's birthday dinner, he exploded and threatened to get out of the car because I wouldn't follow his driving directions. All I could think about was that Bella's feelings would be hurt if he bailed, so I gave in. He did not care at all that he was making me cry on the way to my daughter's birthday celebration. He told me, 'Everyone finds you insufferably bossy. Your kids, do, too,' he'd added. Jesus! He has no idea what my kids think, anyway!"

"True. He's never had kids, so he's not an expert on that. Plus he's not being at all sympathetic or supportive. What else?"

Sara sounded like she was going to keep asking me questions about Jake until even I saw his flaws.

"Well, one of his favorite sayings is 'For every beautiful woman, there's a man who's tired of fucking her.' He says it almost every day."

I heard Sara suck in her breath over the phone.

"Leslie, that's not unkind, it's cruel. Can you hear the threat in that? You're the beautiful woman he's going to tire of one day."

No wonder I hated it every time he said that. Why could Sara see so much that I couldn't?

"Leslie, why are you putting up with this? You need a man who wants to be with you, one who doesn't run away from problems, who solves them. The way you do. You can't settle for less, no matter how long you've known him. No matter how hot the sex is."

I thought of how Jake made me come in the sunshine of Tulum and in front of the fire in Southampton. I *needed* that Jake.

"We're a 'We' now, Sara. I want his imperfections. I want to let him see mine. That's part of commitment. Right?"

"I get that, Leslie. That ability to love wildly is one of the best parts of you. But it doesn't sound like Jake is capable of returning that acceptance, that fierce love. He sounds terribly emotionally fragile to me. At times like this, it's wise to check yourself, to slow down."

My head couldn't argue with her. My heart felt differently.

"You know, it sounds to me like Jake is your burn ointment. Your sexual healing after years of Marty's sabotage. But that doesn't mean he's your soul mate. Each man you date now is a building block for your self-esteem. Not the foundation. Don't confuse the two."

I knew she was right. It didn't make a dent in how much I wanted, and needed, Jake in my life. And my bed.

The first Tuesday in March, Rittenhouse Square was exploding with pink dogwood blossoms, orange and yellow daffodils, and fresh young grass. Early one morning, I spotted a female wood duck, far less glamorous than the males with their metallic purple-green heads, paddling peacefully in the children's pool near the *Duck Girl* statue. I thought wood ducks mated for life. I looked around, but her drake was nowhere to be found.

Jake and I had known each other for thirty-four years.

Our six-month anniversary was in twelve days.

He was turning fifty in ten days.

Jennie was fading. She would leave him soon, no matter what he did.

Were these milestones to Jake, too? I wasn't sure.

Jake's key turned in my brownstone door, and he walked in, looking like he hadn't showered or shaved yet today. He was lugging Jennie's food and dog bed. She wobbled behind him. She hadn't needed a leash in weeks.

He didn't look me in the eye. He didn't hug me. Or kiss me. Even after he put down all Jennie's supplies.

My chest seized.

While he went back out to his Jeep, I got Jennie a bowl of fresh water and gave her skinny ribs a pat as I figured out how to proceed. Should I ignore Jake? Wait for him to bring up whatever was troubling him? Marty had withheld his emotions for so many years, the silent treatment had become intolerable to me. *Withholding emotion is a form of manipulation*, Sara had told me. Jake had pulled enough vanishing acts. My last therapy session had convinced me: I had to know if he was all in.

"Hey, Jake, what's wrong?" I asked as soon as he came inside. I stood next to him in my white-paneled foyer. He dropped his backpack, heavy with his computer.

"Nothing," he said, looking down and sighing, still not meeting my eyes.

"Sit," I said, moving to the Italian silk couch next to the fireplace. The same spot where he'd first kissed me six months before. "Tell me. I want to know."

"Come on, Leslie. Later." His voice chafed with irritation. Irritation with me. "Let's talk about this another time."

He was still standing, a few feet in front of me, his hands on his hips. This person did not seem like Jake.

The cold feeling in my chest got colder. But not knowing what was wrong, feeling invisible, would devastate me. I deserved better.

"No," I said, reaching for his hand. My mouth was dry. "Talk to me. Please."

He pulled his hand back. He stood a good yard from me, stiffly, like a child facing a reprimand. He crossed his arms over his chest. His eyes were a cloudy, cataract gray.

"I've been thinking. This past week, it was nice to have a break from you."

My head jerked as if he'd slapped me. The week before we'd gone to Tulum, he'd confessed that the maximum he could stand to be apart from me was seventy-two hours. He pivoted his jaw, his upper torso, away from me. But the look on his face before he turned away was full of hurt and yearning, as if he actually wanted to be closer to me, to be assured that I needed him.

I stared at Jake, wearing his usual button-down oxford and jeans, speechless.

"It was nice to not feel jealous, for a change." He was spitting the words at me. "You're so intense. And inflexible. You always make me come to you."

He surveyed the living room where we'd first kissed and made love six months before. He glared at the fireplace, the bookshelves filled with Shakespeare, Anne Lamott, Jon Krakauer, Cheryl Strayed. My favorite writers. He looked down at the handwoven Persian carpet. He looked everywhere but at me. He sounded like a stranger. A furious one.

I sank into the love seat, stunned. Me, inflexible? The intense part, damn straight. But Jesus, so was he. We both were. It was something I loved about us.

My brow furrowed and my mouth hung open as I looked at him, trying to decipher his body language. That body I'd come to know so well. What was all this *you you you* talk? Why couldn't he say *I*?

Jake was still speaking.

"You make all your decisions without thinking about me. You and your kids are totally dominating my life."

What the hell? My kids? He barely saw them.

Who was he talking about? None of these qualities described *me*. It felt like he was talking about an invented character, rather than his lover, his friend since we'd been teenagers. Jake had once told me that his ex-girlfriend required him to call her at eleven o'clock to check in. Every night. No matter where he was or what he was doing. Maybe Jake equated that kind of mutually controlling, mistrustful relationship with love. I could never live that way. Although I had my flaws, I never came close to being possessive or calculating. It seared me to hear Jake paint me as a strict, unforgiving woman.

But underneath the anger, I could sense panic. He paced around the room in a circular swoop, like a bird trying to find its way out of a barn. Was he embarrassed about his irrational jealousy over the helicopter pilot? Was his birthday freaking him out? We'd been planning a ten-day skiing trip to Colorado with his family and a motley crew of friends later in March to celebrate. Jennie was dying. Was the juxtaposition between growing older too much for him to absorb? Was this some kind of male midlife crisis, incomprehensible to me, despite how well I thought I knew him?

This conversation was moving too fast. I wanted to hit pause. I didn't know how, because his words, and the fury behind them, ripped me apart like an ax splitting firewood. Tears slipped down my face. He made no sense. I sat motionless on the couch, my palms cupping my face, watching him, afraid to even blink.

"I think I need some time apart from you," Jake said. "I *know* I need some time apart from you."

Sara's advice and KC's words came zinging back to me: like the abuse victim I'd been in my twenties, I was still willing to pay too high a price to feel loved. I'd made progress, sure, by vowing to never put up with physical abuse again. But Jake, like Marty, like my first husband, was turning my insides into black tar. Was this another chapter in the seemingly endless story of how I failed to protect myself from men I loved?

I had to take a stand, right then on the love seat salvaged from my failed marriage.

"Okay, Jake, then go," I said through my tears. I stood up. "I love you. I love us. But I can't take this kind of pain and distance from you. Either you have to leave right now, or I will."

By this time I was crying too hard to say anything more. Somehow we made it to the foyer. I squeezed my arms around his body in a fierce embrace, trying to connect with him physically one final time. Then I sank to the cold marble floor and crumpled into myself, hugging my knees to my chest. Jake put on his leather jacket and picked up his backpack. He whistled to Jennie. She came to him slowly, tottering by me sobbing on the floor, and they both walked out my front door.

––––––––––

The next morning I texted KC. And Winnie. And Sara. I had the mailman's cell, and I felt like using it, so he wouldn't ask why I wasn't getting any more chicken-scratch love letters. That's how bizarre I felt.

I sent everyone the identical message.

> Hi. Jake and I broke up last night. I don't know why. I don't want to talk about it.

Thank God I only had to type the words once, and then copy and paste without having to read them or think about what they meant.

I needed my girl crew to know what had happened, even if I didn't want to discuss it yet. I felt like a Civil War general summoning the cavalry to be at the ready for battle. In case I fell apart. Which I did, over and over, during the next six weeks. Thank God they were all there, waiting to catch me.

KC sat on a high stool at the coffee shop, kicking one heel in the air. She had on a black Tahari suit and shiny black kitten heels. I had on black yoga pants covered in cat hair and a white T-shirt covered in yellow streaks of dried snot.

"I never loved anyone so much," I said through tears.

KC took a sip of her grande iced cold brew, emblazoned with a green mermaid. She raised her eyebrows at me. Starbucks was empty except for a lone male barista. He was grinding coffee and cleaning out the espresso machines behind the counter, pretending he didn't have a wailing customer on his hands.

"What do you love about him, Leslie?" KC asked intently, sounding like Dr. Phil, as if she were humoring an audience member missing three dozen IQ points.

Dammit, she understood exactly why I loved him. I'd written her the world's longest text messages explaining why.

I answered anyway.

"He makes me feel so sensual, and smart, and loved," I howled, as quietly as I could.

KC raised an eyebrow.

"Really? 'Cause that's not what it looks like from my view, right now."

I froze, imagining how I looked to KC. My face was wet. My eyes were red and swollen from crying. Jake Bryant wasn't making me feel especially hot or loved at that moment. In fact, he was directly responsible for more tears, mucus, and self-doubt than I'd ever experienced. As I knew damn well, but had temporarily forgotten, I was the only one responsible for whether I felt sexy, cherished, and loved.

I looked KC in the eye and burst out laughing, shaking the ice in my Starbucks cup.

"Only a true friend tells you what you hate hearing," I managed to blurt out.

She nodded with relief and covered my hand, cold and wet from clutching the iced coffee in its plastic cup, with her warm fingers.

"I was afraid you were gonna marry him, girl. I totally get the wanting/yearning. But you can't end up with someone that vindictive, that immature. No guy is so great a lay to put up with that kind of coldness and betrayal. Honey, you've come too far for that. He's not the one for you."

I wiped my face with a scratchy Starbucks napkin from the table. I reached into my purse for my favorite love note, folded and refolded so many times that the paper felt like soft cotton. *I want to cover you in my love*, Jake had written. I handed it to her as proof.

"I'm never going to find someone else, KC. Not as smart or eloquent as Jake. Not as erotic. I can't settle for anything less."

I felt like the only person on the planet who'd ever been broken up with.

"Oh, girl, you can't see it now, but you'd be settling by staying with him. He's never going to be ready for the kind of relationship you want. You're too independent, too confident. He'd always be punishing you because of his jealousies. Which is twisted. And unfair."

As I watched, appalled, KC tore Jake's note in half.

"You know about 'unsafe' personality types, right?"

She ripped the note again. My eyes welled with tears, but she had my full attention with her words.

"Abandoners?"

Another rip.

"Men like Jake are great at starting relationships. Can't stick with them. They're turned on by pursuit, by convincing women to trust them, but they always, *always* leave when you need them most. Like Lance Armstrong ditching Sheryl Crow when she got breast cancer. Jake probably has some kind of attachment disorder from being abandoned himself as a kid. Or he's a narcissist. He'd never make you happy over time. This phase of your life is about finding *you*, discovering what makes you happy over time. Jake is probably the most important one of the boyfriends—because he's shown you, more than anyone else, what you *don't* want in a man.

She collected the shreds of Jake's love note, walked over to the trash, and threw them away. She came back wiping her hands with finality.

I opened my mouth to protest, to explain Jake's flaws, to remind her of how kind, sweet, and gentle he had been with me, so many times. KC put her hand on mine again to stop me from defending him. She smiled ruefully at me and shook her curls.

"Jake sucks at adulting," she said pithily. "Honey, I know he's not all bad. But bottom line: from my perspective, Jake seems like a cowardly, immature, hypocritical hoarder who abandoned you emotionally. And also, sweetie, maybe you were not so good at adulting, either. Maybe you needed to be a sex-crazed teenager again, as part of getting over Marty. The only thing that really worked between you and Jake was sex. And an intense erotic connection is not the same as a functioning relationship that lasts."

My throat constricted. She was right. That didn't make me miss Jake any less. God, sometimes I hated KC.

"Jake's got a magic feel for beginnings, and the written word. He's certainly in touch with his sexuality. And yours. His superpower is overpromising at the start of a relationship, and then underdelivering over time. Falling in love is easy, Leslie. Staying in love, once you figure out your angel's got feet of clay? That takes a grown-up. How would a man like that ever have been enough for you?"

Great question. I had no idea how to answer.

"I've gotta head back to work, girl," she announced, standing up and throwing her cup in the Starbucks recycling bin. I stood up, she hugged me, and I watched her outside the glass picture window, checking her phone as she power-walked up the street to her office, feeling like I'd never again walk up any street as confidently as KC did.

———————

After suffering through six weeks of phone, text, and email embargo, one word, *Jake*, lit up my phone late one Sunday night. I lunged for it, and all three cats exploded off the bed to get out of my way. I had been under the covers, crying into the sheets for the third or fourth time that day, surrounded by the cats and Tigger. The kids were with Marty, so I'd had no reason to hold back the waterworks all weekend. Observers might have assumed I was training for the Olympics of crying in public. I cried Saturday in the Whole Foods cookie aisle when I saw they had Jake's favorite kind of Tate's, which, in case you're curious, is Chocolate Chip Walnut. Coming home from the market, I wept behind the wheel of my car, circling the block looking for parking, because I couldn't call Jake to help me unload the groceries. Brushing my teeth after dinner an hour before my phone rang, I noticed my left eyeball was threaded with red spiderwebs, a burst blood vessel, a nice topping for my perennially swollen face. I was too exhausted from crying to care that I looked more like a real-life zombie than a fifty-year-old divorced, brokenhearted mother of two who had gone from five to zero boyfriends in six months.

It was ridiculous. I was ridiculous. Which made me howl even more.

Despite obsessing over our relationship for the past month and a half, I had almost no idea why we'd broken up. Instead, I experienced a jagged combination of self-pity and self-fury. How had I been blind to Jake's self-destructive patterns? I couldn't even get mad at him. I felt bizarrely sorry for him as well as myself, although there was zero evidence that he felt sorry for himself or me. His Facebook pictures from his birthday ski trip showed him with a huge smile pasted on his face, as if relieved to be free of me. My sadness, on top of the confusion, made me feel like I was trying to grab fog with my bare hands.

"Jake? Hi. Is it really you?"

For a second, I tried not to sound desperate to talk to him, or like I'd been sobbing for six weeks straight. I lacked sufficient energy to manufacture fake cheer, though. I slumped back into the mess of my pillows and the comforter, clutching my phone.

"Yeah. It's me," he slurred. He sounded a little drunk. "I broke two ribs biking in Central Park today."

"Oh no! Are you okay? How was your birthday? How was your birthday trip?"

"I'm fine. Juiced up on painkillers. Colorado was great. Thanks for your birthday text. It was nice to be in vacation mode. Great skiing, too. We had a great time."

Without me, I felt like adding.

"Ah, so well, um, I have something to tell you."

My stomach tensed as if a Boy Scout were pulling it tight with a drawstring. I rolled over and looked at myself in my mirror headboard, trying to brace myself for whatever he had to say. It sure didn't sound like good news. My face looked as lumpy as if I'd had my wisdom teeth taken out.

"Before that last time I came to see you? Well, actually a while before that. While we were in Tulum. When I was jealous about the helicopter pilot? You left your computer behind when you went hiking. I did a terrible thing. I'm not proud of it."

I tried to keep breathing.

"Okay, Jake, it's okay. Go ahead and tell me."

I went onto your Facebook account and your text message history. To look for something about the helicopter guy. And . . . um . . ."

What reason would anyone have to spy on me? Why hadn't he told me at the time? When I got back to our beach hut, we'd made love, divvied up entrées at dinner, and slept with our arms wrapped around each other in the same bed. Jake had never said anything.

He paused, like Simon Cowell on *American Idol*, about to deliver the big reveal.

"And, uh, I found all those messages to Chris Bailey."

All those messages? What was he talking about? He failed to mention he'd found *nothing* about the helicopter pilot or anyone else. Because there was nothing to find.

"Chris Bailey? My friend who's in Marine Special Operations Command? The one who's been in Afghanistan for the past six months?"

"Yeah. The one you said you wanted to give a big hug to the next time you see him. The one you kissed. And lied to me about. I found it all in your text history."

"Jake, I've seen Chris Bailey two times in my life. Not once since last summer. I kissed him once or twice. What are you talking about?"

"Don't laugh at me, Leslie! Are you laughing?"

"No, Jake. I'm stunned. I was kind of snorting. Not laughing."

Fresh tears slid down my cheeks. Sure, I got all flirty with guys whom I'd kissed once. I loved that, too—since first grade, I'd been a boy chaser. Jake knew that about me. He *liked* that about me.

"*This* is why we broke up?" I asked.

A warning snaked through my swollen brain. Wait a cotton-picking minute. My fifty-year-old boyfriend had dug into my Facebook account, broken up with me without telling me the real reason, let me suffer for six motherfucking weeks without knowing why he'd bolted, and now *he* was mad at *me*? How could he not feel guilty for hurting me, for concealing his insecurity and jealous paranoia, or for making me feel invisible? I'd never lied to Jake, or hidden anything from him, or even *looked* at his phone. Because if you respect someone, you respect their boundaries. In my world, at least. Jake sounded like my possessive, abusive first husband. Jake's lack of introspection took my breath away. How could a grown man be this irrational? Suddenly, KC's words hit me like a baseball bat: no baggage equals no empathy. How had I fallen for this, despite years of therapy?

"We broke up because I kissed a man who is practically a stranger, someone who means nothing to me? Bullshit, Jake. You broke up with me because you were terrified of how close we were getting. Because you don't want to admit that I love you. Goddamn you, Jake."

The phone was slick with tears. It felt supergoddamnfantastic to let him know how much he'd hurt me. To be furious with him for destroying us.

"I hate how insecure I am, Leslie," he said with venom. "How jealous I get."

His voice dropped to a whisper; he sounded like a six-year-old boy. "I'm completely unlovable, Leslie. You don't want to be with me."

He said it like a warning, as if he were pleading with me not to get too close to the septic tank of his soul.

"Jake. I love you." With two fingers, I wiped away a deluge of snot. "Let me show you how lovable you are. No one is perfect. Why couldn't you talk to me about this?"

I was begging. It felt humiliating. I couldn't stop myself.

"Well." His voice hardened, despite the emotion of what I was saying, of how vulnerable I was making myself to him. Or maybe because of it.

"It's not only what I found on your computer. There are other reasons, too. You make me feel so insecure, so jealous all the time. It's not just the helicopter pilot. Or the Special Ops guy. I felt like I could never leave you alone." Jake made it sound as if I were independent specifically to torture him. "When I went to Canada. When I went to South Africa. I worried the whole time about you cheating on me. You were always so hard to hold on to."

Jake sounded as insecure as a shy, nerdy ninth grader. He was so wrong about me. In both my marriages, even at their nadir, I'd never once stepped out on either husband. As far as I could tell, my personality ran pretty much the opposite of cold, unfaithful, and controlling. My therapist, my kids, and probably even Marty would tell you I was too open, too loving, too passionate, too truthful. None of Jake's accusations described who I really was.

"Why didn't you tell me this before, Jake? We could have gotten through it. Together. You always told me you liked it that other men found me attractive. Why didn't you talk to me about feeling jealous?"

"Well, I guess I was embarrassed. I didn't want to be that guy. That jealous guy. That insecure boyfriend."

The cats had crept back onto the edge of my bed. Anger and grief coursed through me like alternating ocean waves. Jake sounded like a teenager, not an adult.

"But Jake, sabotaging our trust, ending our relationship, breaking my fucking heart, was better than that? Better than working it out with me? Because *you* didn't want to admit to being 'that guy' who was paranoid and insecure? You let me *twist* for the past six weeks, torturing myself over why you ended things, with my therapist and friends on speed dial, wondering how I could have been in love with someone who one day turned off all his feelings for me like a faucet?"

Silence. He still had not said anything approaching an apology. There had been no *I'm sorry I hurt you, Leslie. I'm sorry I went onto your computer and spied on your life and destroyed a great relationship with the woman of my dreams.*

I deserved all of those words, and more.

"Well, uh, there are a few other things, too," he said.

Fuck.

"Like what?" I asked anxiously.

Jake hesitated. Whatever it was, he didn't want to tell me. Had he stolen money from me? Installed a GPS tracker on the TT?

"Well, you always pour the first cup of coffee for yourself."

Oh my God. Was he ten years old? His hostility gutted me. How could the man who in January had written *Is it OK if I love you in some way for the rest of my life?* now be angry about the first coffee pour-over? Did Jake *want* to sabotage what we had? Did he expect me to never get angry, to never disappoint him, to never let him down in any way?

I squeezed my phone tight. An ambulance siren howled down the street out front. I tried to make my voice sound normal.

"Okay, thanks for telling me all this, Jake. Your honesty is really . . . helpful. I love you."

It was true. Maybe it always would be. No matter how much he hurt me. God, sometimes I hated being a heterosexual female.

"I have more to tell you, Leslie. You're not going to like it."

Well, it wasn't as if I'd *liked* what he'd told me already.

"I feel badly about how things ended," he said, with a hint of a question mark in his voice, as if he wanted me to ask what he meant. I stayed quiet. I was devastated by the fact that things ended, but not by *how* they ended. What did he mean?

"Ah, I was seeing someone else while we were together. Hannah. I feel bad about that."

I dropped the phone as if I'd grabbed a hornet's nest with my bare hand. Did he think this information would help me somehow? No. His goal was to hurt me and to salve his guilt-ridden conscience. I couldn't speak. I knew he was telling the truth; I remembered the sneaky smile on Hannah's face at the Halloween party, the times Jake wouldn't answer my texts for days when he was in New York working. As part of my shock, all I could think of was the many diseases he'd possibly exposed me to via Hannah and her Calvin Klein boyfriend and all the women *that* guy slept with. I heard Jake's voice coming from the phone on the floor, saying "Leslie? Leslie?" increasingly angrily, until the phone finally went silent.

I'd worked so damn hard, in therapy and other places, to become an adult. That meant being honest, and transparent, and vulnerable with the people I loved, my kids, my friends, my editors, everyone in my life whom I cared about. I needed the man—or men—in my life to be the best version of themselves as well. The whole time I'd been with Jake, I'd been waiting for the grown-up version to arrive, the mature, forgiving, communicative man, that guy I thought I loved and trusted.

There was clearly no grown-up version of Jake on his way to me.

There never had been.

My heart cracked open.

I started to cry again. Knowing what Jake had kept from me, how damaged he must be inside, how unkind he could be, how naive I'd been about a man once more, stung even more now that I knew the truth. Our intense sexual connection, the passion of his love letters, our entire relationship together, had been nothing more than a mirage of shimmering palm trees and sapphire-blue water that evaporated when I got too close to him. We'd never truly been a *We*.

I fell asleep in bed with the lights on. When I woke up in the middle of the night to turn them off, my pillow was still wet. I had a considerable measure of salty Jake tears left in me, but I knew one thing for certain: Jake Bryant never deserved me. Any part of me. The spell was broken. "We" were done forever.

In my tear-stained bed the next morning, I texted a recap of Jake's confessions to KC. There was too much for me to figure out alone. How could KC have seen, more clearly and far earlier than I had, that I was letting myself down again, falling for a man who couldn't love me the way I wanted to be loved, who couldn't even be honest with me or faithful? I would never let myself be blinded like that again.

I was down in the kitchen, dismally making coffee for one instead of two, when my phone lit up with her response. I loved/ hated it when, in reaction to one of my three-hundred-word soul-searching missives, KC shot back the perfect breezy retort in fewer words than my opening sentence.

Hey girl!

KC was probably dodging traffic into her office and dictating to Siri.

You never really know a guy until he breaks up with you. Your computer??? Cheating the whole time on you when he was accusing you of cheating?!? Classic cheater profile. Good riddance. I promise, you will survive!

I threw down the phone on the couch. Losing Jake—or whom-ever I had thought he was—felt like heroin withdrawal. If I had ever used heroin. Which I haven't, thank Holy God.

What was KC talking about when she wrote "classic cheater profile"? Even though I suspected Marty had stepped out, I'd never been especially curious about infidelity, since our other problems dwarfed it. I turned once again to the online universe. What I found wasn't pretty. A psychology magazine explained that cheaters were narcissists, unable to get enough attention in one relationship. Cheaters constantly questioned partners and frequently accused them of infidelity, because being unfaithful makes them paranoid, and they assume their partner must be betraying them also. I had felt sorry for Jake, because he was so insecure and unable to see how deeply I loved him. I felt like a fool.

Then I realized, like biting down on a rock: Jake was the fool here. He had told me his past two relationships ended because both girlfriends had been unfaithful, one allegedly with a colleague, the other with a waiter at the bar near his building. Now I wondered: did those women actually cheat on him? Maybe their betrayals had been as illusory as mine. Maybe Jake had, in some way, *wanted* to believe we were all cheating on him, because he was cheating on us. You know a relationship is over when you start sympathizing with the exes.

Sara was even more blunt. "This is the behavior of a socio-path," she said during our emergency session that afternoon. "I don't normally allow myself to get this angry in my professional sphere, Leslie. But cheating on you, while accusing you of cheating on him, and now sharing the infidelity as if he's proud that he hurt you? That is using infidelity as a weapon to annihilate you. He's not merely troubled. I worry that he could be toxic to you and all women who cross his path. This is emotional abuse, Leslie, poten-tially as serious as the physical abuse you endured. The manipula-tion, the betrayal, the withholding of facts, then springing it on you, is among the most puzzling postbreakup tactics I've come across in my thirty years of psychotherapy."

I crawled through the afternoon. I made myself go for a neighborhood walk, pondering what she said. I waited in a daze at two different traffic lights that had turned green. Isn't it surprising, looking back after a relationship ends, how you can see the red flags you ignored at the beginning? Memories of Jake's paranoid possessiveness and strange preoccupation with infidelity flooded back like shower water suddenly turned ice cold. In one of the first letters he'd written me, the night after our Atlantic City tryst, he'd told me the truth himself, writing, *I'm probably being an incredible hypocrite because I spend time with other women, and you've been very clear about your feelings, which is all that should matter.* The first present he'd given me was a copy of Junot Díaz's book *This Is How You Lose Her*, which included a short story about a man who cheated on his fiancée with over fifty women and then got discovered when she broke into his computer and read his emails.

Why hadn't I paid attention? This was part of what Sara and KC were trying to get me to see. My instincts about men were good. I just had to listen more assiduously.

I looked up, lost in thought. I was in front of my own front doors. Tigger and all three cats were looking woefully out the kitchen window, as if they'd survived without food for a week when I'd been gone for less than an hour.

Later that night, when I thought I was crying quietly in my bedroom, I heard a knock on my door.

"Come in," I said, wiping my face on a corner of my sheet.

Timmy walked in, followed by Bella.

"Hi, guys," I said. "What's up?"

I patted the bed. They stood there, afraid of my sadness.

"Mom," Tim said. "We know you're upset about Jake. We can hear you. You don't have to hide the fact that you are crying from us."

Which, of course, made me burst into fresh tears.

"Oh, you two are so sweet," I managed to say.

They climbed under the covers on either side of me. Bella looked at Timmy expectantly, like they'd discussed what to say.

"Mom, he wasn't good enough for you," Timmy said. "He

wasn't . . . nice to you. Bell and I never really liked him, anyway. Don't worry. You'll fall in love again."

There are few things as profound as getting a pep talk about love from your own teenaged kids. I took each of their warm, soft hands.

"Thank you both. I know you're right. I'm just sad now. I miss Jake so much."

Bella finally spoke up. "Mom, someone great is going to find you and love you the way we do."

God, I hoped she was right.

After walking Tim and Bell back to their rooms and tucking in each one, I lay under the covers in my own soft bed. My own kids could see my value. KC and Sara could, too. At times, I still couldn't. Part of this journey was, obviously, that I had to learn and relearn that the way I allowed men to treat me was up to me, and only me. I had to thread a particularly challenging needle: to find validation from men while not allowing them to steal my self-confidence. The tricky part was finding the right balance, to open up to the men in my life without completely giving myself over to them. Men could be healers, as well as destroyers, and it was at times surprisingly hard to tell the difference between the two.

The truth is, despite the heartbreak he wrought, I got what I needed most from Jake. Hope that I could love deeply again. More fabulous sex in six months than I'd had in the thirty years prior. Hope and great sex? Who wouldn't be grateful for that, at fifty or at any age? I'd taken what I wanted from Jake and the other men in my life. And, as Sara had prophesized, I'd paid for it.

I may have gotten unlucky with the men in my life, but Jesus, I had the world's best girlfriends, a brilliant therapist, and the most compassionate kids. Which all felt far more dear than five boyfriends right then.

Jennie finally died on a Sunday in May. I was leaving for a domestic violence conference in western Canada the next day, but after seeing the news on Jake's Facebook page, I decided to send a care package, to take the high road despite his betrayal. I rushed around buying his favorite coffee from La Colombe. I took his favorite framed photo of the two of them and wrapped it in teal-blue tissue paper. I added a glossy pack of Crane's note cards embossed with the silhouette of a coonhound. Lastly, I stopped at the liquor store and bought the most expensive bottle of tequila they had. I packed it all up in a small mountain of blue tissue and trucked it to the post office early Monday morning before catching my flight to Vancouver.

The conference fascinated me, especially a long, intense dinner with two Canadian police detectives and the chairman, addressing the latest technological tools to prevent stalking, trafficking, sexual assault, and relationship abuse. When I returned home Friday, Jake still hadn't mentioned the box. I knew he was probably heartbroken, so I let it go. But eventually, I texted him to find out if he had gotten it. Maybe it had been lost somehow, or confiscated by an overzealous postal employee because I'd snuck in booze.

This was Jake's reply:

> Yes, thanks for the package, Leslie. Hannah has actually been great to me during these sad days. We're getting along wonderfully and she's seeing me through.

Nice touch, Jake. Thanks so fucking much.

––––––––––––

> Hey Leslie!

Marc's text, one night when I was home alone in bed with three purring cats and Tigger sprawled across my bedroom threshold, felt like a gift from the God of Younger Men.

I imagined Marc, in all his adorable hotness, coming over for an evening of crazy-hot adventurous sex. Walking in the door, taking off his jean jacket, pushing me up against the living room wall, bending me over the couch, watching himself screw me in front of the mirrored walls in the dining room.

I answered his text, smiling to myself, with a simple Yes, sir? He replied immediately.

I'm a single man again, Leslie. Let's have fun.

I wanted to drop the phone like a hot cookie sheet. Though I was appalled by the realization, I had zero desire to see him. So, instead of telling Mr. Fuckable Junior to hustle on over *stat* and charge his ride to my Uber account, I sent Marc a response that probably shook him as much as it did me.

Hey, Marc, thanks for your text. Fun is good, as Dr. Seuss says. But I'm actually looking for more these days. (And I'm sorry about the breakup. Never enjoyable. You're a great guy and it's her loss for sure.)

Me, saying no to a night of crazy sex with a man twenty years younger because I wanted "more"? What the hell had happened to me? The five-boyfriend plan was *broken*.

To my surprise, it felt good to say no. Because saying no meant saying yes to something better. Better than staying in a dead marriage. Better than unforgettable one-night stands with men twenty years younger. Better than Jake cheating on me. At least, that's what I *hoped* it meant.

I wanted my mermaid back. I didn't know for sure where Jake had her, but my best guess was that after Christmas, he'd taken her to his cabin in Connecticut. She was probably on the front porch, covered in dust, pollen, and spiderwebs. I couldn't bear imagining her alone there. In late May, due to a coincidence that didn't feel like coincidence, I had a family reunion at a resort thirty minutes away. I'd only been to Jake's cabin once, years before, but the layout of the rough-hewn, two-room place was simple enough to navigate, even if I had to poke around inside. There was no alarm; I couldn't remember if there was even electricity. I emailed Jake to let him know I was taking her. He shot back a terse email: **Wasn't that a gift for me?** I reminded him of his agreement that he'd return her if we broke up. I could sense his pout, like a child forced to share a toy, when he asked for the hotel address, writing curtly that he'd drop her off there instead.

As I drove to the reunion, I thought about what I'd learned from Jake and a year of men in my life.

First of all, divorce, or any breakup, hurts like hell. The only person who shares your despair is usually the one person you can't talk to anymore. But going at life alone is worth the anguish, because, over time, being treated as invisible, or being loved inadequately, by a person you adore can be as painful as being hit.

Second, I'd had a great year, despite the fact that I was still single. By leaving a husband who no longer cherished me, navigating a variety of lovers at once, and rejecting a beloved but self-destructive boyfriend, I rediscovered the best parts of myself. My skin may have gotten more wrinkled, but I was more comfortable in it than ever. I could admit now what the feminist in me didn't want to acknowledge at nineteen. Since I was a little girl, I've loved boys. The way they look, and smell, and make me feel.

As I'd been packing my car for the reunion, a man had stopped on the sidewalk and said, "Dang, girl, you still got it. Will you marry me?" In my second half century, I'd rather hear that than get a hundred Instagram likes. Only a man can rock me in that primitive, sacred, physical way.

I'm not suggesting all women need men in this blatant fashion. But in my case, male energy revitalizes how I view parenting, work, money, death, sex, and myself as a woman. Men show me who I am, in ways that my female friends, as much as I rely on and adore them, do not. The key is to keep an open mind, and to not expect or demand things men won't ever be able to give me.

I hit the hotel check-in bell around ten o'clock. The night clerks, a young man and woman who looked like high school students working their first jobs, smiled eagerly as they entered my credit card information. Their enthusiasm made me wonder if they were anxious to get rid of me so they could go back to making out in the supply closet.

"Did anyone drop off a statue under my name?" I asked, wondering how odd my request sounded. The clerks broke into synchronized smiles. "You're the one picking up the mermaid?" the girl asked. "She's so beautiful."

Sure enough, there she was, in the fluorescent light of the storage room behind the counter, listing slightly sideways next to a computer printer on a patch of indoor/outdoor carpeting. She was covered in silky cobwebs but still dignified in her armor of gray-green scales. I smiled when I saw her pretty copper face, her voluptuous breasts, and her wide hips flaring into her mermaid tail.

"Was there a note?" I asked the girl. Her face fell, as if she was disappointed for me. "Um, sorry, no, he just wrote down your name." The news hurt like a bee sting, but without the surprise of one.

I brushed off my mermaid's cheeks. I picked her up with both arms in an awkward hug (her curved metal tail was a pointy, potentially lethal weapon). I gingerly carried her to the TT and strapped her into the front seat before going up to my room. Three days later, after hugging my relatives farewell, I drove back to Philly with her as my passenger, imagining she was whispering her thanks for the rescue.

Driving home, flicking through rock stations, I took a vow to keep chasing boys. While it may seem contradictory, I also promised myself I wouldn't search for that one perfect man. The times I've believed one person was going to complete my life, I inevitably panicked, mistakenly believing, with claustrophobic certainty, there were no available substitutes. But the problem isn't a lack of men.

There are men *everywhere*. (And women, too.) At every age of our lives. On sidewalks, in airports, supermarkets, and yoga studios. The problem comes, for me at least, when I choose a frame that's too narrow, closing my eyes to potential partners, to the uniqueness of romance, sex, and love.

Even when passion comes into our lives, it can slink away unexpectedly. Both my marriage, and my postdivorce year of dating, confirmed that lasting intimacy can prove as elusive at fifty as when I chased boys on my elementary school playground. It's outside my control whom I catch, how long I keep them, who they turn out to be over time, and whether or not they want to be with me. No matter how tough I grow, how fiercely I absorb life's sly lessons, how wisely I choose.

I hope that one day, I'll find someone I love as deeply, or even more deeply, than I did all of my boyfriends and husbands combined. Maybe I will find a great man who will stay forever, treat me right, and hold my hand while I die.

Maybe not.

Sometimes, happily ever after doesn't happen. But happier than ever before can, and does. Perhaps the most priceless lesson my year of five lovers taught me is that self-love is, in fact, far more important than the perfect partner.

Spending my life seeking soul mates taught me this: finding true love is rarely a good measure of how much you deserve it.

That gift, you give yourself.

And if anyone, including Jake, ever asks why I wanted my mermaid back, I'll say I brought her home to someone who deserves her.

Me.

THE NAKED TRUTH
CHEAT SHEET

1. Forget everything everyone ever told you about meeting men* and dating.
2. Go to where the men are. Don't expect men to magically come to you. They won't. Men are *everywhere*. In airports, restaurants, the supermarket, Starbucks, yoga class, the local dog park, online dating sites, you name it. But you have to see them. And make them see you.
3. Don't play hard to get. You're a grown-up; be confident and go after what you want. If you like someone, flirt with them. If someone you like flirts, flirt back.
4. Go out solo as much as possible; being alone makes you more approachable than being in a group or with a friend. Sit at the bar, on a bench, or next to an empty seat whenever you are out alone. Never order room service and always walk or take the subway—you will never meet someone in your hotel room, in a taxi, or in an Uber. Well, except the driver; and if the driver is cute, well, lucky you.
5. Revel in your sexuality. Whatever that means to you. Discover what makes you swagger and then don it like a magic cloak even when you take out the garbage.

---

* My viewpoint is from the perspective of a heterosexual woman, because I am one. But change the gender identification and/or sexual orientation to whatever works for you, and let me know if the same advice holds true. Thank you.

6. Be transparent. Wear as little makeup as possible; don't disguise who you are or how old you are (it doesn't work). Great hair is more important on an older woman, anyway.
7. Make eye contact with every person who catches your eye. Smile. Even if you're never gonna see them again. Even if they are twenty years younger.
8. Make yourself easy to approach. Sit next to people. Get off your phone. Wear clothing that prompts an easy opening line, like a splashy dress, an unusual hat, or crazy shoes.
9. Get their name and number (even if it kills you).
10. Smile, be nice, and look for niceness in other people. Friendliness is the sexiest quality on earth, whatever age you are.

ACKNOWLEDGMENTS

My kids will always top the list of people I'm grateful to for supporting me as a mom and a woman.

Thank you to Alice Fried Martell, dear friend, literary agent, truth teller, and cheerleader extraordinaire. Thank you Christine Pride, Priscilla Painton, and Lashanda Anakwah, for believing in this book and championing it, and to everyone at Simon & Schuster who understood that a book about sex could also explore an emotional journey. The team at Gail Davis Speakers in Dallas, including Gail Davis, Julie O'Keefe, Brooke Farmer, Dana Swan, Kelley Copeland, Abi Ferrin, Amanda Lindhout, Kathryn McCoy, Drusilla Blakey, Adrienne Metzig, and Megan Withers—you show that women rule the world. Bruce Vinokour and Sonya Rosenfeld at Creative Artists Agency, thank you for bringing my stories alive visually.

Despite the . . . umm . . . *unique* role of men in my life, friendships with women are my true and enduring romance. Special thanks to the maids of dishonor Elin Cohen, Brooke Evans, Lila Leff, Jeri Curry, Leslie McGuirk, Carolina Martinez Pitarch, Jennifer Brown, Michele Dreyfuss, Jodi Dehli, and Jackie Walker. To the best honorary girlfriends I could ask for: Bradford Richardson, Jeremy Norton, Randolph Adams, Ian Horneman, and Harry Lerner. Thank you to Heath Kern Gibson and Camilla Peterson for being insightful and invaluable early readers.

Shoutouts to my crew of family and friends, old and new: Perri Morgan, Dick and Patty Simon, Susan Cheever, Sarah Tompkins, Chris Appleby, Scotty and Patty Ivey, Jack Davies and Kay Kendall, Sonya Bernhardt, Ruth Marcus, Carol Hansen, Sally and Bob Caiola, Scott Weiss, Sam Pelham, Visko Hatfield, Pam Sherman, Pat Walsh, Regan Ralph, Linda Lourie, Sonya Lawrence Green, Christine Courtois, Bobby Grossman, Nanci Bramson, Kevin Burns, Alex Calingaert, Paul and Elizabeth Centenari, John Lesko, Niki Allen, Rolf Grimsted, Kennett Marshall, Alice Fuisz, Nassim Assefi, Jennifer Weis, Susanna Porter, Gerry and Rhonda Wile, Sarah Woolworth, Soraya Chemaly, Annie Clark, Andrea Pino-Silva, Charlie Esposito, Debbie Brenneman, Page Evans, Carrington Tarr, Dorie Fain, Laurie and Ray Goins, Brett and An Groom, Xiomara Pineda, Shelly Hall, Michel Martin, Jolene Ivey, Dani Tucker, Susan, Alex and Chessy Prout, Linda Konner, Scott Owens, Sarah Nixon, Laura Putnam, Jan Sidebotham, Deborah Wagner, Paul Caiola, Katherine Kendall, Bobby and Mary Haft, David and Katherine Bradley, Ginny Grenham, Phil Klein, Kelly Griffith, Elena Burch, Dave and Val McGloin, JP and Kara Dowd, Mark and Beth Odom, Tom Bryant, Aaron and Dana Martin, Susan Mathes, Gay Cioffi, Jill Sorenson, Sharon Langoff Robinson, Kim Anspach Rutkowski, Brooke Boardman, Skippy Redmon Banker, Kyra Tirana, Katie Hood, Seanna Bruno Crosby, Nancy and Larry Goldstone, Angie Firestone, Maria Bowling, Elsa Walsh, Tim Morgan, Randy Eder, Ann Hunter Lepkowski, Marcia Thayne, Mary Lee Brighton, Hermine Dreyfuss, Paul Zevnick, Jan and Walt Connor, Bob Wickham and Carmel Sauvageau, Nancy and Mickey Lincoln, Julie Gunderson, Grant and Ruth Harmon, Linda Baquet, Willie Joyner, Trista and William Farrell, Helen Harmon, Sara Glenn, Kit Gruelle, Leonard and Betty King, Laura Oradei Bayz, George Harmon, Loulie Harmon, Chris and Jody Parrish, Bill Parrish, Susan Swayze, Jim and Amy Lohr, John and Leslie Fuchs, Julie Harmon and Hugo Machuca, Bunkie Harmon, Miriam Harmon,

Louise and Jake Warner, Anderson and Michelle Kressy, Sue and Roger Smith, Anne Oman and Marcus Williams, Matt and Kara Kressy, Edie Kressy, and everyone at The One Love Foundation, Knock Out Abuse, Windhorse Korrals, Longacre Farm, Gilly's, and the *Washington Post*.

ABOUT THE AUTHOR

Leslie Morgan is the *New York Times* bestselling author of *Crazy Love*, *Mommy Wars*, *The Baby Chase*, and more than four hundred columns for the *Washington Post*'s parenting blog. Her first essay appeared in *Seventeen* when she was a senior at Harvard College, and she financed an MBA from The Wharton School by writing for *Glamour*, *Money*, and other magazines. She is a frequent media guest and speaker on women's leadership and overcoming adversity. Her TED Talks have been viewed by more than four million people in forty countries. She lives in the District of Columbia, New York, and New Hampshire.